SUNKEN REALMS

A COMPLETE CATALOG OF UNDERWATER RUINS

Karen Mutton

Other Books Of Interest:

TECHNOLOGY OF THE GODS
LOST CONTINENTS AND THE HOLLOW EARTH
AXIS OF THE WORLD
PIRATES & THE LOST TEMPLAR FLEET
MAPS OF THE ANCIENT SEAKINGS
THE PATH OF THE POLE
ATLANTIS IN AMERICA

SUNKEN REALMS

A COMPLETE CATALOG OF UNDERWATER RUINS

Adventures Unlimited Press

Sunken Realms
A Complete Catalog of Underwater Ruins

ISBN: 1-931882-96-7
ISBN 13: 978-1-931882-96-5

Published by:
Adventures Unlimited Press
One Adventure Place
Kempton, Illinois 60946 USA
auphq@frontiernet.net

www.adventuresunlimitedpress.com

Sunken Realms

A Complete Catalog of
Underwater Ruins

PERMISSIONS

I would like to thank these people:
Graham Hancock for permission to quote from his book *Underworld*. Dr Greg Little for permission to quote from his articles and the use of his photographs. David H. Childress for permission to quote from his books *Lost Cities of North & Central America; Lost Cities of Atlantis, Ancient Europe & the Mediterranean; Lost Cities of Ancient Lemuria & the Pacific.*
My family for their patience.

Dedicated to the memory of my father,
Richard James Carfoot
Who passed on January 5, 2007

TABLE OF CONTENTS

ANCIENT RUINS OFF INDIA: PART 2
GUJARAT-DWARKA
GULF OF CAMBAY
THE SARASVATI RIVER
ANTEDILUVIAL CITIES OF SUMER

TABLES

Measurements provided in this book are either in imperial or metric depending on the original source. To find the equivalent, use the following table:

1 inch   = 2.54 centimeters
1 foot   = 0.30 meter
1 yard   = 0.91 meter
1 mile   = 1.69 kilometers
1 acre   = 0.40 hectares
1 square mile = 2.59 square kilometers

1 centimeter = 0.3937 inches
1 meter = 39.37 inches/ 1.094 yards
1 kilometer = 0.621 miles
1 hectare = 2.471 acres
1 square kilometer = 0.386 square miles

GEOLOGICAL ERAS AND PERIODS IN THE CENOZOIC

Era	Period	Time (millions of years)
Cenozoic	Holocene	100,000 (0.1)
	Pleistocene	2
	Pliocene	5
	Miocene	25
	Oligocene	38

PREHISTORIC TIME PERIODS (IN EUROPE AND MIDDLE EAST)

Palaeolithic—Old Stone Age from 4 million years to about 10,000 years BC. Generally a period of hunting and gathering.

Mesolithic—Middle Stone Age from 10,000 years to about 7,000 years BC. Hunting and gathering with more sophisticated tools called microliths.

Neolithic—New Stone Age generally from 7,000 years to about 4000 BC when polished stone was used, agriculture invented as well as animal herding.

Bronze Age—beginning from about 3000 BC when Bronze was invented for weapons and tools.

Iron Age—around 1000 BC in Asia and the Middle East when iron became the main metal for weapons and tools.

Please note these periods pertain only to the old world. Cultures like the Australian aborigines did not develop technology beyond the Mesolithic period.

AUTHOR'S FOREWORD

Sunken cities—the words fill the imagination with images of lost Atlantis, mystical Avalon or volcanic Mu. My own interest in these sunken legends harkens back to my teen years when I was exposed to the mystical writings of T. Lobsang Rampa and Edgar Cayce. Books by alternative historians who supported the idea of lost antediluvian civilizations such as Charles Berlitz, Brad Steiger, Andrew Thomas and Raymond Drake also provided a lot of inspiration.

After obtaining a Bachelor's degree in Ancient History from the University of Sydney, my academic training enabled me to look at the claims of alternative historians with a sympathetic but critical eye. Sadly, most of their claims turned out to be baseless. No irrefutable evidence of Atlantis, Lemuria or Mu has been presented, but mysterious submerged sites do crop up occasionally and deserve to be studied. Such enigmatic sites as Bimini, Yonaguni and the Gulf of Cambay in India which are easily dismissed as natural formations by archeologists because they fit into no historical time period, nevertheless show some artificial features.

Underwater archeology only came into prominence with the invention of SCUBA by Jacques Cousteau in the mid 20th century and to date well over two hundred sites in the Mediterranean Sea alone have been discovered. These sites, including towns, harbors and villages have also been surveyed and photographed by underwater archeologists. Many of the more famous sites such as Alexandria, Apollonia and the Bay of Naples are featured in this book.

However, this book also discusses the controversial claims, including those linking alleged discoveries with Atlantis and Mu. My intention is to open up the reader to all possibilities and not discount a site because it should not be there. The oceans, seas, lakes and rivers which cover 70% of the Earth's surface could contain all kinds of artifacts and even structures. Since the last Ice Age the oceans have risen almost 400 feet, inundating possibly countless settlements. As we have barely scratched the continental shelves with exploration, who knows how many sunken settlements exist around the world? Who knows which legends of lost lands will turn out to be factual? Who knows how much of our unknown history lies at the bottom of oceans, seas and lakes?

GLOSSARY

ANTEDILUVIAL — Before the flood (generally the Biblical Flood of Genesis.)

ATLANTIS — A mythical island in the Atlantic Ocean first described by the ancient Greek philosopher Plato.

BC — Before Christ (also Before Common Era — BCE)

BERINGIA — The now submerged land bridge linking Alaska to Siberia.

BP — "Before Present," as opposed to "Before Christ."

BREAKWATERS — Artificial harbors made of huge stones.

BRONZE AGE — A time period after the Neolithic when bronze tools and weapons were manufactured. It occurred at different times in different areas.

CATASTROPHISM — The study of rapid, catastrophic geological changes as opposed to uniformitarianism which is the study of gradual geological changes.

CRANNOG — An artificial island created in prehistoric times in Britain.

EUSTATIC — The geological process whereby land and sea levels are changed gradually.

HYPERBOREA AND THULE — Mythical northern Atlantic islands according to the Greeks.

ICE DAMS — Huge dams composed of ice at the end of the Ice Age.

ISTOSTACY — The process whereby land and sea levels are changed dramatically.

KERGUELEN — A large landmass which sank in the Indian Ocean 20 million years ago.

KUMARI KANDAM — A mythical landmass to the south of India according to the Tamil Indians.

LEMURIA — Mythical continent in the Indian Ocean first named by geologist Phillip Sclater.

LGM — Last Glacial Maximum when the Ice Age was at its height locking millions of litres of water into ice caps and glaciers from 22,000 to 17,000 years ago.

LITHOSPHERE — The Earth's crust and upper portion of the mantle.

LYONESSE, YS, HY BRASIL — Mythical sunken Celtic lands.

MAGNETOMETER — An instrument that measures the earth's magnetic field intensity.

MESOLITHIC — Middle Stone Age lasting until about 3,000 BC in most places. Flint was used for tools and weapons.

MID ATLANTIC RIDGE — An underwater mountain chain running the length of the Atlantic Ocean.

MIOCENE — A geologic epoch within the Tertiary period (about 26 to 5 million years BC).

MU — Mythical continent in the Pacific Ocean.

MUDALU — Mythical Pacific continent according to Taiwanese.

NEOLITHIC — New Stone Age, generally classified as a time when agriculture developed as well as pottery and early urbanism.

PALAEOMAGNETISM — Study of magnetism in rocks to determine the intensity and direction of the Earth's magnetic field in the past.

PLATE TECTONICS — Popular theory explaining volcanism, continental drift, seismicity in terms of slow movements of the earth's lithospheric plates.

PLEISTOCENE — Geological period from about 1.6 million years ago to 10,000 years ago when ice sheets covered huge portions of the northern hemisphere.

ROV — (Remote Operated Vehicle) An unmanned undersea vehicle remotely controlled from a vessel or offshore platform. It is equipped with manipulator arms to perform simple operations.

SAHUL — A large continent comprising Australia, New Guinea and Tasmania.

SIDE-SCAN SONAR —A technique of nautical

archeological survey which helps map the seafloor.

SPARTEL — A submerged island between Spain and Morocco.

SUBDUCTION ZONE — According to the theory of Plate tectonics this is an area on the Earth's crust in which the edge of an oceanic continental plate is being pushed under another plate.

SUNDALAND — A large Ice Age continent in South East Asia comprising Indonesia, Malaysia, Thailand and parts of the Philippines.

TARTESSOS — A semi mythical town in Spain that disappeared during classical times.

TSUNAMI — A huge coastal wave or waves formed by earthquakes or undersea avalanches.

YOUNGER DRYAS — A period known as the little Ice Age when the ice sheets advanced after retreating for a few millennia.

INTRODUCTION

Sunken cities, legends of lost lands such as Atlantis, Lemuria and Thule have excited people for thousands of years. We are fascinated by the possibility that a town, city or whole civilization can disappear without trace and often without warning. The 2004 Indian Ocean tsunami only too clearly illustrated that the forces of nature are able to obliterate thousands of lives and submerge cities despite our modern technology. Such destructive forces as earthquakes, volcanoes, tsunamis, hurricanes and landslides have been threatening humans since before the dawn of civilization and are responsible for the loss of many settlements. Rising seas which occurred at the end of the last Ice Age inundated countless other human habitations, some of which are being discovered in this century.

The main objective of this book is to provide a survey of submerged settlements from around the world, including inland seas, lakes and springs. There are at least two hundred sites in the Mediterranean alone, from Israel to Spain, which have been discovered and studied by underwater archaeologists. The most fascinating recent discovery has been of the sunken cities of Menouthis and Canopus off the coast of the Egyptian city of Alexandria. India also has its ruins off the coast of the city of Dwarka, with others possibly existing near Mahabalipuram and in the Gulf of Cambay. Underwater archaeology in Britain, Scandinavia and the Americas has also revealed artifacts consisting of wood and other organic material from settlements in the Mesolithic Age.

The second aim is to examine the controversial discoveries that have been reported off the coasts of Spain, Japan, Taiwan, India, Cuba and the Bahamas. These stone formations, which have been classified as natural by many archaeologists and geologists, nevertheless possess artificial features like symmetry and structure. Such formations as can be found at Yonaguni, Bimini and in the Gulf of Cambay, have led other scientists to believe they are man-made. The problem with the man-made theory is one of age — none of these features was above land less than six thousand years ago, the conventional age for the genesis of urbanisation. To acknowledge that sophisticated structures were being built up to ten thousand years ago during the Palaeolithic or Mesolithic era would totally upset the prevailing historical timeline.

The third aim is to examine the legends of sunken lands such as Atlantis, Lemuria and Mu and whether there is any credence in the numerous claims of their discovery. Atlantis has been 'discovered' on nearly every continent and there are hundreds of theories pinpointing its existence, from Spain to the Antarctic. Some of these theories will be discussed, particularly those supported by archeological evidence, although it is not the purpose of this book to identify any particular area.

Finally, this book looks at the mechanisms which have created sunken sites. These mechanisms vary from flooding to earthquakes and tsunami inundation. Many villages in modern times have been deliberately flooded to create dams and reservoirs. Other coastal settlements have been destroyed by subsidence over the centuries. Yet other towns like Helike in Greece were struck by an earthquake and tsunami which totally obliterated them.

The controversial ruins (with the exception of those off Cuba) have all been discovered in areas on the continental shelves which were above sea level during the last Ice Age. Because vast expanses of water were locked up in the huge icecaps that covered much of Europe and North America, the levels of the oceans were up to 400 feet lower than at present. The following map of how the world appeared during the Ice Age reveals that many areas of the world once possessed much larger coastlines. This is particularly evident in the now lost South East Asian continent of Sundaland, and greater Australia, which formed the Pleistocene continent of Sahul. The Persian Gulf was totally above water, and areas like Japan, Yucatan and Florida were much larger.

The coastline of the Mediterranean was dramatically different; islands like Malta, Cyprus and Sardinia had larger territories while other sunken islands like Spartel were above sea level.

The meltdown that occurred at the end of the Ice Age, about 12,000 years ago, must have been dramatic and possibly catastrophic. Research indicates that a huge body like the Black Sea was formed in only a few years, if not much sooner. Sundaland fractured into Indonesia and the Malay Peninsula when the continental shelves were inundated by the encroaching waters, destroying any human settlements that may have existed. Virtually every culture has the legend of a devastating flood that may have originated from this distant time. Probably the most famous and enduring inundation legend is the 2,500-year-old story of Atlantis as recounted by the Greek philosopher Plato.

The 21st century is proving to be a fascinating time for underwater archaeology. Discoveries are being reported on a monthly basis, not only in the Old World but also in the New World and Asia. Lakes and inland seas are also providing fertile ground for archaeology. It is very likely that the greatest archeological discoveries of the 21st century will not be made in jungles, deserts or mountains but on the continental shelves which surround the landmasses.

PART 1
THE DISCREDITED SCIENCE OF CATASTROPHISM

**SUPERFLOODS, VOLCANOES, EARTHQUAKES
AT THE END OF THE ICE AGE
PLATE TECTONICS VS SUNKEN CONTINENTS
ANCIENT CONTINENTS
KERGUELEN, SUNKEN RIDGES, LAND
BRIDGES AND ISLANDS
THE GAS BELT HYPOTHESIS
IMPACTS FROM COMETS, ASTEROIDS OR
METEORS?
ANCIENT TSUNAMIS
FLOOD MYTHS FROM AROUND THE WORLD**

This chapter explores the possibility that lost civilizations, unknown to archaeologists, could have existed and been destroyed by natural cataclysms during the last Ice Age.

CATASTROPHISM
SUPERFLOODS, VOLCANOES, EARTHQUAKES AT THE END OF THE ICE AGE

At the height of the last Ice Age, (known as the Last Glacial Maximum or LGM) from 25,000 to 18,000 years ago, the oceans were hundreds of feet lower than at present, exposing millions of extra square miles around the continents. The water was locked up in the huge ice caps which covered most of North America, Europe and the poles to a depth of up to two miles (four km.) These sunken lands could easily have supported human populations or even unknown civilizations. The possibility that unknown civilizations could have been inundated has failed to excite mainstream historians, although alternative writers and scholars have been searching for such sunken lands as Atlantis since the nineteenth century. The most concerted effort to examine submerged ruins belongs to author Graham Hancock, whose seminal book *Underworld, Flooded Kingdoms of the Ice Age* describes his diving excursions to ruins on at least three continents.

Prior to the adoption of Darwin's Theory of Evolution by academics, two main schools of thought about the Earth's prehistory and geology fought for dominance: Catastrophism and Uniformitarianism. Catastrophists, led by Cuvier, believed that massive and cataclysmic events such as earthquakes, volcanoes and tsunamis helped shape the landscape of our planet. They also generally believed that God had been responsible for such catastrophes as the Noachian flood, although Cuvier was not interested in divine cataclysms. The Uniformitists, particularly Lyell and Hutton, rejected religious intervention and accepted the Darwinian doctrine that changes had occurred gradually over long periods of time.

The dominance of Darwinism in such disciplines as Geology, Science, Prehistory and Anthropology has relegated Catastrophism to the back burner, although scientists are now acknowledging that cataclysms such as comet impacts, mega quakes, tsunamis and super volcanoes contributed to the mass extinctions which took place at various intervals in the Earth's history. The Indian Ocean tsunami of 2004 which claimed over a quarter of a million victims also forced scientists to look for past events of a similar magnitude, resulting in the discovery of huge tsunamis in the ancient Pacific, Atlantic, Indian Oceans and Mediterranean Sea.

Palaeontologists and Prehistorians have always studied human evolution within Darwinian parameters and simply refuse to acknowledge the possibility that humans could have developed civilizations in areas now inundated by the oceans. It is thought provoking to realise that at the height of the last Ice Age, the Earth's surface differed in these areas:

10

• Alaska and Siberia were connected by a land bridge across the Bering Strait called Beringia. Archeologists have determined that the first Americans, the Clovis people, crossed Beringia during the Ice Age.

• Southern England was joined to northern France where the English Channel now lies.

• Mediterranean islands and coastlines were much larger than today. Malta was joined to Sicily and Italy while Corsica and Sardinia were one island. Cyprus was much larger.

• Various shelves and shoals in the North Atlantic were above land, such as the Celtic Shelf and Dogger Bank in an area known as Doggerland.

• The Black and Caspian Seas were mainly dry land.

• The Persian Gulf to the Strait of Hormuz was dry with the exception of three large lakes 17,000 years ago.

• India's coastlines extended and Sri Lanka was joined to the south. The Maldives were much larger.

• A huge continent known as Sundaland comprised Indonesia, Malaysia, Thailand and parts of the Philippines.

• China was much larger, with Taiwan attached to the mainland. Japan formed a peninsula joining greater Korea to Siberia.

• The continent of Sahul incorporated Australia, New Guinea and Tasmania as well as many areas to the north of Australia.

• Many Pacific islands formed a larger archipelago.

• The Grand Bahama Banks were above water.

• Florida and the Yucatan were larger in area.

From 18,000 to 7,000 years ago the massive ice caps melted, raising the ocean levels by up to 300 feet (130 meters.) Twenty five million square miles, or five percent of the Earth's surface was swallowed by the rising sea levels during this time. Most scientists assume that the sea levels rose gradually, perhaps half a meter per century in a process known as the eustatic rise.

However, this assumption fails to take into account the process of istostacy, whereby land and sea levels are changed dramatically and extensively. One agent of istostacy was the weight of the icecaps which forced the earth's crust into basin like depressions beneath. Eventually when the ice melted, the pressure was removed and the basin floor rebounded. This is still occurring today in areas such as the Baltic Sea which are rising about a meter every century. Furthermore, istostacy occurs more frequently in certain areas. Around this zone of 'post glacial rebound' is a 'peripheral zone of submergence' — which, simply, is a larger area of rebound. For instance, while the Scottish highlands might be rising, other areas of Britain are sinking.

Other more recent theories, such as Professor Emiliani's ice dams, postulate that the post Ice Age flooding may not have been gradual at all. He believes that huge ice dams holding up massive lakes and melting water were breached during this time, causing catastrophic floods. One such super dam collapsed in the American northwest 13,500 years ago, causing a massive amount of water to raise the sea level at least sixty meters. Other glacial lakes such as Agassiz in Canada and the Baltic Ice Lake collapsed, releasing huge volumes of water across the land and into the oceans. The Black Sea was also transgressed by waters from the Mediterranean, as Robert Ballard's underwater excavation verifies.

Another theory, the superflood, is proposed by geologist Professor Shaw. He has traced three superfloods:
1. 15,000-14,000 years ago.
2. 12,000-11,000 years ago.
3. 8,000-7000 years ago.

These superfloods could have been easily caused by the collapse of the ice dams or from increased volcanism which occurred during those times. Indeed, tephra from heavy volcanism has been discovered on the Mediterranean bed from the period of 17,000 until 6,000 years ago. Furthermore, huge earthquakes, such as the one which created the Parvie 'rock tsunami' in Sweden, occurred during this period, as well as a rapid increase in world temperatures.

Author Graham Hancock, who assessed the impact of these events in his book 'Underworld' wrote: "Marine archaeologists have barely even begun a systematic survey for possible submerged sites on these flooded lands. Most would regard it as a waste of time even to look. In consequence, whether in Australia or Europe, the Middle East or South East Asia the enormous implications of the changes in land-use and rising sea-levels between 17,000 and 7,000 years ago, do not appear ever to have been seriously considered by historians and archaeologists seeking the origins of civilization." (pp 54-55)

However, since the new millennium, research has been undertaken off the coasts of America, Europe, India and Cyprus, yielding new information about populations at the end of the Ice Age. While this research is mainly revealing evidence of thriving Mesolithic communities, controversial discoveries in India are providing tantalising clues to a lost pre Harappan civilization which is now underwater.

REFERENCE: G. Hancock, 'Underworld, Flooded Kingdoms of the Ice Ages'.

PLATE TECTONICS vs SUNKEN CONTINENTS

During the nineteenth century many prominent geologists accepted the idea that continents had been submerged by seismic activity in the distant past. This idea waned in the twentieth century when the theories of Continental Drift and Plate Tectonics firmly denied the possibility of large landmasses rising or sinking to the ocean floor.

The theory of Continental Drift underpins the current geological paradigm of Plate Tectonics. Alfred Wegener, who invented the phrase in 1912, published the hypothesis that the continents, once part of a singular land mass, had somehow drifted apart by the centrifugal force of the Earth's rotation. Like others before him, he noticed how the shapes of the continents on both sides of the Atlantic Ocean seem to fit together. Of course, this theory allows for no sunken continents.

Although initially ignored by many geologists, Wegener's Continental Drift theory gained momentum with the discovery of seafloor spreading whereby new oceanic crust is apparently formed through volcanic activity at the mid-ocean ridges.

The theory of Plate Tectonics, which encompassed both Continental Drift and Seafloor spreading, was developed in the 1960s by geologist Harry Hess to explain large scale motions of the Earth's lithosphere (crust and upper mantle). This lithosphere is broken up into tectonic plates which ride on the asthenosphere, a solid structure which can flow like a liquid over vast time scales beneath the Earth's surface.

The Earth's tectonic plates

These plates are about 60 miles deep (100 km) and consist of both continental (sial) and oceanic crust (sima). Each plate adjoins another along a plate boundary, areas commonly associated with earthquakes, volcanoes and oceanic trenches. A subduction zone occurs where two tectonic plates move towards each other and one slides underneath the other towards the mantle. Without the process of subduction, plate tectonics could not exist. It also causes the formation of oceanic trenches as it is in subduction zones that one plate begins its descent beneath another. The most devastating and deepest earthquakes, such as the one which produced the Indian Ocean tsunami of 2004, occur on subduction zones.

The main continental plates are the African, Antarctic, Australian, Eurasian, North American and South American while the Pacific Plate is oceanic. The movement of these plates caused the formation and breakup of continents over billions of years, including the supercontinents Rodinia, Pangaea, Laurasia and Gondwana.

By the 1960s and 70s the theory of Plate Tectonics, which incorporated both Continental Drift and seafloor spreading, had been totally embraced by the scientific community. However, since then there still have been some dissenting voices, particularly as the number of observational anomalies has increased. Some of these anomalies are:

> • Seismic research shows that under the oceans there is no continuous asthenosphere, and the oldest parts of the continents extending up to 600 km have no asthenosphere beneath.
>
> • Seismotomography does not reveal mantle deep convection

currents.

• Several plate boundaries are purely theoretical and could be nonexistent, such as the North American, Eurasian and southern boundary of the Pacific plate.

• Maps which show evidence of one supercontinent always contain glaring omissions such as Central America which cannot fit into the model. Submarine structures which may be of continental origin are also ignored, such as the Jan Mayen Ridge and Falkland Plateau.

• Palaeomagnetic data which supports the theory of continental drift can be unreliable and produce inconsistent results.

• India, which supposedly drifted from the Antarctic to collide with the Asian plate, has many characteristics which indicate it has always been attached to Asia.

• According to the theory of seafloor spreading, most rocks should be very young in geological age. However, various samples obtained from the Mid-Atlantic Ridge were found to be between 1,690 and 1,550 million years old. Such examples as Bald Mountain are explained away by geologists as glacial remains.

• Plate tectonics dictates that the volume of crust generated at mid-ocean ridges is equalled by the volume subducted. However, there are 80,000 km of mid-ocean ridges supposedly producing new crust and only 30,500 km of trenches.

• Both Africa and Antarctica are surrounded by plates but there is no evidence of spreading ridges and corresponding subduction zones.

•Large scale uplifts and subsidences which have characterised the evolution of the Earth's crust, particularly those in continental interiors, such as marine strata discovered high in the Himalayas, can't be explained by Plate tectonics.

• The vast majority of all sedimentary rocks comprising the continents were laid down under the sea. Because most of these seas on the present continents were shallow, less than 250 meters, they are described as 'epicontinental'. However, this does not account for about one hundred cycles of sea level changes which may have occurred because of slow vertical movements.

• Another problem for plate tectonics is of the many submarine plateaux and ridges scattered throughout the oceans which were once above water. Their crusts are much thicker than the average seafloor crust and their existence cannot be explained in the spreading seafloor hypothesis. Furthermore, shallow-water deposits from the Jurassic to Miocene eras have been found in boreholes drilled in the Atlantic, Indian and Pacific Oceans, indicating that many parts of the ocean floor were once shallow seas, marshes or land areas.

Full discussion of these anomalies can be found at:

http://ourworld.compuserve.com/homepages/dp5/sunken.htm

Another theory, called Vertical Tectonics, is based upon the teachings of Madame Blavatsky, founder of the Theosophical tradition. In the late nineteenth century she wrote in 'The Secret Doctrine 2.787: "Elevation and subsidence of continents in always in progress…The Alps, Himalayas and Cordilleras were all the result of depositions drifted on to sea-bottoms and upheaved by titanic forces to their present elevation. The Sahara was the basin of a Miocene sea…Why may not a gradual change have given place to a violent cataclysm in remote epochs? Such cataclysms occurring on a minor scale even now." (She was referring to the 1883 eruption of Krakatoa which caused a deadly tsunami.)

Another new hypothesis of geodynamics is Surge Tectonics by Arthur Meyerhoff, which rejects both continental drift and seafloor spreading. It postulates that all major features of the Earth's surface are underlain by shallow magma chambers and channels known as surge channels. These form an interconnected worldwide network which is characterised by micro-earthquakes and high heat flow. Surge tectonics postulates that the main cause of geodynamics is lithosphere compression, generated by the cooling and contraction of the Earth.

REFERENCES: Wikipedia articles on Plate Tectonics,

Continental Drift
http://ourworld.compuserve.com/homepages/dp5/sunken.htm

ANCIENT CONTINENTS

According to the theory of Continental Drift, the Earth originally had one large continent called Rodinia during the Precambrian age, up to 650 million years ago.

- By 514 million years ago Rodinia had broken up into Laurentia, Siberia and Baltica while a large continent called Gondwana existed in the southern hemisphere. Australia, South America, India, Africa and Antarctica were all part of this great southland.
- By the late Carboniferous era about 306 million years ago, the continents that make up North America collided with Gondwana to form the western half of the super continent of Pangaea. Much of Gondwana was covered by ice.
- 240 million years ago, during the Triassic era, Pangaea and Gondwana formed a huge landmass stretching from the North to South polar areas. The Tethys Ocean separated it from north and south China.
- 195 million years ago the continent of Laurasia begin to split between North America and Asia.
- By the late Jurassic period, 152 million years ago, Pangaea was breaking apart, Eastern and Western Gondwana were separating while the Central Atlantic Ocean was beginning to separate Africa from North America.
- During the Cretaceous, about 94 million years ago, parts of Northern Africa and North America were beneath water. India had separated from Gondwana, which now consisted only of Australia and Antarctica.
- By the Miocene, 14 million years ago, the continents had assumed their modern shape, Antarctica was covered by ice and India had joined Asia, causing the Himalayas to rise. Florida and parts of Europe were covered by water.

Other continents are now submerged under the sea which

were once dry land such as Sundaland, Kerguelen and Zealandia. Sundaland is the area now comprising Indonesia and the Malayan peninsula which formed a huge continent until large parts were inundated during the last Ice Age. Zealandia, also known as Tasmantis, sank after breaking away from Australia about 80 million years ago and Gondwana about 130 million years ago.

Zealandia, which was 3,400,000 km 2 in area, stretched from New Caledonia in the north to New Zealand's sub-antarctic islands in the south (about 19 to 56 degrees south.) Major parts of Zealandia are the Lord Howe Rise, Norfolk Ridge and Chatham Islands.

KERGUELEN

In 1999 the Joint Oceanographic Institutions for Deep Earth Sampling (JOIDES) discovered a huge continent sized plateau about 3,000 km to the southwest of Australia. This plateau, about a third the size of Australia, was the remains of a lost continent which sank beneath the ocean about 20 million years ago. Core samples revealed fragments of wood, spores and pollen in sediment 90 million years old, as well as many volcanic rocks.

The Kerguelen Plateau contains sedimentary rocks similar to those found in Australia and India, indicating that they were once connected.

Scientists know that Kerguelen extends for over 2,000 km and now lies about two km beneath the surface of the ocean. They believe that it was a remnant of the supercontinent of Gondawanaland which broke up many millions of years ago. Today a few scattered islands are all that remain of the Kerguelen group, including Grand Terre, Heard and Macdonald islands.

SUNKEN RIDGES, LAND BRIDGES AND ISLANDS

A land bridge is a narrow area which links two larger land masses. Such bridges existed during the Ice Age linking Siberia to Alaska at Beringia, Britain to France, Denmark to Sweden, India to Sri Lanka and the Philippines to Sundaland, to name but a few. These areas are ripe for underwater archeological excavation and are yielding valuable clues about life at the height of the Ice Age in both Europe and North America.

Ridges, seamounts, guyots are all underwater mountain features which exist throughout the oceans. The most famous ridges are the Mid Atlantic and Mid Pacific Ridges, areas of intense seismic and volcanic activity.

The Azores, Canaries and Madeiras are all mountain tops of the Mid Atlantic Ridge which extends from pole to pole. The Atlas Mountains in northern Africa extend into the Atlantic where a land bridge must have existed between these islands and the continent until about 17,000 years ago. For more information on the Mid Atlantic Ridge see page 93.

In July 1976 the Deep Sea Drilling Project discovered an underwater mountain range connecting southern Greenland with Ireland and Europe.

The Azores-Gibraltar Ridge, a plateau of a sunken landmass connected to the southern Iberian coast, was once a land bridge from Europe to a large Atlantic island which sank on the Vema fault, possibly only 7,000 years ago.

Other ridges are : 1. The Atlantic-Indian Ridge, East Pacific Rise, Explorer Ridge, Gakket (Mid Arctic) Gorda, Juan de Fuca, Mid-Indian, Nazca, Pacific-Antarctic, Reykjanes, Central Indian, Southeast Indian, and South West Indian Ridge.

Seamounts are submarine mountains that do not reach the water's surface. They are usually extinct volcanoes which are often found rising from the seafloor at depths of 1,000 to 4,000 meters. There are about 30,000 seamounts around the world. The shallowest, the Bowie Seamount, rises within 24 meters of the surface off the coast of British Columbia. Some seamounts may have been above land during the Ice Age. Various Atlantic seamounts such as the Horseshoe, Josephine and Ampere which can be found directly across from the Straits of Gibraltar were targeted for exploration by Russian Atlantologists during the Soviet era. Another sunken bank, the Dogger, which is part of the Celtic shelf, has also been suggested as the location of Atlantis by a Russian researcher.

The Emperor Seamounts are an extension of the Hawaiian islands, formed millions of years ago by volcanism.

The north Atlantic Rockall Plateau is another elevated area adjacent to the Rockall Trough. The Anton Dohrn Seamount is a

19

submarine elevation on the Rockall Trough halfway between the tiny island of Rockall and the Outer Hebrides.

THE GAS BELT HYPOTHESIS

In the decades before Plate Tectonics was adopted as the dominant theory concerning the composition of the Earth's crust, the idea of the 'gas belt system' or 'travelling volcanism' attracted adherents such as James Churchward, famous for his 'Mu' books.

Churchward believed that the Earth is traversed by deep gas belts lying about 12 to 18 miles beneath the surface. When a blockage develops along the belt, earthquakes result if this blockage is not alleviated by a volcanic eruption along a gas line. These gas chambers undergo catastrophic collapses at various times, causing subsidence and submersion of lands. This collapse caused the submersion of the Pacific continent of Mu, with the loss of 64,000,000 souls, according to Churchward.

Churchward cited examples of various earthquakes and volcanoes occurring along the same gas belt line. For instance, when San Francisco experienced its devastating quake in 1906, Mt Etna in Sicily erupted. Mt Etna has also erupted simultaneously with quakes in Vanuatu (1976), and Indonesia in 1979 because they were all points on the S. Great Central Belt. Furthermore, three days before the catastrophic quake tsunami hit the Indian Ocean in late 2004, a huge earthquake occurred in the Southern Ocean, although, fortunately, no-one was injured.

Edgar Cayce, the 'sleeping prophet', also spoke of this phenomenon of travelling volcanism in some of his readings. He warned, "If there are greater activities in the Vesuvius, or Pelee, then the southern coast of California, and the areas between Salt Lake and the southern portions of Nevada, may expect, within three months following same, an inundation by earthquakes." (Reading #270 35)

Mt Pelee, on the Caribbean island of Martinique, is, according to Churchward, "The most dangerous spot in the world…It's on the active Great Central Belt, and at this area it runs only a few miles below the surface: it's mentioned in the Troano MS, having submerged lands long ago." (J. Churchward, 'Cosmic Forces')

20

Although Churchward's theory is discredited today, methane chambers are now acknowledged to exist beneath the Earth's crust and seabed. Dr Thomas Gold of Cornell claims methane gas deposits lie deep in the Earth in huge chambers and can, under certain conditions, convert into oil. It is also feared that such chambers may constitute a potential hazard to humans and animals as occurred when Cameroon's Lake Nyos out gassed deadly methane and carbon dioxide in 1986.

REFERENCES: http://www.bibliotecapleyades.net/arqueologia/esp_churchward02.htm

J. Churchward, 'Cosmic Forces'

IMPACTS FROM COMETS, ASTEROIDS OR METEORS?

In the late 19th century the theory arose that Atlantis and other continents were sunk when a huge comet or asteroid smashed into the Earth. Originating with Ignatius Donnelly's book 'Ragnarok, Age of Fire and Gravel', the comet theory was championed by cosmologist Martin Hoerbiger and author Henry Bellamy. German rocket scientist, geologist and prehistorian Dr Otto Mück in his 1950s book 'Alles uber Atlantis' believed that a huge meteor, known as the Carolina Meteorite, hit the western Atlantic in 8498 BC. This meteorite formed numerous craters and bays such as the Carolina Bays. His book was published in English in 1978 as 'The Secret of Atlantis'.

Mück dates this event by comparing it with the Mayan calendar which he alleges commemorated the destruction of Atlantis. This 'asteroid A' crashed into one of the thinnest regions on the Earth's crust—the Mid-Atlantic Ridge, where it created the Puerto Rico Trench. The impact caused craters, deep sea holes, massive earthquakes and tsunamis which were remembered in myths and legends from around the world as the Great Flood. Anomalous oceanic features such as the Blue Holes of the Bahamas and Carolina Bays were scars from this catastrophic event.

Mück's carefully crafted thesis discussed the probability that the impact caused every volcano across the Atlantic Ocean to erupt. This had the effect of 30,000 hydrogen bombs exploding in unison. A 'juncture line' (subduction fault line) encircled the Azores Plateau, which was sitting on a 'platelet' of its own. The pressures from asteroid strike caused huge amounts of magma and gases to erupt all around this 'platelet', causing the sea floor beneath to subside. With a dramatic reduction of pressure underneath, the island of Atlantis was submerged with the platelet, leaving only the Azores and its mountain Pico Alto.

Huge amounts of water vapour were ejected into the sky and fell down as rain which caused flooding throughout the world. Furthermore, the sinking of Atlantis caused the Gulf Stream to form which in turn resulted in the warming of Northern Europe. The great ice caps of Europe melted, releasing so much water that the ocean levels were raised by about four hundred feet, creating an island now known as Britain.

Mück calculated the date at 8498 BC because on that day the sun, moon and Earth were in conjunction with each other. This created a gravitational pull which drew the comet into earth orbit.

Another scholar, Professor M. Kamienski of Krakow University, believes that in 9546 or 9540 BC a portion of Halley's comet fell into the Gulf of Mexico, causing catastrophic floods and natural disasters.

Contemporary scholars such as Andrew Collins have also theorised that a comet broke up over the Atlantic about twelve thousand years ago, causing the land of Atlantis to sink. His book 'Gateway to Atlantis' in 2000 proposed that a comet rained down on the Caribbean at the end of the Pleistocene era, causing massive fire storms across North America which killed off many species such as camels, mastodons etc. This comet, striking from the northwest, had disintegrated into pieces, causing catastrophic disasters from the Yukon to Florida. It also caused the onset of the Younger Dryas, or mini Ice Age, after the ice sheets had been steadily retreating.

In 2007 this theory suddenly became acceptable to researchers of various disciplines who proposed that an extraterrestrial object, probably a comet, exploded above North America nearly 13,000 years ago. For the first time this theory was discussed publicly in a May 23 news conference of the Joint Assembly of the American Geophysical Union in Acapulco.

The impact of the comet had a catastrophic effect upon North

America and the world. Scientists from the University of California at Santa Barbara believe that the comet was originally about four km across and either exploded in the atmosphere or had fragments hit the Laurentide ice sheet in the north east. The ensuing firestorms killed off vegetation which in turn caused the extinction of large mammals such as the woolly mammoths. The Clovis culture also disappeared from the archeological record soon after, possibly from starvation caused by the collapse of the food chain.

Although the impact crater has not been discovered, high concentrations of iridium, usually associated with meteorites and comets, have been found in more than a dozen archeological sites in North America. The scientists also found metallic microspherules containing nano-diamonds which could have originated in a comet. Large depressions in the Great Lakes and Hudson Bay are suspected of originating from an extraterrestrial impact, as are the Carolina Bays.

The Santa Barbara team concluded that the impact of the comet destabilised a large portion of the Laurentide ice sheet causing a massive amount of freshwater to flow into the Atlantic and Arctic Oceans, thus disrupting the ocean's circulation. This in turn led to a cooling of the atmosphere and the Younger Dryas period.

http://www.physorg.com/news106410997.html

Such discoveries have vindicated Collins who wrote in *Alternative Perceptions Magazine* Issue 113, June 2007:

"The cataclysm I proposed that caused the destruction of Atlantis is identical to that being cited by the 25 strong scientific team at the American Geophysical Union last week. Using available evidence on the structure and dating of the Carolina Bays, a knowledge of the firestorms recorded in sentiments across the United States, as well as details of the flow of ice melt waters and the mass extinction of Pleistocene animals, I concluded that a comet had come out of the north-western skies and disintegrated into pieces, causing multiple aerial detonations across North America. This resulted in wide scale firestorms, massive explosions, tens of thousands of elliptical craters from the Yukon down to Florida, as well as the onset of the Younger Dryas, or mini Ice Age. This in turn led eventually to the end of the last Ice Age, with the drowning eventually of large areas of the Bahamas and Caribbean."

In July 2007 the findings were published in the 'Proceedings of the National Academy Sciences', with a mainstream segment on the National Geographic Channel.

The Topper site at a South Carolina river bluff, excavated by archaeologist Al Goodyear and geophysicist Allen West, provided evidence of Clovis artifacts, nano-diamonds, glasslike carbon and concentrations of iridium. This site drew international attention in 2004 when stone points sharpened by humans were carbon dated to nearly 50,000 years ago, much older than acceptable dating.

Goodyear found there were four times as many Clovis points as Redstone points at similar sites. Because archaeologists believe that the Redstone culture developed from the Clovis culture, this suggests that a huge population drop from Clovis to Redstone cultures was possibly caused by a natural catastrophe like a comet.

West has commented about the comet theory: "It has been pretty quickly embraced. People weren't comfortable with the existing theories on the disappearance of the large mammals and the Clovis people."

http://www.contracostatimes.com/nationandworld/ci_7110996?nclick_check=1

REFERENCES: 'Comet Could have Exploded Over North America 13,000 years Ago' http://www.physorg.com/news106410997.html

Contra Coastal Times

http://www.contracostatimes.com/nationandworld/ci_7110996?nclick_check=1

ANCIENT TSUNAMIS

The catastrophic Indian Ocean tsunami of late 2004 claimed up to 300,000 lives in the space of 24 hours. Prior to this event, few scientists were interested in studying tsunamis as they believed that they were very rare events. An exception is Ted Bryant of Wollongong University who has discovered that many such events occurred on the Pacific coast during Australia's prehistory. The following summary is of a selection of tsunamis which have occurred during the era of human habitation and may have been responsible for millions of deaths around the world.

MEDITERRANEAN:

A large earthquake and tsunami devastated the Mediterranean about 12,000 years ago, inundating small islands like Spartel. See page 40.

8,000 BP

In November 2006 scientists reported that a massive tsunami, triggered by a debris avalanche from Mt Etna in Sicily, ravaged the eastern Mediterranean about 8,000 years ago. The Mt Etna avalanche sent six cubic miles of rock and sediment tumbling into the water at more than two hundred miles per hour. Pummelling the seabed, it transformed thick layers of soft marine sediment into jelly, triggering an underwater mudslide. Researchers at the National Institute of Geophysics and Volcanoes in Italy used sonar equipped boats to survey the Ionian Sea floor sediment displaced by the avalanche.

They suggest that the tsunami reached heights of up to 165 feet in Sicily and Italy within fifteen minutes of the avalanche. At speeds of 450 miles per hour, the tsunami would have swamped Greece and Libya with 43 feet (13 meter) waves an hour later.

After devastating the Greek islands and Turkey, the waves would have reached Egypt and Israel in just over three hours.

Eight thousand years ago the shorelines of the Mediterranean were about 30 feet (10 meters) lower than at present, which compromises the identification of such tsunami deposits. However, a sunken Neolithic site in Israel, Atlit, which was suddenly abandoned eight thousand years ago, has been identified as a possible victim of the tsunami.

Any settlements on the coasts of southern Italy, Malta, Tunisia, western Greece or Libya would have been completely annihilated by the towering waves. Many thousands of people must have been killed by this event which was even more catastrophic than the 2004 Indian Ocean tsunami.

SANTORINI – About 1600 BC the explosive volcanic eruption of Thera caused massive tsunamis which inundated the Mediterranean and may have been instrumental in the demise of the

Minoan culture.

ATLANTIC:
NORTH ATLANTIC TSUNAMI circa 6100 BC

In prehistoric times three huge landslides occurred underwater on the edge of Norway's continental shelf causing huge tsunamis in the North Atlantic Ocean. Known as the Storegga Slides (Norwegian for Great Edge), three major underwater landslides caused a massive displacement of water. The first occurred sometime around 30,000 to 50,000 years ago. The second and third occurred about eight thousand years ago when an area the size of Iceland slid into the Norwegian Sea. The dimensions were staggering—a 290 kilometer (180 mile) stretch of coastal shelf, with a total area of 3,500 cubic km (840m3) caused a massive displacement of water which impacted the coasts of Scotland, Norway and the Shetlands.

In Norway, the coast shows evidence of a 10-20 meter tsunami. In Scotland traces of the tsunami have been recorded, with deposited sediment being discovered in the Firth of Forth, 80 kms (50 miles) inland and 4 meters (13 feet) above normal tide levels. Other parts of Britain show an inundation of about 25 meters above the High Water Mark. In the Shetland Islands evidence for this event is widely displayed along peat cliffs and low lying valleys. The greatest force of the tsunami was probably on the exposed headlands, but the greatest inundation was in inlets.

The Storegga Slide was first discovered in the late 1983 when Norwegian scientist Tom Bugge studied the underwater displacement and realised it had happened in three stages. In the 1980s Professor Alastair Dawson of the Aberdeen Institute for Coastal Management noticed a 'very curious' layer of sand in the land along the Scottish east coast. Originally thought of as storm sediment, he became aware of the Norwegian scientists who had done a study on Storegga and realised that the sediments in Scotland were related to this ancient catastrophic event.

INDIAN OCEAN TSUNAMIS

On November 14, 2006 the New York Times published an article called 'Ancient Crash Epic Wave' about a monstrous tsunami which struck the island of Madagascar circa 4,800 years ago. Huge wedge shaped chevron deposits containing sediments from the ocean floor fused with a mixture of metals are as deep as the Chrysler Building in Manhattan is high and twice the area of Manhattan. These chevrons point in the direction of a newly discovered crater at the bottom of the Indian Ocean, 18 miles in diameter and 12,500 feet below the surface.

Burckle crater was discovered in 2005 by Dr Dallas Abbott who estimates it to be between 4,500 to 5,000 years old.

The obvious explanation is that a large comet or asteroid smashed into the Indian Ocean 4,800 years ago, producing a monster tsunami at least 600 feet high. While many astronomers are skeptical that the chevrons were created by impact, scientists from the Holocene Impact Working Group are sure that a major impact occurs every millennium and can leave tell tale signs in chevrons. Dr Abbott uses satellite photography to scan the oceans for tell tale signs of deep depressions, such as changes in the ocean surface which occur when either mountains or depressions are beneath the surface.

Dr Abbott and her team have discovered chevrons in the Caribbean, Scotland, Vietnam, North Korea and the North Sea as well as one on Long Island and another in Connecticut. With colleagues from the Novosibirsk Tsunami Laboratory in Russia, she visited the huge chevrons on Madagascar to study samples. They were found to contain tiny fossils from the ocean floor as well as iron, nickel and chrome fused to the fossils which points to a chondritic meteor as the culprit.

Dr Ted Bryant from the University of Wollongong was the first person to recognise the signatures of mega-tsunamis. Such tsunamis leave deposits containing unusual rocks with marine oyster shells which cannot be explained by natural processes. Speaking of the Madagascar tsunami, he commented, "No tsunami in the modern world could have made these features. Aceh was a dimple. End of the world movies do not capture the size of these waves. Submarine landslides can cause major tsunamis but they are localised. These are deposited along whole coastlines."

Bruce Masse, an environmental archeologist at the Los Alamos National Laboratory believes that the comet fell on May 10, 2807

BC according to information contained in many flood myths from around the world, particularly those mentioning a full solar eclipse which occurred on that day.

REFERENCE: 'New York Times' November 14, 2006. 'Ancient Crash, Epic Wave' **http://www.nytimes.com/2006/11/14/science/14WAVE. html?ei=5090&en=35b395ffd080eb47&ex=1321160400&pagewanted=all**

FLOOD MYTHS FROM AROUND THE WORLD

Flood myths are an enduring theme from different cultures around the world, suggesting that early humans witnessed the devastating meltdown from the Ice Age and immortalised it in their legends.

Most ancient and indigenous cultures had a flood myth. This section summarises the huge variety of stories from around the world.

- The Greeks believed that Zeus had sent a flood to destroy the men of the 'Bronze Age'. They believed this flood was sent by the gods to punish a wicked race of people. The fountains of the deep opened, the rain fell and the seas and rivers rose to kill everyone except Deucalion and his family who built an ark.
- According to the Romans, Jupiter was angered by the impiety of humanity and decided to destroy it. "With Neptune's help, he caused storm and earthquake to flood everything but the summit of Parnassus, where Deucalion and his wife Pyrrha came by boat and found refuge." (Ovid book 1)
- The Scandinavian gods Odin, Vili and Ve slew the great ice giant Ymir and his icy blood drowned most of the Rime Giants.
- When the Welsh lake Llion flooded, Dwyfan and Dwyfach escaped in a mastless ship with animals. They landed in Britain and repopulated the world.
- The Lithuanian god Pamzimas sent two giants, water and wind, to destroy the world.
- The Sumerian god Enlil warned the priest king Ziusudra

of a coming flood and instructed him to build a great ship to rescue the animals. Then the floods covered the world for seven days and nights. Ziusudra survived and was granted eternal life for protecting the animals and seed of mankind.

• The God of the Hebrews set out to destroy wicked mankind, but Noah was righteous and warned in advance. For forty days and nights the floodwaters covered the earth and eventually Noah's ark came to rest on Mount Ararat.

• Ahriman, the evil god of the Persians, caused a flood which covered the whole earth.

• In Africa these tribes had a flood myth: Masai, Cameroon, Komililo, Kwaya, Pygmy, Yoruba, Kikuyu, Ekoi, Mandingo, Ababua, Bakongo Basonge.

• North Siberian tribes such as the Samoyed had a myth where the world was flooded and a handful of people survived.

• Central Asian tribes such as the Altai had a flood myth where a man called Nama and his sons built an ark into which many animals and birds were rescued.

• The ancient Indian Hindus had a myth in which a fish warned Manu, the first human, of a coming deluge. Manu alone of all creatures survived and a woman was fashioned from offerings of butter, whey and curds.

• Other Indian tribes such as those in Assam, Sikkim, Tamil Nadu, Bengal and Bhil had flood myths as did hill tribes in Burma, Thailand and China.

• Tibet was almost totally inundated until the god Gya took compassion on the survivors, emptied the waters through Bengal and sent teachers to civilize the people.

• The Chinese Supreme Sovereign ordered the water god Gong Gong to create a flood to punish wicked humanity. After many years Gong Gong was driven away and rivers were fashioned to channel the floodwaters to the sea.

• Many Asian island cultures such as the Bunum and Ami of Taiwan, as well as the Ifugao of the Philippines, Dayak of Borneo, Toraja of Sulawesi had flood myths.

• Many tribes from Australia, particularly Arnhem Land,

Western Australia and South Australia had stories of flooding waterholes or inundation from storms.

• The Polynesian creator god Tane caused a flood to convince a tribe of his superiority. For eight months the waters rose and only those who had built a large raft survived.

• Pacific Island cultures such as those in New Guinea, Vanuatu, the Carolines, Tahiti, Hawaii, Fiji, Samoa and the Cook islands had flood myths. In Hawaii the god Kane covered all the islands except the peak of Mauna Kea, where two people survived to punish men for their wickedness.

• North American tribes from the Innuit to the Haida, Kwaitukl, Squamish, Yakima, Cree, Blackfood, Obijway, Chippewa, Algonquin, Cherokee, Chocktaw, Lakota, Navajo, Hopi and Zuni all had extensive legends of floods.

• Of all the Central American tribes, the Maya are the most famous. Their flood myth involves an original race of dwarves who were destroyed by god because of their wickedness. The Maya believed they were of the Third Race, the previous others being destroyed by floods.

• There were many flood myths in South America, but the Incans had a legend that at one stage all the mountains were covered in water. The creator, Viroccocha, saved a man and woman who landed in Tiahuanaco. The creator fashioned a new race out of clay, as well as animals and plants.

Detailed studies of these legends can be found on the comprehensive website Flood Stories from Around the World by Mark Issak **http://www.talkorigins.org/faqs/flood-myths.html**

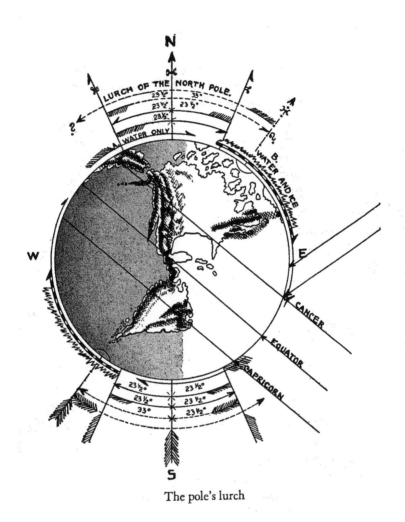

The pole's lurch

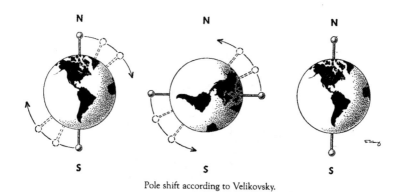

Pole shift according to Velikovsky.

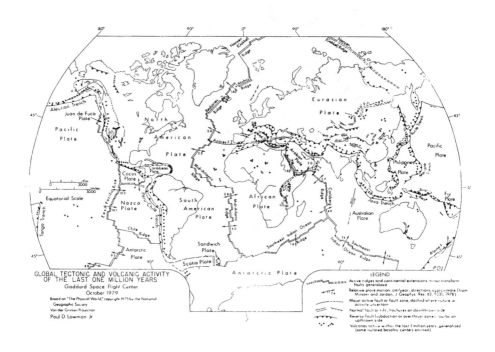

PART 2
PLATO'S ATLANTIS & RUINS NEAR
THE PILLARS OF HERCULES
PLATO'S LEGEND OF ATLANTIS
EARTHQUAKE AND TSUNAMI
12,000 BP—SPARTEL ATLANTIS CLAIMS
LOST CITIES OFF SPAIN
TARTESSOS
CLAIMS OF ATLANTEAN RUINS OFF CADIZ
AND GIBRALTAR
CLAIMS OF ATLANTIS IN CADIZ
RUINS OFF MOROCCO

This chapter looks at Plato's description of Atlantis and some of the alleged discoveries of sunken ruins which have been reported off Spain and Morocco near the ancient Pillars of Hercules.

PLATO'S LEGEND OF ATLANTIS

The legend of Atlantis is one of the most enduring stories of all time and has inspired thousands of writers, mystics and clairvoyants, each with his or her own theory. The original story, as recounted by the Greek philosopher Plato, concerns information given to his ancestor, the Athenian lawgiver Solon, by Egyptian priests in about 600 BC. It was a moral tale which spoke of arrogance, abuse of power and eventual destruction by the gods of Atlantis and its culture nearly twelve thousand years ago.

In addition to providing a moral tale of the abuse of power, Plato also gave many precise descriptions of the topography, architecture, culture, religion and foreign policy of Atlantis and its capital city. These precise descriptions have provoked endless speculation about the reality and whereabouts of this great culture in a way that no other legend has ever inspired.

Rather than discuss Plato's descriptions and speculate on the whereabouts of Atlantis, it is more cautious to merely summarize his works from the Dialogues of 'Timaeus' and 'Critias' which were both written in about 360 BC. Critias was Plato's great grandfather and Solon was his ancestor while Timaeus's identity is unknown. Solon was famous as the great Athenian lawgiver who provided the first Athenian constitution in about 600 BC, setting the city on the path to democracy.

It is beyond the scope of this book to analyse the endless claims about the location of Atlantis. They range from the Antarctic to America, Bolivia and nearly every country in the Mediterranean as well as the Atlantic and Caribbean islands. However, such claims will be discussed if they are supported by evidence of off shore ruins, anomalous underwater formations, legends or elaborately crafted theories. The reader can make up his or her own mind about all the subsequent claims which will be discussed in this book.

Selected quotes from Plato's 'Timaeus':

"There have been, and will be again, many destructions of mankind arising out of many causes; the greatest have been brought about by the agencies of fire and water, and other lesser ones by innumerable other causes."

"When, on the other hand, the gods purge the earth with a deluge of water, the survivors in your country are herdsmen and shepherds who dwell on the mountains, but those who, like you, live in cities are carried by the rivers into the sea. Whereas in this land, neither then nor at any other time, does the water come down from above on the fields, having always a tendency to come up from below; for which reason the traditions preserved here are the most ancient.

"For these histories tell of a mighty power which unprovoked made an expedition against the whole of Europe and Asia, and to which your city put an end. This power came forth out of the Atlantic Ocean, for in those days the Atlantic was navigable; and there was an island situated in front of the straits which are by you called the Pillars of Heracles; the island was larger than Libya and Asia put together, and was the way to other islands, and from these you might pass to the whole of the opposite continent which surrounded the true ocean; for this sea which is within the Straits of Heracles is only a harbour, having a narrow entrance, but that other is a real sea, and the surrounding land may be most truly called a boundless continent. Now in this island of Atlantis there was a great and wonderful empire which had rule over the whole island and several others, and over parts of the continent, and, furthermore, the men of Atlantis had subjected the parts of Libya within the columns of Heracles as far as Egypt, and of Europe as far as Tyrrhenia. This vast power, gathered into one, endeavoured to subdue at a blow our country and yours and the whole of the region within the straits; and then, Solon, your country shone forth, in the excellence of her virtue and strength, among all mankind. She was pre-eminent in courage and military skill, and was the leader of the Hellenes. And when the rest fell off from her, being compelled to stand alone, after having undergone the very extremity of danger, she defeated and triumphed over the invaders, and preserved from slavery those who were not yet subjugated, and generously liberated all the rest of us who dwell within the pillars. But afterwards there occurred violent earthquakes and floods; and in a single day and night of misfortune all your warlike men in a body sank into the earth, and the island of Atlantis in like manner disappeared in the depths of the sea. For which reason the sea in those parts is impassable and impenetrable, because there is a shoal of mud in the way; and this was caused by the subsidence of the island."

More points from 'Critias':

- Nine thousand years elapsed since war between Athens and Atlantis.
- Atlantis was commanded by ten kings.
- Atlantis an island greater in area than Libya and Asia.

• The island was sunk by earthquake and became an impassable barrier of mud to mariners sailing to any part of the ocean.

• In the centre of an island was a plain, very fertile.

• Near the plain and in the centre of the island at a distance of 50 stadia was a low mountain.

• Atlantis was first settled by the god Poseidon who received it as his allotment from his father. He seduced a mortal girl called Cleito, breaking the ground and enclosing the hill in which she dwelt all around making "alternate zones of sea and land larger and smaller, encircling one another, there were two of land and three of water, which he turned as with a lathe, each having its circumference equidistant every way from the centre, so no man could get to the island, for ships and voyages were not as yet."

• Poseidon brought two springs of water for his wife, one warm and one cold as well as abundant food for the island.

• Poseidon and Cleito had five pairs of male twins, and divided Atlantis into ten portions.

• The eldest son was named Atlas and whole island and ocean were named Atlantic.

• The second son had the extremity of island towards pillars of Hercules, facing the country with is now called Gades. (Spain)

• Sons and descendants of Poseidon and Cleito held sway over country within the pillars as far as Egypt and Tyrrhenia. (Italy)

• Atlantis was very rich. Orichalcum, more precious than anything except gold and unidentifiable today, was mined there.

• There were many elephants, wood, fruits, essences, suggesting a semi tropical climate.

• Atlantis prospered, constructing temples, palaces, harbors and docks.

• There were bridges over the zones of the sea surrounding metropolis, making a road to and from the royal palace

• "And beginning from the sea they bored a canal of three hundred feet in width and one hundred feet in depth and fifty stadia in length, which they carried through to the outermost zone, making a passage from the sea up to this, which became a harbour, and leaving an opening sufficient to enable the largest vessels to find ingress. Moreover, they divided at the bridges the zones of land which parted the zones of sea, leaving room for a single trireme to pass out of one zone into another, and they covered over the channels so as to leave a way underneath for the ships; for the banks were raised considerably above the water. Now the largest of the zones into which a passage was cut from the sea was three stadia in breadth, and the zone of land which came next of equal breadth; but the next two zones, the one of water, the other of land, were two stadia, and the one which surrounded the central island was a stadium only in width. The island in which the palace was situated had a diameter of five stadia. All this including the zones and the bridge, which was the sixth part of a stadium in width, they surrounded by a stone wall on every side, placing towers and gates on the bridges where the sea passed in. The stone which was used in the work they quarried from underneath the centre island, and from underneath the zones, on the outer as well as the inner side. One kind was white, another black, and a third red, and as they quarried, they at the same time hollowed out double docks, having roofs formed out of the native rock. Some of their buildings were simple, but in others they put together different stones, varying the colour to please the eye, and to be a natural source of delight. The entire circuit of the wall, which went round the outermost zone, they covered with a coating of brass, and the circuit of the next wall they coated with tin, and the third, which encompassed the citadel, flashed with the red light of orichalcum." There were palaces on the citadel as well as a holy temple to Cleito and Poseidon surrounded by an enclosure of gold.

• Poseidon's temple was a stadium in length and half a

stadium in width of proportionate height. Its exterior was covered in silver with pinnacles of gold, the interior had an ivory roof, wrought with silver, gold and orichalcum. Walls, pillars and floor were also covered in orichalcum.

• In the temple they placed statues of gold: Poseidon on chariot with six winged horses and a hundred Nereids riding on horses. There were also images and statues of ancestors.

• There was a large and magnificent altar as well as:

• Hot and cold fountains with cisterns, some open and some closed for bathing. Separate baths for kings, women and animals. Aqueducts carried water along bridges to the outer circles.

• There were many temples, gardens and places for exercise as well as a racecourse a stadium in width and in length all around the island for horses to race.

• Guardhouses for guards, the most trusted near the citadel.

• Docks full of ships and naval stores.

There was a wall which began at the sea and went all round— 50 stadia from the largest zone or harborand enclosed the whole, the ends meeting at the mouth of the channel which led to the sea. The area had many houses where the merchants lived. There were also canals and harbors full of ships.

"The whole country was said by him to be very lofty and precipitous on the side of the sea, but the country immediately about and surrounding the city was a level plain, itself surrounded by mountains which descended towards the sea; it was smooth and even, and of an oblong shape, extending in one direction three thousand stadia, but across the centre inland it was two thousand stadia. This part of the island looked towards the south, and was sheltered from the north. The surrounding mountains were celebrated for their number and size and beauty …and rivers, and lakes, and meadows supplying food enough for every animal, wild or tame, and much wood."

The plain "was for the most part rectangular and oblong, and

38

where falling out of the straight line followed the circular ditch. The depth, and width, and length of this ditch were incredible, and gave the impression that a work of such extent, in addition to so many others, could never have been artificial. ...It was excavated to the depth of a hundred, feet, and its breadth was a stadium everywhere; it was carried round the whole of the plain, and was ten thousand stadia in length. It received the streams which came down from the mountains, and winding round the plain and meeting at the city, was there let off into the sea. Further inland, likewise, straight canals of a hundred feet in width were cut from it through the plain, and again let off into the ditch leading to the sea: these canals were at intervals of a hundred stadia, and by them they brought down the wood from the mountains to the city, and conveyed the fruits of the earth in ships, cutting transverse passages from one canal into another, and to the city."

   • The men of Atlantis had to do military service in lots, each being 10 stadia square. Total number of lots was 60,000. Leaders were required to furnish part of a war chariot, making 10,000 chariots, also 2 horses, armed soldiers, slingers, javelin throwers and four sailors.
   • The ten kings had absolute control of the citizens, and the laws. Commands of Poseidon were inscribed on pillars of orichalcum at the temple of Poseidon."There were many special laws affecting the several kings inscribed about the temples, but the most important was the following: They were not to take up arms against one another, and they were all to come to the rescue if anyone in any of their cities attempted to overthrow the royal house; like their ancestors, they were to deliberate in common about war and other matters, giving the supremacy to the descendants of Atlas. And the king was not to have the power of life and death over any of his kinsmen unless he had the assent of the majority of the ten."
   • For many generations the kings were obedient to the laws and virtue. Eventually human nature got the upper hand and they became greedy and cruel. Zeus decided to

inflict punishment on the island.

The narrative ended at this critical point leading the world to wonder about Atlantis for over two thousand years.

Not surprisingly this original description of Atlantis had a decidedly Hellenic flavor. It is fascinating to study how the Atlantean myth developed over the next three millennia, particularly influenced by the writings of the Theosophists who elevated the myth to a new level in the late 1800s.

Atlantis explorers usually fall into two categories; those who use Plato's descriptions and those who are influenced by the writings of Madame Blavatsky and Edgar Cayce. The disparity between the two possibly accounts for the huge range of claims proclaiming the 'discovery of Atlantis'. Indeed, in recent years Atlantis has been confidently located in Cyprus, Malta, Santorini, the Azores, Canaries, Bahamas, Indonesia and Turkey to name but a few.

Translations of the 'Timaeus' and 'Critias' by Benjamin Jowett can be found at this site:
http://www.activemind.com/Mysterious/Topics/Atlantis/timaeus_ and_critias.html

EARTHQUAKE AND TSUNAMI c12,000 BP

SPARTEL AS ATLANTIS CLAIMS

A large earthquake and tsunami hit the Mediterranean about twelve thousand years ago at the end of the Ice Age, coinciding with Plato's date for the destruction of Atlantis. This event may have been responsible for the inundation of numerous islands, such as Spartel, now submerged by 175-410 feet (54 to 125m) of water in the Gulf of Cadiz between Spain and Morocco. Contemporary researchers such Georgeos Díaz-Montexano, Jacques Collina-Girard and as Marc Gutscher have hypothesised that Spartel may have been Atlantis, although there is animated controversy as to who originated the theory.

Diaz-Montexano, a Cuban researcher, first published his

Atlantis-Spartel theory in an April 2000 issue of Spanish magazine 'Mas Alla de la Ciencia' and in August 2001 'El Museo' and 'Ano Cero'. As an independent researcher, his Spartel theory did not have much credence until a similar theory was proposed by French geologist Collina-Girard of the University of Aix en Provence. His original article, 'L'Atlantide devant le Detroit de Gibraltar? mythe et géologie.' was published in 'The French Academy of Science' in September 2001.

Atlantis, according to Collina-Girard, was twenty miles (32km) south west of Tarifa Spain, and twelve miles (19km) north west of Tangier, Morocco. He wrote in the 'Proceedings of the French Academy of Sciences', "Atlantis was an island situated in front of the Straits which were called the Pillars of Hercules as Critias tells Socrates."

He was interested in studying patterns of human migration between North Africa and Europe at the height of the Ice Age and constructed a map of the European coastline which was 130 meters lower than at present. His reconstruction reveals an ancient archipelago, with an island Spartel just beyond 'the Pillars of Hercules'. About 11,000 years ago, or 9,000 years before Plato, Spartel was inundated by the rising waters of the post-glacial sea.

Although Spartel was only 14 km wide at its largest, Collina-Girard still argued that Plato had misinterpreted the figures of Atlantean statistics which had been given to Solon by the Egyptians. He also believes that the Greeks invented a story of volcanic eruptions sinking Atlantis to make the story more dramatic than a gradual inundation by the sea.

Hampered by his lack of credibility, Diaz-Montexano doggedly defends his claims that he originated this popular theory on the website 'Atlantis in Gibraltar, Between Iberia and Africa' : **http://usuarios.lycos.es/atlantisiberia/release_news.htm**

In 2005 the Journal 'Geology' published an article by Marc-Andre Gutscher of the University of Western Brittany in Plouzane, France, of a seafloor survey which discovered deposits of 50—120cm resulting from an ancient tsunami.

41

This tsunami, which took place about 12,000 years ago, was caused by a magnitude 9 earthquake.

At first Gutscher's analysis seemed to indicate that Spartel would have been uninhabitable as long as 14,000 years ago, but sediments obtained convinced him that Spartel would have been big enough to be inhabited at the time of the tsunami. He posits that Spartel could have been a candidate for Atlantis even though the island would have been less than five hundred meters wide 12,000 years ago.

Gutscher noticed thick 'turbidite' deposits (sand and mud shaken by underwater avalanches) resulting from sediments that have been shaken by up to eight underwater geological upheavals since the end of the Ice Age. Each earthquake could have resulted in a drop of the sea floor by several meters. The abstract for this article, 'Destruction of Atlantis by a great earthquake and tsunami? A geological analysis of the Spartel bank hypothesis' can be found

http://geology.about.com/gi/dynamic/offsite.htm?zi=1/XJ&sd n=geology&cdn=education&tm=26&f=00&tt=2&bt=1&bts=1&zu =http%3A//www.gsajournals.org/gsaonline/%3Frequest%3Dget- abstract%26doi%3D10.1130/G21597.1

Mapping of submerged Spartel by Dr Gutscher failed to turn up any man-made structures and showed that the island was much smaller than previously believed." I was hoping to find concentric structures or walls of some kind but we didn't," he admitted.

LOST CITIES OFF SPAIN

Spain occupies the unique position of having coastlines on both the Atlantic Ocean and Mediterranean Sea. As such, many Atlantean researchers such as Elena Whishaw, Maxine Asher and Georges Diaz-Montexano have concentrated on this country, particularly the area around Cadiz which lies just beyond the 'Pillars of Hercules' (Gibraltar). Spain also has its own lost city of Tartessos which was well known in ancient times and may have been inundated by an earthquake or the rising sea in classical times.

TARTESSOS

Tartessos was a city in southern Spain which was well known in ancient times by the Greeks and Carthaginians. It was referred to as Tarshish in the Bible. Herodotus mentioned "a city called Tartessos...beyond the Pillars of Hercules." However, Tartessos disappeared in ancient times and still has not been definitely located.

The Old Testament has several references to this Spanish city. In 11 Chronicles 9:21 it says; "For the kings went to Tarshish with the servants of Huram: every three years once came the ships of Tarshish bringing gold, and silver, ivory, apes and peacocks."

A later biblical reference in Isiah 23:1 refers to the destruction of Tarshish in "The burden of Tyre, Howl, ye ships of Tarshish; for it is laid waste, so that there is no house, no entering in: from the land of Chittim (Crete) it is revealed to them." In this quote, Tarshish is associated with both Crete and Tyre in Phonecia (Lebanon).

The Tartessians were traders who were experienced in working with and transporting the tin used to create bronze. One of their trading partners, the Phonecians, built a port nearby at Gades, which is now modern Cadiz.

Greek traveller and writer Pausanias visited the area in the second century AD but did not visit Tartessos which probably had already disappeared. He wrote, "They say that Tartessus is a river in the land of the Iberians, running down into the sea by two mouths, and that between these two mouths lies a city of the same name. The river, which is the largest in Iberia, and tidal, those of a later day called Baetis, and there are some who think that Tartessus was the ancient name of Carpia, a city of the *Iberians*."

In 1923 a quantity of Bronze Age bronzes was discovered off the coast of a city called Huelva, including Irish and Cypriot artifacts.

Archeologists such as Adolf Schultern, O. Jensen and R. Hennig suggested that Tartessos was actually Atlantis and extended across southern Spain to sunken Mediterranean islands and Morocco. Jensen believed that Tartessos-Atlantis vanished because it was conquered by the Carthaginians who left no trace of it and spread the rumour that it had been inundated by a flood. After fifty years of unsuccessfully searching for the lost city, Schultern concluded that it had sunk under the marshes near the Rio Tinto and Guadalquivir Rivers and now exists beneath the National Park of Doñana, an area favoured by modern researchers. He was only able to locate one archeological relic from the site—a ring with undeciphered characters on the inside.

Elena M Whishaw's 1928 book 'Atlantis in Spain' first popularised the location of Atlantis in the area of Niebla with its megalithic fortresses and advanced hydraulic engineering. As Director of the Anglo-Spanish-American School of Archeology, she believed Tartessos was an outpost of Atlantis whose inhabitants were skilled miners and engineers. The Sierra Morena was one of the richest areas for minerals in the ancient world.

Russian Atlantologist Dr Zhirov commented on the theories of Schultern and Hennig linking Tartessos with Atlantis. He claimed that Tartessos was not on the continental coast or in the river estuary but rather on the Island of Ertheia which was about sixty miles from the coast. He wrote, "There are some grounds for equating this with the kingdom of Gadieros, the second son of Poseidon, whose Greek name was Eumelus, and who received 'the extremity of the island (i.e. Atlantis) towards the Pillars of Hercules.' This fragment of Atlantis may have survived the original catastrophe as a small island, which existed by trading with the Spanish mainland for metals and other products. However as it lay in the region of earthquakes and volcanic disturbances it was gradually reduced in size until its conquest from the mainland became possible by the aid of a fleet. The subsequent fate of Tartessos is lost in obscurity, but it must have vanished beneath the waves, possibly about 500 BC, at the time of the great subsidence which took place in the Atlantic at that time."

http://www.geocities.com/MotorCity/Factory/2583/1960.htm

CLAIMS OF ATLANTEAN RUINS OFF CADIZ AND GIBRALTAR

Cadiz is a very ancient city which was once called Gades in Phonecian times when it was divided into different sections. The temples of Ba'al and Astarte are now submerged in the bay off the Santa Catalina near the Punta del Nao according to David Childress. He wrote in 'Lost Cities of Atlantis, Ancient Europe & the Mediterranean'; "The massive ruins of the Temple of Ba'al can be viewed in the water as one walks out to the lighthouse on the San Sebastian causeway. I gazed in wonder at the giant blocks of stone weighing 40 to 80 tons lying in about eight feet of water along the causeway. There were squares with slots and grooves in them to be fitted with other stones. It is believed these were the ancient temple foundations." (p258)

Cadiz has also been popular with those seeking Atlantis. From 1958 Dr Maxine Asher and her colleague Dr Julian Nava began their long search for Atlantis which would take them on over fifty field and diving visits to Spain. She believes that the last piece of Atlantis, as described by Plato, is submerged under two hundred feet of water in and near the Straits of Gibraltar. These ruins, allegedly discovered by a Spanish diving team, are located between Tarifa and Ceuta, close to the Rock of Gibraltar. In 1973 an Ancient Mediterranean Research Association (A.M.R.A) team under the direction of Francisco Salazar Casero estimated that the ancient city to be three city blocks wide and about half a mile long. The team tried to photograph the ruins in 1993 but were hampered by strong currents, killer sharks and Spanish military patrols.

This city, according to Asher, is composed of walls and walkways of brick under which are embedded artifacts partially hidden in the sand. Although there were no inscriptions observed, other expeditions have seen pre-Phonecian inscriptions at the underwater Temple of Hercules at La Calletta, near Cadiz.

Dr Asher has been researching and documenting hundreds of "previously undisclosed sources about Atlantis, written in medieval and archaic Spanish, and housed in the private libraries of Cadiz, including museum collections." These sources reputedly reveal links between ancient Spain and the Hebrews and other claims which are ignored or withheld because of their "controversial nature within the religious and scientific communities."

In an article 'The Lost Continent of Atlantis—Myth or Reality' in the Ancient Mediterranean Research Organisation, she wrote: "The truth is that four cities lie underwater from Cadiz to Gibraltar,

and these cities are submerged at least 120 feet and resting on the continental shelf. Using the yardarm of 10 feet for every 1000 years of recorded history, we can observe highly developed sunken cities, the remains of which are at least 9,000 years old or older."
http://www.atlantisresearch.com/myth_or_reality.html

Dr Asher's website http://www.atlantisresearch.com/ shows that she has a very long association with Atlantis and is the founder of the Ancient Mediterranean Research Organisation. The website comments, "In June 2004, satellite photos were taken over the waters of Cadiz, Spain, definitely proving the existence of Atlantis." She is currently involved in a Hollywood film called 'The Atlantis Conspiracy' which details her four decades of ignored archeological work.

Dr Asher's website has brief footage of ruins lying 120 feet down on the continental shelf off the coast of Spain. She believes them to be vestiges of Atlantis dating from about 9000 BC.
http://www.atlantisresearch.com/film.html

In 2004 another claimant to the Atlantis in Spain 'discovery', Cuban Georgeos Diaz-Montexano emerged complaining of plagiarism by Collina-Giraud who made headlines with his Spartel theory. Most of the website information on this epigrapher consists of badly translated Spanish or sensationalised headlines about his 'original' satellite discoveries of Atlantean ruins off the coast of Cadiz. Such statements led Dr Asher to legally claim her discovery of Atlantis in Spain in 2004.

Diaz-Montexano reports of underwater expeditions to coastal areas of Spain and Gibraltar, providing photos of large stones with metal connectors. Unfortunately the photos come from a long pdf document in Spanish which provides no information on their context or use, so it is impossible to determine the age or function of these stones. The article can be found at:
http://club.telepolis.com/gadeiros/atlantologia/library/atlantisnews.pdf

Another badly translated website http://www.freerepublic.com/focus/f-news/1011563/posts discusses an expedition in 2003 which focused on the off shore area between Gibraltar and Cadiz. Montexano's expedition consisted of Juan Naval Luis (historian), Gem Tirado and Maria Fdez-Valmayor (investigation and documentation), Antonio Font (engineering and architecture) Raul Mensalvas (submarine archeology) Antonia Dazo and Estaban Wheat Marquez (geologists) and underwater archeologists Beatriz Lumbreras, Marsal Grifa, Manuel Santana, Miguel Aragon and Naval Filomeno.

According to this website they located pillars, slabs, paving stones, pools and wheels between 10 to 30 meters of water from Gibraltar to Huelva. Some impressive photographs of rectangular blocks and stones as well as a pure copper tool are presented on this site which links to another site in Spanish — **http://Atlantologica. com/**

It is extremely difficult to find independent information on Montexano and his expeditions in English. Dr Greg Little, an Atlantis researcher and explorer has made insightful comments about Diaz-Montexano and his acerbic spokesperson Maria Fdez Valmayor on the site 'Atlantis Insider.'

He observed, "Perhaps the most interesting information that has emerged from this comes from what purport to be actual expeditions to the underwater coastal areas of Spain and Gibraltar. Photos have been taken of large metal connectors and stone, but most of the metal 'artifacts' appear to be modern remains of dumping. The stones are interesting, but their context and use is not known. Montexano has made use of these photos on several websites, but others are credited as taking the photos...."

http://www.mysterious-america.net/atlantisinsider.html

CLAIMS OF ATLANTIS IN CADIZ

Dr Rainer Kuehne, from the University of Wuppertal, was obviously influenced by the theories of Adolf Schultern and Maxine Asher and thinks that remnants of Atlantis can be found in the Doñana National Park near Cadiz. Today this park is a large wetland wilderness, 543 km², of which 135 km² are a protected area.

His theory is that Atlantis was destroyed by a devastating flood between 800 and 500 BC which led the terrified inhabitants to believe they were sinking beneath the waves. A single satellite photo of a marshy region known as Marisma de Hinojos near

Cadiz purportedly shows two rectangular structures in the mud and parts of concentric rings that surrounded them. He believes that this ties in with Plato's description of an island of five stades (925m) diameter that was surrounded by several circular structures or concentric rings. Furthermore, he thinks that the rectangular features could be the remains of a temple devoted to the sea god Poseidon and a 'golden' temple devoted to Cleito and Poseidon as described in Plato's 'Critias'.

Kuehne's controversial findings include:

- A rectangular structure of size 230 meters x 140 meters which he believes to be remnants of the 'silver temple of Poseidon'. The geographical coordinates of this structure are 36°57'27" +/- 6"N and 6°23'06" +/- 8"W.
- A rectangular structure of size 280 meters x 240 meters located 500 meters south-west of the first structure, possibly a remnant of the 'golden temple of Poseidon and Cleito.'
- These two structures are surrounded by parts of concentric rings which sound like the rings of earth and water described in Critias 115e-116a.
- A chain of lakes located north-west of these structures which could be a remnant of the channel which ranged from the capital of Atlantis to the sea.

These features were initially discovered by Werner Wickboldt, an Atlantis enthusiast who was searching for signs of Atlantis with satellite photography. He believes it fits Plato's description, although the Greeks must have confused the word coastline for island during transmission of the Atlantis story. The 'buildings' are also of a larger size than Plato's descriptions, although Kuehne cheerfully concedes that the original measurement of 'stade' must have been larger than originally thought.

Kuehne used other topographical features, such as the plain extending from the coast to Seville, the Sierra Nevada Mountains and the copper mines of Sierra Morena to support his theory.

Unfortunately for him the site is in the Doñana National Park which may make it difficult to excavate. There have also been no reports that he has even visited the area, although a BBC article mentioned how he was trying to achieve funding for such an excavation. Furthermore, Tony Wilkinson an expert in the use of remote sensing in archeology at the University of Edinburgh was less enthusiastic as the alleged rectangular ruins have not been dated.

Dr Maxine Asher has enthusiastically endorsed Dr Kuehne's theory on her website as it supports her belief that parts of Atlantis can be found around Cadiz.

This original article appeared in June 2004 online article of 'Antiquity' 'Location and Dating of Atlantis' which also mentioned the Spartel-Atlantis theory.

REFERENCES:

Atlantisite.com
http://www.geocities.com/MotorCity/Factory/2583/1960.htm
Ancient Mediterranean Research Association
http://www.atlantisresearch.com/myth_or_reality.html
http://club.telepolis.com/gadeiros/atlantologia/library/atlantisnews.pdf
'The Atlantis Between Spain and Morocco'
http://www.freerepublic.com/focus/f-news/1011563/posts
http://Atlantologica.com/
Alternative Perceptions Magazine Issue # 82, August 2004
http://www.mysterious-america.net/atlantisinsider.html
E. Whishaw, 'Atlantis in Spain'

RUINS OFF MOROCCO

Millions of years ago before the Mediterranean Sea began its incursion into the basin, Spain and Morocco were joined. There have been claims of ruins off the coast of Morocco which are supported by photographic evidence. In his book 'Mysteries from Forgotten Worlds' Charles Berlitz, linguist and Atlantologist wrote, "Enormous walls composed of blocks 8 meters long and 6 meters high, at a minimum depth of about 14 meters were found on the bottom in Moroccan waters on the Mediterranean side of Gibraltar by Mark Valentin in 1958, while free-diving in pursuit of fish, and were eventually traced for a distance of several miles. The general construction of these walls, surrounded by smaller stones, bears a striking resemblance to prehistoric cyclopean stonework on the coasts of the Atlantic and Mediterranean islands that are still above water." (D. Childress, 'Lost Cities of Atlantis, Ancient Europe & the Mediterranean.')

These megalithic stones have been compared to the massive foundation stones of the temple of Baalbek in Lebanon.

REFERENCE: D. Childress, 'Lost Cities of Atlantis, Ancient Europe & the Mediterranean.'

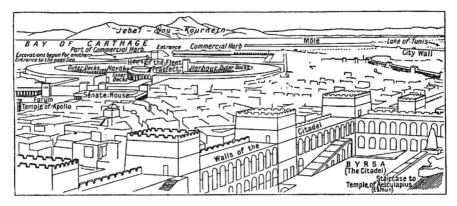

The layout of ancient Carthage and the harbor area.

Sketch of an underwater wall off Morocco. It is reported to be 9 miles long!
Courtesy of William Corliss and the Sourcebook Project.

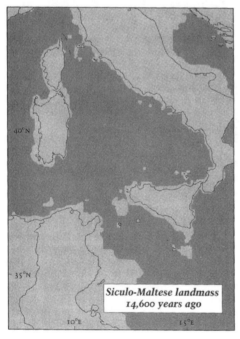

Siculo-Maltese landmass
14,600 years ago

Top: A diver views on the Egyptian statues found in the Mediterranean of Alexandria. Below: A map of the ocean levels around Sicilly and Malta 14,600 years ago. Courtesy of Graham Hancock.

PART 3
THE MEDITERRANEAN
SANTORINI ERUPTION c1600 BC
HELIKE 373 BC
RUINS IN ALEXANDRIA
THE BAY OF NAPLES, ITALY
LIBYA
MORE UNDERWATER
MEDITERRANEAN SITES
PRE NEOLITHIC, NEOLITHIC
& BRONZE AGE SITES
PHONECIAN & EGYPTIAN SITES
GREEK & ETRUSCAN ERA SITES
ROMAN ERA SITES
CONTROVERSIAL RUINS
YARMUTA, LEBANON
CLAIMS OF ATLANTIS IN CYPRUS
CLAIMS OF ATLANTIS IN MALTA

With over 200 confirmed sites, the Mediterranean is the most promising body of water for underwater archaeology.

SANTORINI ERUPTION circa 1650 BC (1639-1616 BC via Radiocarbon dating; 1628 BC dendrochronologically; 1530-1500 BC archeologically.)

During the Bronze Age of the Aegean civilization, a huge

53

volcano erupted on the Greek island of Thera (Santorini), causing widespread tsunami and ash devastation across the Mediterranean. The waves on the island itself might have been over 100 meters high, whereas in Israel, on the other side of the Mediterranean, the waves would have reached about 5-7 meters high. Geologists have learned that the volcano erupted and then collapsed into a caldera about 380 meters below sea level over a period of months.

The town of Akrotiri on Thera was buried by a thick layer of pumice. Originally excavated by French vulcanologist Ferdinand Fouque in 1866, a Bronze Age settlement was discovered in Akrotiri. When further excavated in 1967 by archeologist Spyridon Marinatos, it was revealed to be a Bronze Age settlement of the Minoan culture. Thera appears to have had a thriving Minoan economy based upon intensive trade throughout the eastern Mediterranean. Surprisingly, no skeletons of people have been discovered, leading to the conclusion that the population escaped from the island before the main eruption.

There is evidence that Cretan settlements like Amnisos, Malia, Ghoumia and Zakros were inundated by a tsunami at that time. Anaphi island, closest to the eruption, shows evidence of inundation and pumice deposits to 50m above sea level although the waves must have been much higher on the other side of this island.

"On the west cost of Turkey, just north of the island of Rhodes, is an area of shoreline facing Thera which is shaped like a funnel. The shock wave from the volcano created a mountain of water about eight hundred feet tall which penetrated thirty miles inland. Huge boulders were dislodged, and yet in other areas of the Turkish coast, the wave was only about twenty feet high." (Charles Pellegrino, '*Unearthing Atlantis*' p.87)

Recent archaeological research by a team of international scientists in 2006 has revealed that the Santorini event was even more massive than previously thought. It expelled 61 cubic km of magma and rock into Earth's atmosphere compared to previous estimates in 1991 of only 39 cubic km. The eruption took place in about four distinct phases, with the fourth being the most violent. Pyroclastic flows at 300 to 350°C flowed over the islands and into the sea, leaving deposits up to 40 m thick on Thera. Huge amounts of volcanic material lie on the sea floor. The collapse of the cone into the sea drove out a large amount of water, which then receded back into the sea and crashed upon the walls of the caldera, creating a huge tsunami.

Many historians now believe that the eruption at Thera formed the basis for the Atlantis legend. This hypothesis was first postulated in a paper published by K.T. Frost, Professor of History at Queens University in Belfast in 1913 titled 'The Critias and Minoan Crete.' In 1909 he wrote in 'The Times' of London about the need to reconsider Mediterranean history in the light of recent discoveries on Crete. "The whole description of Atlantis which is given in the 'Timaeus' and 'Critias' has features so thoroughly Minoan that even Plato could not have invented so many unsuspected facts." Such facts included the great harbour, shipping, elaborate bathrooms, stadium and the bull sacrifice which can all be found in Minoan archeology.

Frost's theory was dismissed by academics because the timing and location of Crete bore no relation to Plato's description. It was revived in the 1930s by Professor Marinatos, the distinguished archeologist who excavated the Persian war sites of Thermopylae and Marathon as well as older sites at Pylos. He also excavated Amnistos in Crete, discovering substantial Minoan ruins such as a palatial villa. In an article entitled 'The Volcanic Destruction of Minoan Crete' in the British journal Antiquity in 1939, Marinatos wrote how he had discovered pumice stone in Amnistos and evidence of a tsunami in Crete. He was the first to deduce that the source of this cataclysm was the small volcanic island of Thera, (Santorini) 75 miles north of Crete. In 1950 he published an article supporting the thesis of a Minoan Atlantis which expanded upon Frost's original arguments. Believing that the cataclysm at Santorini was the source or inspiration for Plato's story on Atlantis, he excavated the Minoan era town near Akrotiri on Thera.

In the 1960s the Atlantis theory really took off with a series of articles by seismologist A.G Galanopoulos. He argued that almost everything in Plato's Atlantis could be made to fit Minoan Crete. Ignoring inconvenient details like the extensive ports and cisterns described by Plato, he claimed that Plato overestimated the age of the eruption by tenfold so that rather than occurring in 10,000 BC, it really occurred in the first millennium BC.

Professor Archibald Ray of Glasgow University commented, "Professor Galanopoulos, the volcanologist, suggested that an additional zero had been added in translation to all large numbers. Consequently, the date would be more like nine hundred years before Solon's visit to Egypt. If so, we apply the same logic to population and island size, produce a more acceptable description more in accordance with Minoan Crete and its destruction by the explosive eruption of Thera." ('Lost Civilizations', A. Atkinson p65)

Galanopoulos also claimed that the 'Pillars of Hercules' referred to two promontories on the south coast of Greece, facing Crete as well as the more familiar Strait of Gibraltar. He believed that the island of Thera was the centre of Minoan life and Crete was its larger adjunct. The slopes of the volcanic island must have been adorned with majestic temples and palaces which were buried during the cataclysmic eruption.

Attempts have been made to detect submerged harbors and canals at Thera using sonar equipment. In 1965 a team composed of Dr James Mavor of the Woods Hole Oceanographic Institution, Professor Galanopoulos as well as geophysicists and engineers, were given permission to search the bay with the research vessel 'Chain'. Unfortunately Dr Mavor was unable to utilise the deep sea submersible 'Alvin' which he had designed. Although they made significant discoveries about the depth of the caldera and volcanic deposits beneath the sea using a magnetometer and seismic profiler, the evidence to support Galanopoulos's theory was not forthcoming.

Mavor planned a second land based expedition concentrating on diving and survey work as well as land excavations. However, he discovered upon his arrival that Marinatos was not entirely cooperative, and matters between them became very strained when a member of his team was accused and then acquitted of stealing antiquities. While Marinatos used the team to help excavate the site of Akrotiri, achieving personal acclaim in the process, Mavor's contribution was forgotten beyond his book 'Voyage to Atlantis'. Unfortunately Mavor's underwater license and support from the Athens Archeological Society were withdrawn after he gave a press release entitled 'A Minoan Pompeii and the Lost Atlantis.'

The Atlantis-Thera theory is now favoured by the majority of historians, but it is not without its critics. Detractors of this popular theory are quick to point out that Santorini is in a different direction from the Platonian island of Atlantis. No Minoan excavations have discovered ruins matching Plato's elaborate descriptions of Atlantis. Furthermore, the eruption of Thera occurred at least a century before the cataclysm which devastated the Minoan places of Crete. It is also unlikely that the age of the inundation could be overestimated by tenfold. Without this 'convenient' overestimation of times and sizes, Marinatos's theory does not have much merit. Surprisingly, this theory – that Santorini was the source of the Atlantis legend—is the most accepted by archeologists despite its many shortcomings.

The BBC news on April 20, 2007 carried a story 'The wave that destroyed Atlantis' about a group of scientists who discovered that the eruption of Santorini occurred at the same time as the disappearance of Minoan culture—suggesting a direct causal link between the two events. Professor Hendrik Bruins of the Ben-Gurion University of the Negev in Israel said, "The geo-archeological deposits contain a number of distinct tsunami signatures. Minoan building material, pottery and cups along with food residue such as isolated animal bones were mixed up with rounded beach pebbles and sea shells and microscopic marine fauna. The later can only have been scooped up from the sea-bed by one mechanism—a powerful tsunami, dumping all these materials together in a destructive swoop. An event of ferocious force hit the coast of Crete and this wasn't just a Mediterranean storm."

Canadian archeologist Sandy MacGillivray has been excavating Minoan settlements such as Palaikastro on the eastern edge of Crete for twenty five years. With colleague Hugh Sackett he has excavated seven blocks of Palaikastro, discovering a house dusted with powdery grey ash from the Thera eruption. However, the ash was found only in areas where it could have gathered after a flash flood or other inundation by water. Moreover, a horizontal band of gravel about a foot long which was composed of broken pottery, ash, rocks and organic matter was found on the beach—a tsunami signature. He discovered that tsunami deposits can be found at least 15 meters above sea level and many buildings show evidence of missing walls on buildings facing the sea, whereas side walls were left intact.

The evidence pointed to the probability that a giant wave had struck the Palaikastro Bay while the freshly fallen ash from Thera was still lying about. This tsunami had inundated the town for miles inland, streaking it with strange patterns of ash.

MacGilllvray consulted Costas Synolakis, an earth scientist from the University of Southern California who specialised in pioneering tsunami models on computers. In 2000 Synolakis had concluded that the eruption of Thera had only produced waves at most nine feet high when they hit Crete and could not have devastated the Minoan civilization. However, after observing the debris patterns produced by the huge tsunami which hit Banda Aceh in 2004, he visited Palaikastro with MacGilllvray and was stunned to report: "A blanket of cultural debris, broken dishes, broken glass, bits of done, people's belongings scattered everywhere, It looked exactly like that kind of debris carpet, and you don't get it in a smaller tsunami. The presence of this chaotic deposit suggested that the tsunami was at least three to four meters (10 to 13 feet) at the shoreline."

http://discovermagazine.com/2008/jan/did-a-tsunami-wipe-out-a-cradle-of-western civilization/article_view?b_start:int=2&-C=

Further layers of chaotic debris were discovered 90 feet above sea level. Synolakis's new model determined that the tsunami was about 15 meters high (50 ft) when it hit Palaikastro and other towns like Mallia. Although Minoan culture survived for another generation after the disaster, the main towns and palaces of Crete were ransacked and vandalised and eventually the Mycenaean occupied the Palace of Knossos.

REFERENCES:

BBC News Friday 20 April, 2007   http://news.bbc.co.uk/2/hi/science/nature/6568053.stm

'Did a Tsunami Wipe Out a Cradle of Western Civilization?'
Discover,
   http://discovermagazine.com/2008/jan/did-a-tsunami-wipe-out-a-
   cradle-of-western-civilization/article_view?b_start:int=0&-C=
   Wikipedia article on the Santorini eruption
   'Lost Civilizations' A. Atkinson
   'Unearthing Atlantis: An Archeological Odyssey' C. Pellegrino,
Random House, NY, 1991

HELIKE 373 BC

In 373 BC a catastrophic earthquake of magnitude 7 followed
by a tsunami destroyed and submerged the ancient Greek city
of Helike, a principal city on the southwest shore of the Gulf of
Corinth. At the time of the catastrophe Helike was part of the
Hegemony of Sparta, and there were ten Spartan warships in the
harbor on the night of the quake. As the tsunami, probably caused
by an underwater avalanche, occurred during the night, everyone
in the city perished under waves of about 35 feet high, as did the
Spartan warships. News travelled fast and the Achaians sent two
thousand men to help but they were too late to rescue anyone, nor
could they recover any bodies.

Helike, founded in the Bronze Age, had established colonies
like Priene in Asia Minor and Sybaris in Italy. Its destruction was
discussed by Greek and Roman authors who ascribed the disaster
to the wrath of Poseidon, god of earthquakes and the sea. It may
have influenced Plato to discuss the destruction of Atlantis a few
decades later.

The sunken city gradually silted over although various ancient
sources documented its destruction and provided clues of its
location. Pausanias, a traveller who visited the site in 174 AD
reported, "This was the type of earthquake, they say, that…leveled
Helike to the ground, and that it was accompanied by another
disaster in the season of winter. The sea flooded a great part of
the land, and covered up the whole of Helike all round. Moreover,
the tide was so deep in the grove of Poseidon that only the tops

of trees remained visible…the tidal wave swallowed up Helike and every man in it… the ruins…are visible but not plainly now as they once were, because they are corroded by the salt water." ('Lost Civilizations' Austin Atkinson)

Greek geographer Strabo wrote (8.7.2) "For the sea was raised by an earthquake and it submerged Helike and the temple of Helikonian Poseidon….The submersion took place by night and although the city was twelve stadia (2km) distant from the sea, this whole district together with the city was hidden from sight; and two thousand men who were sent by the Achaeans were unable to recover dead bodies."

Historian Diodoros of Sicily was even more graphic with his description in 'The Histories'. "The blow came at night, so that…the majority who were caught in the ruined houses were annihilated, and when day came some dashed from the ruins, and when they thought they had escaped the danger, met with a greater and still more incredible disaster. For the sea and the wave rose to a vast height, and as a result the inhabitants together with their land were inundated and disappeared. Two cities in Achaea bore the brunt of this disaster, Helike and Boura." (15.48)

The Roman writer Aelian (On Animals 11.19) wrote: "For five days before Helike disappeared, all the mice and martens and snakes and centipedes and beetles and every other creature of that kind in the city left in a body by the road that leads to Keryneia. And the people of Helike seeing this happening were unable to guess the reason. But after these creatures had departed, and earthquake occurred in the night; the city subsided; an immense wave flooded and Helike disappeared while ten Spartan vessels which happened to be at anchor were lost altogether with the city."

Eventually Helike disappeared without a trace, leaving the ruins intact and free from looting.

Professor Spyridon Marinatos, Director General of Antiquities for Greece and discoverer of Akrotiri on Santorini, pursued the search for ancient Helike, believing it would contain an intact site. However, a trial magnetometer survey of the seabed carried out at his request in 1966 failed to discover any traces of the city.

In 1988 the Helike Project was launched by Greek archeologist

Dora Katsonopoulou and Steven Soter, a scientist from the American Museum of Natural History in New York. Dora puzzled over the word 'poros' which had been used to describe the area where Helike had sunk. The general consensus was that 'poros' referred to the Gulf of Corinth, but she was thinking that 'poros' could also refer to an inland lagoon. A side-scan of the seafloor southeast of Aigion was taken by geophysicist Paul Kronfield showing sonar images of seismic disturbances but no evidence of a city on or below the seafloor. However, he found ten anomalies under the seabed which suggested that they might be the Spartan warships.

The Helike Project decided to search the adjacent coastal plain, as the delta had been lifted by seismic forces to become dry land again. Earthquake expert Iain Stewart believed that a large quake could have created the inland lagoon as well as liquefaction on a large scale. Liquefaction is where the ground literally turns to water beneath your feet and can be seen in some earthquakes. Large quakes can also cause underwater landslides which can result in a tsunami.

From 1991 they drilled bore holes on the coastal plane and discovered many ceramic fragments from ancient to Byzantine times. In 1994 they carried out a magnetometer survey of the plain and discovered a Roman building which had been destroyed by a quake in the late fifth century AD. Excavations were carried out yearly and in 2001 the Helike Project brought to light the first traces of the lost Classical city, buried under deposits of an ancient lagoon. To their astonishment, the explorers also discovered nearby an entire Early Bronze Age town, dating from about 2400 BC, in an extraordinary state of preservation. An earthquake apparently caused the submergence of this Prehistoric town twenty centuries before a similar fate led to the disappearance of its Classical successor.

Subsequent investigations discovered Hellenistic ruins including a large 'industrial complex' consisting of cisterns, basins, workshops and kilns.

The Classical age ruins were the most interesting for the archeologists. At three meters depth they discovered under thick lagoonal deposits the remains of Classical buildings which were destroyed by the quake of 373 BC. Analysis of microfauna in sediment samples suggests that the lagoon covered the ruins of these classical buildings and later silted over. Thus the city did not sink into the depths of the Corinthian Gulf as had been believed, but was submerged by an inland lagoon.

The Early Bronze Age ruins from 2600-2300 BC also provided excitement for the archeologists. About one kilometer from the present shore, the buildings were discovered at a depth of three to five meters below the surface. This prehistoric 'Helike' had rectilinear buildings, cobbled streets, pottery and luxury items like precious metal ornaments. These sediments also show that the ruins were submerged in seawater for some time, suggesting that the settlement may have been destroyed and submerged just like the later Helike.

http://www.helike.org/paper.shtml

According to Soter, "Our sonar survey revealed a large narrow rectangular structure extending out from the shore. It's covered by sandy silt and may be natural but, unlike the normal bottom sediments, here, it's opaque to the penetrating sonar and therefore looks dense, like stone. It might be an ancient harbor mole or breakwater. To expose it would require special equipment to remove the silt..."

According to Paul Kronfield, "We also found what appeared to be the remains of the harbor wall. It looked man made, very regular about 159m (492feet) long with the characteristics of a jetty under 15m (49ft) of water...Just to show you how sonar can mislead you, we also found a large circular structure about 10m (33ft) by 60m (197ft) across. One could imagine it to be an ampitheatre, but Steven identified the feature as a giant submarine 'pockmark', the result of gas bubbles which break the surface during earthquakes, leaving a calcified ring around what is, in effect, a hole in the sea floor." (Atkinson, ibid p 8)

REFERENCES: 'Lost Civilizations' Austin Atkinson

'The Lost Cities of Ancient Helike' http://www.helike.org/paper. shtml

62

RUINS IN ALEXANDRIA

The once great Egyptian cities of Menouthis and Heraklion (also known as Heracleum or Heracleion) now lie buried beneath twenty one feet of water in the Bay of Aboukir (Abu Qir) about 15 miles (25km) from Alexandria. In 1859 a French engineer called Larousse was the first to find remains in the Bay. Gaston Jondet, the Chief Engineer of the Department of Ports and Lighthouses, discovered the Old Port of Pharos in 1910. In his paper 'Les Ports submerges de l'ancienne Isle de Pharos' he described the colossal breakwaters and structures submerged at depths of about 8 m below the surface. These structures formed the ancient breakwater extending 2.36 km (1.46miles) from Abu Qir rock to the western edge of Anfouchy Bay at a depth of 4.5 m (14.76 ft).

In 1933 archeologists, led by Prince Omar Tousson, noticed a number of underwater buildings in the shape of a horseshoe and the remains of a huge structure with 43 columns. They salvaged a statue of the head of Alexander the Great.

Egyptian Abdul-Saadat in 1961 discovered a huge statue of Isis and other artifacts in the Eastern Harbour. The Eastern Harbor contained the ruins of the famous lighthouse at Qait Bey Fort, on Pharos Island, and El-Silsilah (Cape Lochias) with its royal palaces to the east.

In 1996 a Franco-Egyptian team were searching for Napoleon's lost fleet in the Aboukir Bay. They found the flagship 'L'Orient' along with two other ships, 'Las Serieuse' and 'L'Artemise' and recovered many objects like crockery, swords, navigational instruments etc from them. They also found traces of what could be a sunken city, including a headless black granite statue of Isis.

In 1998 French marine archeologist Franck Goddio searched for these legendary cities in the Bay of Aboukir with a nuclear resonance magnetometer attached to a boat which scoured the bay. The team detected granite columns lying beneath the sand as well as the patterns of buildings. After making detailed maps, the divers swam down to remove five feet of sand. Divers uncovered buildings, temples, columns, streets, sphinxes, jugs, sculptures statues and jewellery.

The coins were not minted after 740 AD so it is likely that

Menouthis sank quickly during the great earthquake of 740 or 41.

In 2000 Goddio turned his attention to the second area with an odd magnetic pattern, suspecting that Heraklion was buried there. Heraklion, sister city of Menouthis, was on one of the seven Canopic branches of the Nile in the delta region. They discovered ruined houses, temples, a port and statues. The temple dedicated to the god Hercules and the Egyptian god Amun was from the Ptolemic era. Among other discoveries was a stele of pure gold with Greek script, bronze coins, sixteen jetties for vessels, indicating a flourishing maritime trade, and a bronze statue of the goddess Bastat. The statues had all tumbled to the south west.

The excavation team comprised ten Egyptian archeologists and a number of divers from the European Institute. Alaa Mahrus, Director of the Underwater Antiquities Administration said that the salvaged items were undergoing chemical treatment to remove salts. The finds confirm that life was able to continue in Heraklion until the Byzantine era.

Scientists are divided as to what caused the submergence of the two cities. In Heraklion partial skeletons were found in houses and household objects were very well preserved. Elsewhere people appeared to be killed by falling masonry and the temple had collapsed in one direction. Coins showed that Heraklion was a thriving city until the 8th century AD. Alexandria is not on an active earthquake zone, so it is possible that the quake occurred elsewhere but caused liquefaction of the sandy foundations. Other scientists believe that deadly floods occurred during 740 AD rather than an earthquake.

LIGHTHOUSE OF ALEXANDRIA ON PHAROS

During 1994–1998, a Franco-Egyptian team of thirty divers conducted a salvage inspection of the submerged ruins of the famous ancient lighthouse of Alexandria on the island of Pharos over a period of twelve months. Preliminary documentation had been provided by Kamel Abdul-Saadat in 1961 and a UNESCO mission in 1968, but generally the site, beneath a medieval sunken wall, had lain undisturbed.

The famous lighthouse, built in the mid third century BC,

was embellished with marble and bronze. The lighthouse was a graduated eight stories high, the ground floor being 60 meters high. It had 300 rooms for workers. The top floor contained a permanent firepole with a massive mirror which reflected the whole city.

The lighthouse remained functioning until the Arab conquest of 641AD. In 673 Hajira, King Berbars visited Alexandria and ordered its restoration. He built a mosque on the upper part. In 1100 a strong earthquake hit Alexandria and the lighthouse collapsed except for the square shaped ground part. Another earthquake in the 14th century destroyed the remaining part of the Pharos.

Team leader Jean-Yves Empereur is a director of research at the French Centre National de la Recherche Scientifique with a doctorate in classical literature and archeology. He has directed underwater excavations in Greece and Cyprus and in 1990 established the Centre d'Etudes Alexandrines to study the city's history, especially through underwater salvage excavations at Qait Bay fort from 1994-8. His mission was to evaluate the importance of the site lying under six to eight meters of water that was being threatened by the construction of a modern concrete breakwater.

The team discovered that the site was over 2.5 hectares and consisted of 2,500 pieces of stonework including columns of all sizes, sphinxes, statues and some immense blocks of granite which probably came from the famous lighthouse which had been a wonder of the ancient world. In all, over one thousand archeological artifacts were charted and marked.

Although Alexandria was not founded until the 4th century BC, there were sphinxes and pharaonic monuments from earlier eras. The twenty six sphinxes, of various sizes, belonged to different pharaohs and probably came from the ruined city of Heliopolis which was destroyed in the time of the Greek Ptolemies. This sacred city was used as a quarry for Alexandria and contained many obelisks, sphinxes and other pharaonic elements. Empereur was at pains to point out that these older monuments are not evidence of a pre-Greek settlement. "Nothing has changed the traditional image we have of the Egyptian fishing village, which no new archeological discovery at the terrestrial excavations can put in doubt."

http://www.unesco.org/csi/pub/source/alex6.htm

Fragments of five colossal statues, including Ptolemy as pharaoh, were found. With a total body height of about 13 meters, this head rivaled the statue of Isis which had been found at the same site by Kamel Abdul-Saadat in 1962. The statue of Ptolemy represented one of the three royal couples whose images stood at the foot of the Pharos.

Besides the statues there is a series of granite blocks that are over eleven meters long and weighing 75 tons each. Twenty or so of them are arranged in a line starting from the Mameluke fort and running for 60 meters to the north west. As some are broken into two or three pieces, it indicates they fell from a height and probably were part of the original lighthouse. The remaining blocks were of Aswan granite, whereas any marble or limestone blocks were probably salvaged to be used in other buildings.

PRE GREEK RUINS IN ALEXANDRIA?

Rumours of Egyptian, Minoan or even Atlantean submerged blocks in the harbor of Alexandria have been circulating for almost a century. Not only is there a rumoured Temple of Poseidon, but author Stephan Schwartz claimed in his 1983 book 'The Alexandria Project' that his scuba team had discovered huge stone blocks including 'The Crown of Osiris' from a statue of the Egyptian god. They also reported finding huge granite pedestals for statues with sockets in them.

In his seminal 2002 book 'Underworld' Graham Hancock tackled the controversial question of pre Greek ruins in Alexandria. His Egyptian contact Ashraf Bechai, former leader of the Maritime Museum underwater team, disputed the claim that the large blocks discovered by Empereur belonged to the Pharos. As the lighthouse was reportedly 128 meters tall, it must have used at least 100,000 blocks of stone, and yet, according to Empereur, there are only about 3,000 blocks on the sea floor. Furthermore, ancient texts said that the lighthouse was built of white limestone and not granite which had to be quarried from Aswan, almost one thousand miles away.

Bechai mentioned two more sites with megalithic blocks of ancient origin- Sidi Gaber and the Kinessa. Off shore from Sidi

Gaber, he saw "hundreds of huge sandstone or limestone blocks laid out in three rows, each two courses high, that had been exposed on the sea bed at a depth of about six to eight meters. The blocks appeared to be of identical dimensions- four meters wide by four meters long by two meters high. They were stacked up on an underwater ridge of some sort, because there was deeper water between them and the shore. All around there were hundreds more blocks of similar size that were heavily eroded, or damaged, or had fallen out of line." ('Underworld' Graham Hancock, p18)

Due to poor visibility, Bechai had not located the ruins again, but claimed they were well known to local fishermen. Eventually he dived with Graham Hancock and they located a "Carpet of gargantuan stone blocks in an advanced stage of erosion, completely unconnected to any of the known marine archeological sites in the vicinity, covering a huge area of the sea bed at 10-12 meters water depth." (ibid, p627)

Another building which he had never seen personally, was known by local fishermen as 'Al Kinessa'- the church or temple. While Hancock did not describe this so called structure, he quoted from a 1910 report by Gaston Jondet that there were huge megalithic walls and causeways some distance off the coast of Alexandria beyond the island of Pharos which are now up to eight meters below the sea.

In July 2007 the discovery that underwater traces of a city which existed centuries before Alexandria had been built was announced. Seven rod shaped samples of dirt gathered from the seafloor of Alexandria's harbor suggest that a flourishing urban centre may have existed three thousand years ago. Coastal geoarcheologist Jean-Daniel Stanley of the Smithsonian Natural Museum of Natural History and his colleagues extracted 3 inch wide rods of sediment 6 to 18 feet long (2 to 5.5 m) from 20 feet of water (6.5 m). They were originally trying to understand what caused later buildings to be submerged by water when the surprising discovery came to light.

Ceramic sherds, building stones imported from other areas of Egypt and lead used in construction were all retrieved. The discovery of metallurgy proves that significant human activity was occurring in the area in 1000 BC.

Stanley commented, "Alexandria was built on top of an existing and perhaps quite important settlement, maybe one that was minimised in importance because we can't see it now. Nothing really concrete about Rhakotis has been discovered until now. Virtually nothing is known about the people who would have lived there."

http://news.yahoo.com/s/livescience/20070724/sc_livescience/hiddencityfo undbeneathalexandria&printer=1;_ylt=At0UQpEEoQZOjKjzeoHD.5Wz vtEF

Mohamed Abdel-Maqsud, from Egypt's Council of Antiquities, was cautious, saying the work on uncovering Rhakotis was only just beginning. "There are signs of a flourishing settlement going back to Pharaonic times, but it's too early to say anything about it."

This latest discovery gives credence to Hancock's theory that Alexandria was built upon an earlier city which used megalithic construction materials and whose ruins can still be found in the harbor and off the coast.

REFERENCES: Underwater archaeological investigations of the ancient Pharos

http://www.unesco.org/csi/pub/source/alex6.htm
http://news.yahoo.com/s/livescience/20070724/sc_livescience/hiddencityfo undbeneathalexandria&printer=1;_ylt=At0UQpEEoQZOjKjzeoHD.5Wz vtEF

Drawing of harbor by Abdul-Sadaat
http://www.unesco.org/csi/pub/papers2/alex10.htm#morcos00

THE BAY OF NAPLES, ITALY

An extensive complex of sunken Roman era structures lies off the coast of the Bay of Naples in Italy. As far back as 1495 Guillaume de Villeneuve described this sunken city. "From Naples at the port of Baiae ... is a distance of seven miles, and in times gone by there was a great city there. It was the most beautiful city in the kingdom, but because of the wickedness of the people, and the prevalence of sodomy, the city was destroyed and sunk into the sea." (N. Flemming, 'Cities in the Sea' p 26)

Guiseppe Fazio, Sir William Hamilton and naturalist Sir

James Forbes all dived in this area in modern times. Fazio, who explored the ruins in the 1820s .found evidence for submergence of 12 to 16 feet. In 1902 Professor Robert Theordore Günther of Oxford University decided to do an exhaustive survey of the Bay of Naples, including the islands of Capri and Ischia. With the help of fishermen and sponge divers, he systematically surveyed the coastline and all the submerged ruins. He paid particular attention to the area between Posilipo and Pozzuoli, where he found evidence of a Roman road beneath the sea bordered on each side by luxurious villas.

The best preserved Roman house in **Posilipo** is the Casa degli Spiriti which has a lower floor 10 feet below sea level. Beside the ruins of Günther's House of Pollio is a flight of steps which starts and finishes below sea level, pointing to submergence of about 12 feet.

Pozzuoli, with its natural harbor, was the chief Italian port for overseas cargoes. In 1750 antiquarians excavated a building at Pozzuoli which is now known as the Temple of Serapis. They discovered that the columns stood on a marble floor which was then two feet below sea level. Seven feet under was another older mosaic floor. The columns were smooth to a height of twelve feet; above that they were deeply perforated with holes from marine borers. In the nineteenth century British geologist Sir Charles Lyell concluded that the coast of Pozzuli had sunk into the sea from 500 to 1300 AD. A volcanic eruption from Vesuvius had covered it with protective ash and then raised it about 1538.

Until recently a strange arched mole, known as Caligula's Causeway with fifteen pillars rising from the water and joined just above the water by rounded arches, could be seen at Pozzuoli. Unfortunately it was included in a modern concrete breakwater at the turn of the 20th century.

In 1962 Nicholas Flemming dived at **Misenum** where the great Roman port was once located. He immediately noted concrete blocks in a straight line rising 20 feet almost to the surface. "There were two rows of pillars, one opposite the gaps in the other, so that no large waves could enter the harbor, but the water could continue to circulate and prevent silting." He found something beneath the cliff on the headland. "I sank and saw a narrow submerged corridor 3 feet wide and about 6 feet high passing straight through the headland. I swam slowly into clouds of minute black and silver fish and emerged on the other side into a glowing cavern. Below me there was a square basin cut in the rock which opened towards the sea through two short tunnels. I swam down and out through one of the tunnels, which opened into a channel sloping into deep water." In the cavern were piscines in an excellent state of preservation. (N. Flemming, ibid p 141)

Günther explored the ruins of **Baiae** which are spread over 50,000 square meters and reach to depths as great as sixty feet. In 1959 a team of divers under Dr Gianni Roghi who were working from the 'Daino' started a survey of the ancient city. Despite the notoriously murky waters of the Bay of Naples, the team discovered a mole and a Roman road with a portico of columns.

Baiae apparently sank slowly after the fourth century AD and was not rediscovered until the 1920s. Sunken villas, including that of the infamous Lucius Calpumius Piso, abound, with collapsed wall fragments, red porphyry imported from Egypt, and fine staircases. Today glass bottomed boats, such as the 'Cymbra' take tourists to see the streets, storehouses, villas and mosaics of ancient Baiae. Underwater ruins of Port Julus, a naval base established in 37 BC and sunk by seismic activity, can be also be seen.

Günther also explored the island of Capri with its mysterious Blue Grotto. Although undiscovered until modern times, this grotto contains steps which continue about 20 feet underwater and were built in Roman times. The partially submerged Baths of Tiberius showed that the island had been both submerged and tilted.

REFERENCE—N. Flemming, 'Cities in the Sea'

LIBYA

In 1958 Nicholas Flemming, a Cambridge graduate student, began a survey of North African ports which engaged divers for the next decade. At Apollonia, the ancient port of Cyrene in Libya, Flemming found a mile long stretch of underwater works, including what may have been shallow pools for the raising of fish and shellfish. He wrote, "I reached a low, square building 100 yards from the shore, which had three complete walls, and in one place the masonry rose to within inches of the surface. The long waves swirled and boiled over the stonework, driving clouds of bubbles down into the clear water...I swam slowly around the building, drawing its outline on the plastic board, the wall which joined it to the shore, and the other walls leading off from it towards the unknown. I followed the faint traces of a thin wall eastwards into the city until it met a crosswall. I sketched the junction and swam left." ('Cities in the Sea' p 97)

Other buildings discovered and mapped were the 'Prong Building' and a complex they named the 'Grid Building' as well as numerous walls. There were also slipways and two solid towers guarding the entrance to the harbor called the 'Block Forts'.

Other students, using only inflatable rubber boats and scuba gear, explored harbors along the coasts of Algeria and Tunisia.

In 1959 Flemming returned to Apollonia with two colleagues to study the fish tanks (piscine), investigate the gaps between islands in the harbor, search for the remains of a lighthouse and survey the local coastline for other submerged ruins. They discovered a system of channels and sluices which once controlled the flow of water through the pools.

Today **Apollonia** is ruined and much lies 2 to 2.5 meters (6-9 feet) underwater. Around the harbor can be seen an extraordinary range of structures including the best preserved set of slipways in the Mediterranean. All ten are undamaged but completely submerged and were covered by stone walled huts or houses in ancient times. Even in 600 AD the slipways, quays and other structures were still above water, forming a circular formation around a harbor. Completing the harbor circuit is a massive wall of dressed blocks, some joined with lead dovetail dowels.

Beyond the harbor rock had been quarried to make wave traps which still work. A rubble breakwater linked the harbor to East Island where the foundations of a large round tower suggest that a lighthouse stood. The second breakwater is now in 8 meters of water, and huge blocks scattered nearby on the sea floor suggest the remains of a large tower guarding the entrance.

Flemming's mission was to find out whether the ancient Mediterranean ports had sunk and if so what had caused the submergence. He concluded that Sidon and Tyre had been eroded by the storms and waves of many centuries, whereas other places like Kenchreai and Apollonia had sunk and the buildings were still visible.

Phycus was the port of Cyrene which had fish tanks and unusual structures such as a carved chamber with a domed roof which can only be reached from the water. Flemming who visited it wrote, "Further into the bay is a group of rock-cut tunnels, tanks, and silos of various ages, as is demonstrated by the fact that some features are cut clear through others. The rock in this area is, at most, two or three meters above sea level. There are several roofed tanks each about 3 meters square and lined with hydraulic cement, with short channels leading into them The roofs are of solid rock but only about 10 centimeters thick. There are a great number of beehive shaped silos of two distinct sizes…Many of the silos have been broken across by man-made channels cut at a later date." (Flemming, ibid p 117)

Sabratha Harbor was a natural outlet to the Mediterranean Sea which is partly submerged. It was explored by Nicholas Flemming's Cambridge team from 1966. Its layout is very similar to that of Apollonia. The reef is capped with Roman concrete while the western end has large numbers of sunken squared blocks, possibly from a tower. To the north lie ruins of docks and a breakwater, whereas on the beach to the east are the foundations of what may have been a lighthouse. A large area in the lee of the reef contains ruins of walls and columns. Lines of walls defined a triangular area stretching 100 yards from the shore in about 6 feet of water.

The harbor was large, extending westwards from the triangular quay past the reef and into a second basin protected by the rubble breakwater. The western end of the second basin had a series of blocks in the shallow water, suggesting another quay.

Sabratha Harbor was one of the main outlets from the Sahara desert and one of the main routes to Rome on the Libyan coast. Slaves, ivory and exotic animals were transported along this route, while the symbol of this town was the elephant.

The Cambridge team also successfully surveyed other North African submerged sites at Al Jezirah, Gigthis, Thaenae, Achulla, Sullectum, Thapsus, Horrea Caelia, Neopolis, Misua and Carpis.

REFERENCE : N. Flemming, 'Cities in the Sea'

MORE UNDERWATER MEDITERRANEAN SITES

It is known that there are more than two hundred sunken sites, and possibly many more, across the Mediterranean Sea. Many are the remains of ancient harbor works such as at Sidon and Tyre in Lebanon and Apollonia in Libya. Some are villas or the floors of temples such as Posilipo on the Bay of Naples or at Kenchreai on the Gulf of Corinth. Others are entire waterfronts of lost cities with roads leading into the water. These ruins date from the Neolithic to late Roman era, incorporating Phonecian, Greek and Etruscan cultures.

HARBORS AND BREAKWATERS

The most common structures discovered underwater in North Africa and the Mediterranean are harbors and breakwaters, including moles, quays and cothons.

A breakwater is a protective structure of stone or concrete extending from shore into the water to prevent a beach from washing away. A mole a massive structure, usually of stone, used as a pier, breakwater, or junction between places separated by water. A cothon is an artificial, protected inner used by the ancient Phonecians and Carthaginians. A quay is a wharf used for docking and unloading vessels.

Tabbat Al-Hammam is a mound in Syria. The beach revealed a jetty or breakwater made of massive masonry blocks the size of a man. The structure is over 200 meters (650') long and 15m (50ft) wide. Its outer edge lies in more than 4 meters of water and it dates from the ninth century BC. This is probably the earliest example of a breakwater.

PRE NEOLITHIC, NEOLITHIC
& BRONZE AGE SITES

ASPROS, CYPRUS

In July 2007 archeologists and divers located pre-Neolithic artifacts off the coast of Cyprus. Aspros, an archeological site discovered in 2004, is thought to date back more than 10,000 years, before permanent settlement on the island.

The most significant finds were located in water about 10 m (33 feet) deep and about 100 meters offshore. These new discoveries indicate that ancient Aspros was much larger than the landward section which is 250 meters along the top of a cliff on the north side of the ancient Aspros River bed.

"All of what we see on the land is just a tip of the iceberg of what is in the water," said director Albert Ammerman, of Colgate University in Hamilton New York.

Aspros, with another site at Agia Napa, was used by seafaring foragers who frequented Cyprus well over 10,000 years ago, before the first permanent settlers in 8200 BC. The era in question coincided with a climatic cold snap known as the Younger Dryas (12,800 to 11,600 years ago) when the sea level was 60-70 meters (200-300 feet) lower than today.

ATLIT, ISRAEL

During the Neolithic period when the Mediterranean was about 20 m lower than it is today, a large coastal plain existed off the coast of Israel. At a depth of twelve meters, about 400 m from the shore of Atlit, an 8,000 year old Neolithic village with well preserved dwellings and artifacts, was discovered under a layer of sand.

Twelve structures with paved courtyards and plazas between them have been excavated. A long brick wall at the edge of the village was probably built as protection against flooding from the nearby wadi. Water was provided from a 5.5 m deep well cut into the sandstone, its upper part lined with stones. Between the village houses were several stone lined pits, two or three meters in diameter which served as silos for storing food. Fifteen tombs, some within the houses, were also found.

Many flint and bone artifacts were salvaged from the seabed, as well as stone bowls used in this pre-pottery period. Animal bones found indicate that the village's economy was based on farming and herding, hunting and fishing.

In Phonecian times, Atlit possessed one of the earliest breakwaters in the Mediterranean, dating from the 7th to 6th centuries BC. The breakwaters were built of straight walls enclosing a natural bay. The foundations consist of large ashlar blocks laid on the rock of the seabed and along a small islet offshore. A wall which included a gate separated the harbor from the city.

PAVLO PETRI, GREECE is a Bronze Age underwater site in Greece discovered by geologist Nicholas Flemming who recounted its discovery in his 1971 book 'Cities in the Sea.'

In 1968 the ruins were surveyed by a team of divers from Cambridge University who used a camera suspended from a balloon to photograph the site from the air and a draughtsman, Mike Walton, to draw up plans. Then they marked the sea floor with a grid of white plastic sheets placed every 20 meters over the whole site to draw up a detailed map of the ruins which were the largest ever mapped.

According to Flemming, "The Mycenaean city of Elaphonisos – or Pavlo Petri, as it is now called, was no palatial or capital city. It was a provincial commercial port which drew its wealth from its important position on the trade route to Crete and from the fertile plains around Vatike Bay. The oldest material was found on the island of Pavlo Petri itself, showing that the site was occupied in the Early Helladic Period, before 2000 BC, but most of the ruins and pottery were Mycenaean, dating from between 1500 and 1000 BC. The ruins are mostly of houses and streets and these stretch back from Pavlo Petri, across the basin towards the shore..." (Cities in the Sea, p 59)

The ruins, dating from before 2000 BC to Mycenaean times, consist mainly of intact uncemented stone walls although many had collapsed. An exhaustive search of the underwater site revealed no buildings below 3 meters down (10'). Two main streets were mapped as well as 15 complete homes and 37 tombs. It is suggested that the town had been covered by earth and sand after people abandoned it during submergence, before gradually sinking below the sea.

As no pottery has been recovered which is dated later than Mycenaean times, it is possible that the city was overwhelmed by the cataclysmic volcanic eruption of Santorini, although there is no evidence to support this.

REFERENCE: N. Flemming, 'Cities in the Sea' Doubleday, 1971

PHONECIAN & EGYPTIAN SITES
SIDON AND TYRE, LEBANON

Tyre was already a mighty Phonecian city built on an island when Alexander the Great besieged it in 332 BC. After defeating the Tyrians, he built a mole which joined the island of Tyre to the mainland. Reports from visitors in the 14th century indicated that the harbor was still in use, but by 1697 when Henry Maundrell arrived, the moles and reefs were indistinguishable.

Frenchman Father Antoine Poidebard arrived in Lebanon in 1934 and decided to survey underwater Phonecian sites off the coast, particularly in Tyre and Sidon. In Tyre he saw no sign of the great port. He made the first use of aerial photography with pilot Lieutenant Loquinaire to study the harbor of Tyre. His photographs guided divers to survey the harbor. Poidebard used a sextant to plot the ruins and took many photographs, as well as tape recordings on a 35 mm camera.

The southern or Egyptian harbor was enclosed by a wall 2,500 feet long and 25 feet thick built of 10 feet long stones, bounded with iron and reinforced with concrete. The western wall was of similar design but over 35 feet thick. The eastern end had a shipbuilding yard and repair basin as well as a fresh-water tank.

The northern or Sidonian harbor was smaller and more strongly fortified. The Tyrians reinforced the southern reef with two extra walls formed of blocks weighing 15 tons each.

Poidebard's underwater surveys at Sidon and Tyre had practical value for the French administration in Lebanon. A modern breakwater in Sidon had silted up immediately, whereas Poidebard's surveys revealed that the ancient breakwaters had sophisticated systems of sluice gates that allowed the silt to wash through.

Recent surveys conducted in Lebanon have enabled geologists to map out the former coastlines that have been buried by sediment. Sidon has extended to the sea through the buildup of silt while Tyre, which was once an island, has been joined to the mainland by silting. Much of the old settlement has sunk beneath the waves.

Nick Marriner of the European Centre for Research and Teaching on the Geosciences of the Environment (CEREGE) in Aix-en-Provence, France, and his team set out to drill beneath modern city centres to determine how the coastlines have changed over the centuries. Because of the civil war which only ended in 1990, little excavation has been carried out in Lebanon. Marriner said, "At Tyre there are presently no large-scale excavation sites, and much of our knowledge derives from work undertaken during the nineteenth century to the early 1970s."

Recent discoveries by Marriner's team suggest that Poidebard discovered an urban section of ancient Tyre, rather than the submerged southern harbor.

Marriner, who has drilled forty cores throughout Sidon and Tyre, discovered that the cities have been occupied since about 3000 BC. His examination of the soil shows that the rate of coastal silting multiplied by tenfold during the Roman occupation. The Romans and Byzantines must have been forced to dredge the harbors.

The survey indicates that the old harbors lay beneath today's urban centres. Marriner expresses concern that the archeological sites will be lost in the current rapid urban expansion and hopes they will be protected.

REFERENCE: BioEd Online January 6, 2006 http://www.bioedonline.org/news/news.cfm?art=2253

N. Flemming, 'Cities in the Sea'

CARTHAGE, TUNISIA which was destroyed by the Romans in 146 BC and later rebuilt, also has some underwater harbor ruins. Two enclosed harbor basins, called cothons, are now stagnant lakes in the suburbs of Tunis. Nicholas Flemming and his wife Natalka visited this area and "saw at once the irregular areas of stones projecting from the water which have puzzled archeologists and historians for over a hundred years. On existing evidence, it is not clear whether they are the remains of an external port which was enclosed by breakwaters, or large solid quays against which ships were berthed, or whether it was a part of the town built out into the water on artificially reclaimed land. We swam for hours over the huge tumbled blocks of masonry, some of them several yards square, but apart from establishing that the ruins extended to a depth of more than 20 feet of water, which was unexpected, we could find nothing certain about their origin or purpose. The water was a dark brown-yellow, containing much silt from the shallow waters of the bay...which reduced the underwater visibility to a few feet, and in the deeper water it was impossible to continue the survey without extensive equipment."

REFERENCE: N. Flemming, 'Cities in the Sea'

LEMTA, TUNISIA

In 1966 a team of divers from Cambridge under the leadership of Bob Yorke and Mike Dallas surveyed a large number of sites on the Tunisian shore. They discovered a strange linear structure off the coast of Lemta, ancient Leptis Minor, but were unable to dive it. The Flemmings explored the area and discovered a solitary wall which enclosed a ridge of gravel and rubble which was raised above the seafloor. It turned out to be a mole or jetty 600 yards long, faced on each side by a stone wall.

MOTYA, SICILY was built on an island in Carthaginian times and destroyed by the Greeks. The causeway built by Dionysius in the siege of 397 BC can still be seen under the water to the north of the island. A mole built by the Romans in the siege of Lilybaeum in 250 BC is found in a lagoon, as well as Roman lead pipes. The ancient Cothon of Motya was explored in 1962 by divers under the direction of Miss Joan du Plat Taylor.

Another harbor on the north of the island of Motya ws formed by breakwaters which are now completely underwater. According to Flemming there is no evidence of water level change in Motya, and the drowned causeway might have occurred because of pillaging of the stone.

NORA, SARDINIA was first mapped in 1904 by Patroni and explored in 1963-4 by an amateur team led by Bill St John Wilkes.

There are roads, buildings and dockside structures submerged under 10 feet of water from the Carthaginian era.

GREEK & ETRUSCAN ERA SITES
CRETAN SITES

Quite a few Minoan sites have been explored in Crete which are partly submerged by a change in sea level of about three feet. In 1925 archeologist Spiridon Marinatos explored the Minoan port at Agaioi Theodoroi near Knossos, where submerged docks were found cut into solid rock. At Chersonisos, also near Knossos, he found a concrete Roman mole complete with mooring bollards. Beyond the Roman mole were the scattered remains of a primitive breakwater which may have formed an earlier harbor. Small harbors were also discovered at Pseira and Mochlos which were over four thousand years old.

According to author David Hatcher Childress "Underwater sites are particularly common on Crete, since the west coastline of Crete has risen a few meters in historical times, whereas the east coast has sunk. For those who like exploring the ancient sunken harbors such as Olous (near Elounda), Limin Chersonisou, Itanos, Mochlos etc are of interest. There are severe penalties for the removal of archeological material...The reason that most ancient Minoan ports are not on maps is that they are generally under water! Crete has lost a great deal of coast just in the last 3,000 years. ('Lost Cities of Atlantis, Ancient Europe & the Mediterranean' pp121-2)

Olous, near Eloundra, was known as the port of Driros in Roman times and still has ruins from that era visible beneath the waves at a depth of up to 3 meters. Sunken traces of harbor installations can be observed although the site has never been excavated.

SYBARIS, ITALY was founded in Italy by Greek colonists from Helike about 720 BC. It flourished as a port for goods exported from Greece and Asia Minor to the Etruscan cities of Italy. Sybaris became a wealthy city and its inhabitants were so renowned for their luxurious lifestyle that the word 'sybarite' became synonymous with decadence and over indulgence.

When Sybaris was attacked by its neighbour Crotona in 510 BC, the Crotonites, Strabo tells us, diverted the river Crathis to flow over the captured city, destroying it completely.

Archeologists searched for Sybaris in the 1960s with magnetometers and probes. Finally they discovered the ruins under 15-20 feet of mud. At some point the coastal dunes on which the city had stood had sunk below sea level, forming a lagoon. Then the site rose again but it was still below sea level and any excavation was immediately filled with water. Its future excavation will be a major undertaking, requiring huge pumps and earth moving machines.

KENCHREAI, GREECE

Kenchreai on the Saronic Gulf near the city of Corinth was excavated thoroughly between 1962 and 1969 by members from the University of Chicago and Indiana University. The site of Kenchreai still bears its ancient name and ruins on both the north and south moles have always been visible beneath the surface of the waves. Part of the ancient city is now beneath the modern village of Kechrees, but the commercial, residential and burial sites lie beneath cultivated land, while there are extensive ruins in the area of the harbor.

Extensive ruins of the harbor moles and excavations beneath the harbor uncovered dense remains related to the ancient maritime industry. Some buildings served maritime purposes such as warehouses and fish tanks while others were lavishly appointed structures such as a temple to Isis and Aphrodite as well as a Christian basilica. All excavated areas produced large amounts of pottery which can be dated to as late as the sixth century AD. A submerged cache of wooden crates containing over one hundred large glass panels depicting scenes of maritime life and great intellectual figures, was discovered by Professor Scranton.

TURKEY

The ancient Lycian town of Kevona in Turkey was called **Simena**. Today it is the fishing village of Kalek. In the second century AD a huge earthquake caused a downward shift in the land which was half sunk beneath the waters, particularly the residential section of Kimena. About half the houses were submerged and staircases still descend into the water. The necropolis was also partially submerged.

Myndos near Bodrum has sunken ruins including walls and spy towers caused by a large earthquake which destroyed the city in ancient times. The walls which linked Myndos with Tavsan island and the building above the artificial harbor sank although both buildings appear to be intact beneath the water.

SICILY

Although an archeological team failed to find any shipwrecks or evidence of sunken structures in **Syracuse** harbor in 1957-8, Nicholas Flemming had better luck. He located broad strips of rubble, broken tiles, and stone blocks. Some masonry was discovered at depths of 100 feet, suggesting that the area suffered from an inundation, rather than subsidence.

ETRUSCAN ERA SITES
PYRGI, ITALY

In 1959 Piero Nicola Gagallo, a skin diving Italian marquis, claimed that he discovered a lost Etruscan city off the coast of Pyrgi, north of Rome. Pyrgi was an early Etruscan settlement which had once extended over ten acres. Although the town was abandoned during Roman Republican times, its port had grown into one of the most important during Imperial times. Local fishermen showed Gagallo a reef where they had fished up relics for sale to tourists. One mile offshore, according to a Time Magazine article 'Drowned Cities' (March 9, 1959) he found weed covered ruins, chunks of cut marble and "Something that looks like a street or pier stretching along the bottom for about 100 feet." He believed the ruins covered 20 acres and were in water 30 to 50 feet deep.

Gagallo worked with the Mediterranean Institute of Underwater Archeology to coordinate his explorations of the site. According to the article about twenty to thirty ruins were known to Italian skin-divers, including a large underwater city near Venice and another, off Mondragone, north of Naples, which has ruins along the bottom for nearly three miles. However, almost fifty years later, little is reported about these underwater sites.

The remaining land portions of Pyrgi itself have been excavated and yielded valuable golden tablets written in both Etruscan and Phonecian. Today the town is famous for its medieval castle which has been transformed into a museum of the area and has tours to the underwater ruins. The museum's website can be found at http://www.museosantasevera.org/engver/index2.html while the Time Magazine article can be viewed at :

http://www.time.com/time/magazine/article/0,9171,825689,00.html

SPINA, ITALY

Until the 20th century, this Etruscan port city on the Adriatic was lost under marshes far from the coast. For decades fishermen had been selling exquisite Etruscan vases which they had recovered from the marshes. The area was drained in 1922 and the necropolis was discovered. Aerial photography revealed the outlines of buildings, roads and drainage canals.

ROMAN ERA SITES

CAESAREA, ISRAEL

Caesarea in Israel was the largest and most impressive port in the Roman Empire when it was inaugurated in 10 BC by King Herod to honor his Roman patron Caesar Augustus. It was constructed of 'hydraulic cement', a mixture of volcanic ash, lime and rubble which would harden in water. The magnificent port took around twelve years to build and the labor of thousands of men.

In the Middle Ages a section of Caesarea disappeared under the waves.

In 1960 Dr Edwin Link took his research ship 'Sea Diver' to Caesarea and discovered many artifacts, including a medal showing the towers at the entrance of the ancient port. Kenneth Macleash, a 'Life' editor who accompanied the Link diving team wrote: "As we approach the crumbling ruin of the jetty it looms dark and formless. At six feet or seven it comes into clear focus... We move on, following the sea-changed ruin toward its end at the harbor mouth... I turn to see Bullitt pointing at a spot on the 20 ton block beside us. He draws his knife from its leg sheath and pokes at it. Turning, I see an odd lump on the block near me. It juts out a few inches from the stone and has an unnatural looking hole in its centre. I tear the moss away and brush it clean with my fingers…The hole is perfectly rectangular, a few inches deep. Its sides do not feel like stone. I move over to where Bullitt is working with his knife. He has found a similar hole. Its edges glow like silver where the blade has scraped them. We swarm all over the block and find that there are seven lumps in parallel lines, all with rectangular holes. On the sandy bottom lies an eighth lump, apparently washed out of the stone by wave action…I grab it up and sink instantly to the sea floor. It is pure lead, about 20 pounds of it." ('Mysteries of the Deep', Joseph Thorndike Jr)

The site has been excavated for the past three decades by the late Professor Avner Raban of the University of Haifa's Recanati Institute for Maritime Studies. In April 2006 it was announced that the remains of Herod's harbor had been turned into an underwater museum where divers could view some 36 different sign posted sites. The park was developed with the financial assistance of the Caesarea Development Corporation.

CAESAREA, ALGERIA was the western base for both the Alexandrian and Syrian fleets in North Africa. It was first described by Thomas Shaw in 1737 as being in "miserable condition" with a cothon and other dilapidated buildings. In the twentieth century Dioble dived around the visible ruins but was convinced that there was a larger harbor concealed beneath the water. His efforts resulted in the discovery of four huge harbor basins, as well as a large mole covered with ruined buildings and another curved mole forming the second basin. He believed that another mole formed the fourth basin but could not locate it.

SALAMIS, CYPRUS

This was originally settled by the Phonecians and was the site of a naval battle between the Greeks and Persians in 450 BC. It was an important Roman era town which was later converted to Christianity. Salamis was destroyed by Arab invaders in the 7th century and became submerged by sand which preserved its buildings during an earthquake. There are well preserved Roman forums, baths and a gymnasium and rumours of similar buildings or breakwaters offshore.

FOSSAE MARINAE, a Roman city supposedly sank east of the Rhone delta in France. Professor Denizot was convinced that legends of this sunken city were true in 1930 but it wasn't until the 1950s that Dr Beaucaire started diving there with amateur assistants.

Fossae Marinae was an important staging point in Roman times and Beaucaire discovered ruins stretching several hundred yards from Pointe Sainte Gervaise into dark muddy water. After four years of removing layers of sand, clay and mud, the foundations of the city were uncovered. The villas uncovered were quite primitive, while the most important structures were the quay and mole. Beaucaire also found several columns and part of an arch lying in 15 feet of water. Due to the massive amounts of sediment brought down by the Rhone River, the whole delta with its Roman roads and quarries has subsided at least 12 feet.

EGYPT

In May 2006 Reuters reported that Egyptian authorities had discovered the submerged ruins of what appears to be a Roman city 20 miles (35km) east of the Suez Canal. They found buildings, bathrooms, a Roman fortress, ancient coins, vases and pottery dating back to the Roman era which lasted in Egypt from 30 BC to 337 AD. They also discovered four bridges belonging to the submerged castle, part of which had been discovered in 1910.

CONTROVERSIAL RUINS

These claims are unable to be verified by conventional archeologists. They may, or may not exist.

> • "In front of Marseilles (France) the passages of an underwater cliff have revealed a series of mine shafts and smelting facilities presumably established at a period when humanity was at the so called 'cave-man level." (C. Berlitz, 'Atlantis The Lost Continent Revealed' p201)

Tauroeis was founded by the Greeks of Massilia, about 20 miles east of Marseille. In 1755 the Abbe Barthelemy excavated the beach near St Cyr and discovered mosaics. In 1781 Lieutenant-General Marin excavated this beach and claimed to have discovered pottery, an aqueduct, theatre, baths, temples, tombs and a quay. He made a map of the area. However, in 1806 Monsieur Millin decided that the ruins had belonged to a large villa belonging to Quinctianus which supposedly covered four acres.

Between 1852 and 1861 Abbe Magloire Giraud carried out excavations and discovered the city of Tauroeis but in a different area from that excavated by Marin. Modern archeologists have concluded that the ruins belong to a villa which toppled from a cliff into the sea.

• Archeologist and skin diver Jim Thorne claims to have discovered an ancient acropolis with columns and radiating roads off the Greek island of Melos. (ibid p202)

• "Captain Jacques Cousteau tells of having discovered a road along the sea bottom of the Mediterranean which he followed until his air supply got low." (ibid)

• Other claims about underwater ruins in Greece are ignored by archeologists according to a blog on website:

http://dancingfromgenesis.wordpress.com/category/submerged-ancient-ruins/

The author, James Nienhuis, believes that the Ice Age ended much later than is ascribed by geologists and that any evidence refuting this claim, such as megalithic underwater ruins, is ignored. He claims that huge sculpted megalithic columns and blocks have been discovered off Alonissos Island, presumably from the submerged ancient Ikos. Nienhuis also mentions that submerged ruins have been reported off Plytra, Abdera, Epidaros, Platygiali, Asakos and Elafonisi but "are avoided like the plague by the mainstream scientific outfits, because they reveal that the Ice Age ended much later than is popularly advertised… and don't want to present this powerful evidence which underlines their timeline for ancient history."

While Nienhuis's geological theories may be suspect, his

claim that Greek authorities ignore submerged ruins should be investigated. Whilst it is difficult to substantiate such claims, another website **http://www.iridescent-publishing.com/msc/msc18. htm** does mention the submerged ruins off Alonissos Island, although no description is given. "A flat, volcanic islet, Psathura lies at the northernmost point of the archipelago. To approaching seafarers it must seem almost invisible since it hardly rises more than ten meters out of the sea. Submerged ruins are all that remain of the ancient town of Alonissos which once stood here."

• Chryse was a small island in the Aegean Sea which was mentioned in legends but had disappeared by the second century AD. Its main feature was a temple to Apollo and its patron deity a goddess called Chryse. The Greek traveler Pausanias wrote: "No long sail from Lemnos was once an island Chryse. The waves utterly overwhelmed it and Chryse sank and disappeared in the depths." ('Description of Greece', 8.33.4)

• In 1960 an amateur archeologist claimed to have rediscovered the island which is now a "sunken mass known as Karos Bank, a 10 square mile area near the island of Lemnos." The Kharos Bank is about 40 feet below the surface and white building blocks were said to be visible on the sea floor.

YARMUTA, LEBANON

Amateur diver and historian Mohammed El-Sarji and Lebanese historian Yossef El-Hourany claimed in 2001 that they had discovered the lost Egyptian port of Yarmuta off the coast of Lebanon. This town, known from the Armana tablets, disappeared from history about 3,300 years ago.

Over ten months from 2000 to 2001 El-Sarji photographed and mapped an underwater region about three miles long and half a mile off the beach after making about six hundred dives to the site. On his survey he photographed paving stones of a central square, the remains of a stairway and dykes as well as statues of Egyptian god Set and goddess Bastet. Some of the streets were over 60 meters long and three meters wide.

"They seemed to go on forever," he said. "So wonderfully preserved. I had never seen anything like it."

Cheryl Ward of Florida State University in Tallahassee who reviewd El-Sarji's photographs commented, "If it is Yarmuta, it is a very exciting find because Yarmuta was one of the cities that caused the Egyptians a lot of trouble. If it is a port, particularly from that early period, it is even more exciting because early port sites are few and far between." However, she did concede that other archeologists were not convinced about the identity of the ruins even though "It is highly likely that the photos illustrate some parts of a submerged site."

El-Hourany responded, "What is worthy to note is our discovery of a very wide field of thermal springs under the water of the sea, near the shore, at a distance less than 10 km (six miles) from our site." Such springs appear in ancient descriptions of Yarmuta. Furthermore, the Egyptian statues gave them the identity of Yarmuta which was an Egyptian political centre of the time. The local name for the area is now Ormitho which was mentioned by Strabo in Roman times.

REFERENCES:
http://farshores.org/amyarmut.htm
Http://www.usatoday.com/news/world/june01/2001-06-28-sunken-cities.htm

CLAIMS OF ATLANTIS IN CYPRUS

Iranian American Robert Sarmast has been fascinated with Atlantis since childhood. He was influenced by the research of Russian and Israeli scientists who found a stretch of sunken land off the Cypriot coast in 1989. His book 'Discovery of Atlantis' argues that Cyprus was the highest peak of a lost continent which was destroyed by rising waters. The Mediterranean basin suffered a catastrophic flood with the destruction of the Gibraltar 'dam' that once closed the Mediterranean sea from the Atlantic about 10,000 years ago. This matches Plato's story of an island 'swallowed up' by a catastrophic flood at about the same time. Unfortunately this date does not tally with scientific evidence which dates the breaching of the Gibraltar dam at about five million years ago.

In late 2004 Sarmast announced that he had found convincing and indisputable evidence locating the site of Atlantis off the coast of Cyprus. As the author of a book equating Cyprus with Atlantis, he persuaded Cypriot government officials, as well as the Cyprus Tourist Agency, to help fund the expedition which employed side-scan sonar. His team spent six days scanning the Mediterranean sea bed between Syria and Cyprus and claimed to have found massive man-made structures, including two straight 2 km (1.25 mile) long walls on a hill.

"The Hill, as a whole, basically looks like a walled, hillside territory and this hillside territory matches Plato's description of the Acropolis hill with perfect precision," he told BBC reporter Tabitha Morgan. "Even the dimensions are exactly perfect, so if all these things are coincidental, we have the world's greatest coincidence going on."

http://news.bbc.co.uk/go/pr/fr/-2/hi/europe/4011545.stm.

"What we have here is a whole city, an ancient civilization, megalithic sites packed full of artifacts. We can expect to find colossal buildings, bridges, roads, canals and stone temples. With no sunlight, heat, oxygen or wind to degrade its remains. Atlantis will be mummified in the cold waters of the deep sea, frozen in time."

Sarmast claimed that he had identified many areas described by Plato, including a rectangular plain, running east to west, containing a metropolis at its centre. "My discovery will vindicate Plato. Within his dialogues Plato provides factual clues as to what Atlantis was like. I have matched all but two of the 45 clues with the area around Cyprus... Plato's account is so detailed that it is possible to make city plans based on his description. These match exactly the antediluvian maps of Cyprus as discovered through oceanographic mapping."

Cyprus in its current form seems to be the mountaintop of what used to be a much larger island. An underwater valley stretching between Cyprus and Syria was probably 'the great plain' of Atlantis and an underwater mountain in the middle of the valley appears to be the Acropolis Hill of Atlantis city. Sarmast claims that the ruins can be found about 80 km from the coast of Cyprus.

Within days of his enthusiastic announcement, scientists were casting doubt on his 'discovery'. German physicist Christian Huebscher of the University of Hamburg stated that he and other scientists, who were experts on the salt layers of the sea floor, had also surveyed the area a year previously on the Dutch research vessel 'Pelagia'. They had been researching volcanic formations called 'mud diapirs'. Huebscher found that Sarmast's acropolis was actually a well known volcanic ridge with mud slides on some of the ancient volcanoes about 100,000 years old.

Such mud volcanoes exist on the bottom of many oceans and occur when the mud which lies beneath the salt layers penetrates through fractures and breaks into the salt layers, thus bulging from the bottom of the sea floor.

Undaunted, Sarmast issued a challenge for his detractors to "prove their claims" even though his sonar images seemed to support the volcanoes hypothesis. He spoke of a 'flat top mountain' and not mud volcanoes. Furthermore, his claim that 'man-made structures' were seen by the sonar images was unable to stand up to scrutiny as side-scan can only show the contours of the sea bed. Only a ROV or underwater camera could reveal underwater structures.

In September 2006 Sarmast and his team sent a second expedition with a Remote Operated Vehicle to film the great wall. On his website **http://www.discoveryofatlantis.com** he gave this less than enthusiastic update of the findings in May 2007: "The second expedition on September of 2006 proved that the anomalies on and around the purported Acropolis Hill, situated in the middle of the rectangular 'great plain' of Atlantis, are natural…The sub-bottom profiler used allowed to view the structure of the seafloor up to about 100 feet, and revealed that the 'wall' at the base of the hill is not man-made. However, it also showed that the anomalies are at least hundreds of thousands of years old. This means that when the underwater valley stretching between Cyprus and Syria was above water, and people began to inhabit the area, they would have found an ideal location for a 'natural fortress.'

"We were able to determine the characteristics of the seafloor by using a sub-bottom profiler which sends a powerful but focused form of acoustic energy (sonar) that penetrates the mud...The problem is that in order to penetrate the mud with sound, the sonar energy has to be focused into a very narrow beam that is used to see large areas of the seabed itself. Therefore, our aim of seeing what is below the mud was severely limited because we could only get a glimpse, a narrow look of about a foot or so under the silt. This meant that if there were man-made structures such as buildings, currently below the mud, it would have been impossible for us to recognize them. We knew this going in, and were hoping that the purported wall was man-made because it was so large that we could find it, cut across it with the sonar in tow, and get a glimpse of what it was made of. We knew that finding regular man-made structures below the mud would be an impossible task since the area has been below water for thousands of years and a lot of sedimentation has happened in that time."

He concluded, "We have exhausted the means available to us, given the technological limitations for deep-sea research, and the results failed to either prove or disprove the Cyprus theory... There is no way to find out without the ability to 'X-ray large areas of the seafloor, to see what's under the mud, and discover whether or not man-made structures are there. Narrow sonar beams that give us foot-wide glimpse of what's under the mud, in a straight line as the sonar device is towed behind the ship, are not going to provide what is needed." He suggested that core samples of the seabed from the rectangular valley could be analysed to see when it was above water.

Sarmast's May 24, 2007 update concluded; "There are several cities hidden under the mud, within that rectangular valley, and finding them is practically impossible for the time being, but we are certain that the only thing standing between us and their discovery is time itself. Plato will yet be vindicated..."

REFERENCES: C. Berlitz, 'Atlantis, the Lost Continent Revealed'

http://news.bbc.co.uk/go/pr/fr/-2/hi/europe/4011545.stm.

Discovery of Atlantis http://www.discoveryofatlantis.com

Photo credit: http://www.discoveryofatlantis.com

ATLANTIS IN MALTA CLAIMS

Hubert Zeitlmair, a retired German real-estate investor, first went to Malta in 1993 where he was inspired by the megalithic temples to conduct his own research. An aerial photograph taken in 1933 convinced him that ruins lay on the seabed off the coast of Malta. On July 13, 1999 he claimed to have discovered the submerged ruins of a megalithic temple. The discovery was announced at a meeting of the Paleo Astronaut Society in Augsberg, Germany, on August 18. A web site, maltadiscovery.com includes the translation of an article from the Maltese newspaper '*iL Mument*' and an interview with Zeitlmair that appeared in '*Maltamag*.'

Zeitlmair's ruins allegedly sit on an underwater plateau about 500-900 meters long. The lowest point of the plateau is more than 25 m below sea level and the highest point is about 7 meters below sea level about one-and-one-half miles off the city of Sliema on Malta's east coast. The temple is said to be similar to Maltese land temples with gigantic stone blocks astronomically aligned, an avenue that goes up the centre of the structure and kidney like rooms orientated to an easterly direction. The walls are said to be preserved to a height of four to six meters (13 to nearly 20 feet).

Graham Hancock, researching his book 'Underworld' flew to Malta to meet with Zeitlmair and dive on the alleged ruins. Upon meeting the enigmatic German, he was surprised to discover that he was visually impaired and had used Maltese brothers Shaun and Kurt Arrigo to dive the site. As Hancock details in 'Underworld', repeated dives with the Arrigo brothers failed to turn up anything resembling a structure, although the famous 'cart ruts' were seen to continue into the sea from the coast. These ruts, resembling cart tracks, have a function which is not understood today. They are affectionately known as 'Clapham Junction'.

On his third visit to Malta in 2001, Hancock dived off the coast of Marfa Point and witnessed these enigmatic 'cart ruts' as well as a constructed canal underwater. He noticed that they were wider and deeper than the ruts at Clapham Junction and ran in parallel pairs as though left by cart wheels. Surprisingly, the ruts rose about 30 centimeters above the surrounding bedrock, like low, parallel walls. The canal like feature was spanned by a 'bridge' which was flat on top and level with the surrounding plain. They spied what appeared to be tool marks on the vertical walls of the canal.

Dr Anton Mifsud, President of the Prehistoric Society of Malta, believes that Malta is presently too small to have sustained the world's earliest architectural civilization; its antecedent civilization is missing and could be under the water. In fact 17,000 years ago the three Maltese islands of Malta, Comino and Gozo as well as Filfla were all joined to one land mass, itself joined to Sicily by a 90km landbridge. As Sicily was joined to Italy, Malta was physically part of Europe at that time. In his book 'Malta, Echoes of Plato's Island', he argues that Malta is a remnant of Atlantis, although he gives the date of this cataclysm of around 2200 BC when the great land bridge joining Malta to Filfla collapsed due to tectonic action. This catastrophic event caused a tsunami across Malta which destroyed the megalithic culture responsible for building the great structures of Tarxien and the Hypogeum.

The current Maltese islands were formed about 10,600 years ago, after earlier inundations had separated Malta from Sicily 16,500 years ago. A huge percentage of the country's landmass was inundated by 10,600, including any human inhabitants. Mifsud believes the underwater ruts and canals to be further evidence that Malta was Plato's island.

Before leaving Malta for the third time, Hancock was shown video footage taken by Shaun Arrigo of the underwater Sliema 'temple' and another site, registered as 'Janet-Johan' which showed large canals and parallel cart ruts much deeper and wider than the Marfa ones. "Some of the canals cut through the bedrock in perfectly straight horizontal lines for more than 100 meters without any break. Then, beyond them the camera came suddenly into an area of huge scattered megaliths. All were fallen except one which stood partially upright leaning at a drunken angle." ('Underworld,' p 448)

The Maltese Museum Department's archaeology curator Ruben Grima has visited Zeitlmair's site, and was unconvinced that the stones on the seafloor are indeed a temple, according to archaeologist Anthony Bonanno of the University of Malta. Bonanno himself is skeptical of the find, noting that even if there is a submerged structure it does not mean the temples need to be re-dated.

Shaun Arrigo was unable to comprehend why the Museums Department had "totally ignored" his findings, as the sites were lying "unprotected" at a depth of about 8 meters off the coast of northeast Malta. Arrigo had found a pottery plate 8 cm in diameter in one of the ruts and forwarded it to the Museums department, together with photographs. In response to the allegations the Museums Department replied that they had received a report by Anton Mifsud and intended to inspect the site in the near future. The department said that "no comment on the recently reported site can be attempted before a complete inspection has been carried out."

Six years later such a report is still not forthcoming.

In 2002 a film crew from Japanese television company TBS Vision Inc filmed archeological underwater sites around the Maltese islands with Anton Mifsud and Chris Aguis Sultana, an underwater photographer. Sultana is a director for Griffin and Crown Foundation for Underwater Prehistoric Research and has dived Maltese coasts since he was 21. He claimed, "The archway I found underwater could not have been made by nature. Its highly mechanical definition suggests that it was made by humans. The People of Atlantis are believed to have had a great knowledge on how to store water. The archway, I believe, used to form part of a water preservation system."

REFERENCE: G. Hancock, 'Underworld'

THE ISLAND OF SANTORIN
and
THE METROPOLIS OF ATLANTIS
AFTER PLATO (KRITIAS, 430 ᴠꟼC)

A map of the island of Thera, also called Santorini, as a possible model for the legend of Atlantis.

A portion of the underwater city of Elaphonisos, in the Aegean.

PART 4
THE ATLANTIC OCEAN
**MYTHICAL LOST LANDS IN THE ATLANTIC
THULE & HYPERBOREA
CELTIC REALMS LYONESSE, YS, HY BRASIL
CANTREF GWAELOD
ATLANTIC ODDITIES—MID ATLANTIC RIDGE
THE LOST CITY
HOLE IN THE CRUST
MYSTERIOUS ATLANTIC ISLANDS
MESOLITHIC SITES
NORTH SEA SETTLEMENTS
ISLE OF WIGHT
SEAHENGE, ENGLAND
DANISH SETTLEMENTS
ATLANTIS ON THE CELTIC SHELF HYPOTHESIS
CARNAC, BRITTANY
GERMAN AND FRISIAN LEGENDS
MID ATLANTIC RUINS?
CANARIES, AZORES
SEARCHING FOR ATLANTIS IN THE ATLANTIC
OTHER LANDMARKS IN ATLANTOLOGY**

MYTHICAL LOST LANDS IN THE ATLANTIC

At least two legends of lost lands existing in the north Atlantic such as Thule and Hyperborea have been circulating since ancient Greek times. The Celtic cultures believed in at least four sunken islands such as Lyonesse and Hy Brasil. Even though the Greeks were aware of the frigid nature of the polar regions, they postulated the existence of warm productive lands in perpetual sunshine existing in the higher latitudes. Hyperborea and Thule have influenced popular imagination, particularly with Nazi groups such as the Thule Society. Although there is absolutely no evidence that a circumpolar continent or island existed in antiquity, there is evidence that a huge tsunami originating from Norway inundated the North Atlantic 8,000 years ago.

THULE

The Greek explorer Pytheas first wrote of Thule in his now lost work 'On the Ocean' after his travels between 330 and 320 BC. It was said to be six days by sea north of Britain, near the 'frozen sea'. Roman writer Strabo, in his 'Geography' quotes from Pytheas saying, "Pytheas of Massilia tell us that Thule, the most northerly of the Britannic islands, is fartherest north, and that there the circle of the summer tropic is the same as the Arctic Circle'. But from the other writers I learn nothing on the subject—neither that there exists a certain island by the name of Thule, nor whether the northern regions are inhabitable up to the point where the summer tropic becomes the arctic circle." (Strabo Book 11, Chapter 5).

Naturalist Pliny the Elder examined Pytheas's claim: "The fartherest island of all, which is known and spoke of, is Thule; in which there be no nights at all, as we have declared, about mid-summer, namely when the sun passes through the sign of Cancer, and contrariwise no days in mid-winter; and each of these times they suppose do last six months, all day or all night'. (Book 1V, Chapter 16)

Polybius in his Histories gave Thule a more mystical description. "Those regions in which there was no longer any proper land nor sea nor air, but a sort of mixture of all three of the consistency of a jellyfish in which one can neither walk or sail, holding everything together, so to speak." (Book XXXIV)

HYPERBOREA

The ancient Greeks also had a legend of Hyperborea, a land of perpetual sun beyond the 'north wind.' Hecateus (about 500 BC) said that the holy place of the Hyperboreans lay "on an island in the ocean...beyond the land of the Celts." Popular accounts believed that the god Apollo's temple of Delphi was founded by individuals from Hyperborea, his homeland. The holy place of the Hyperboreans was built after 'the pattern of the spheres'; a place Apollo would visit on his swan drawn chariot.

Diodorus wrote, "Opposite to the coast of Celtic Gaul there is an island in the ocean, not smaller than Sicily, lying to the North — which is inhabited by the Hyperboreans, who are so named because they dwell beyond the North Wind. This island is of a happy temperature, rich in soil and fruitful in everything, yielding its produce twice in the year. Tradition says that Latona was born there, and for that reason, the inhabitants venerate Apollo more than any other God. They are, in a manner, his priests, for they daily celebrate him with continual songs of praise and pay him abundant honours.

In this island, there is a magnificent grove of Apollo, and a remarkable temple, of a round form, adorned with many consecrated gifts. There is also a city, sacred to the same God, most of the inhabitants of which are harpers, who continually play upon their harps in the temple, and sing hymns to the God, extolling his actions. The Hyperboreans use a peculiar dialect, and have a remarkable attachment to the Greeks, especially to the Athenians and the Delians..."

"It is also said that in this island the moon appears very near to the earth, that certain eminences of a terrestrial form are plainly seen in it, that Apollo visits the island once in a course of nineteen years, in which period the stars complete their revolutions, and that for this reason the Greeks distinguish the cycle of nineteen years by the name of "the great year"..."

The legend of Hyperborea was revived during the 18th and 19th centuries when it was postulated that the 'Aryan' (European) race originated in this sunken northern land. Writers such as Jean Sylvain Bailly, Rev William Warren and H.S Spencer tried to prove that man originated in the northern polar region. Madame Blavatsky, founder of the Theosophical Society, claimed that the 'second root race' originated in Hyperborea. Later root races were Lemurian, Atlantean and Aryan according to Theosophical doctrine.

Indian writer Bal Gangadhar Tilak's book 'Arctic Home' tried to prove that there was once a warm circumpolar continent which subsequently sank. He claimed Indian Vedic texts pointed to a 'realm of the gods' where the sun rises and sets once a year—a reference to the polar regions. With his mastery of the Vedic language, Tilak placed the original Arctic island existing around 10,000 BC, just before the end of the last Ice Age.

Zoroastrian H.S Spencer wrote his book 'The Aryan Ecliptic Cycle' in 1965, claiming that the Zoroastrian scriptures were more ancient than the Vedic and traced the progress of the 'Aryans' from the north to their new homes in Egypt, the Middle East and India. The Hyperboreans became associated with mystical enlightenment, or a paradise on earth.

THE CELTIC REALMS

The legend of a sunken kingdom appears in Cornish, Breton, Welsh and Irish mythology.

LYONESSE

Lyonesse, **Lyoness**, or **Lyonnesse, 'City of Lions'** is a sunken land believed to lie off the coast of Cornwall, near the Scilly Isles. In the Arthurian legend it is was the homeland of Tristram but before he could inherit it from his father, it had sunk beneath the waves. Sometimes it is also associated with the mystical isle of Avalon where King Arthur lies. The <u>Trevelyan</u> family of Cornwall believes its ancestor riding a white horse was the only survivor of the inundation. To this day the family's coat of arms bears a white horse rising from the waves.

It is suggested that the legend of Lyonesse has some factual element as a folk memory of the flooding of the Isles of Scilly and Mount's Bay near Penzance. Locals speak of a sunken forest in Mount's Bay and there is archeological evidence of the petrified tree stumps visible at very low tides. The Cornish name of St Michael's Mount is Carrak Looz en Cooz, meaning 'the grey rock in the wood'.

The Scilly Islands consist of around 100 mostly uninhabited granitic islands with white sand beaches although in Roman times they probably consisted of only one large island known as Siluran Insulam or Ictis. There is evidence of drowned houses, field walls

Sunken Realms

and graves which can be observed at very low tides. Stone huts off the island of Tean and now allegedly seven feet underwater. Furthermore, there are megalithic remains such as chamber tombs and standing stones from before recorded history and possibly many more off shore.

The Saxon Chronicle states that Lyonesse was inundated in 1099 while another legend states that Lyonesse disappeared in the year 1089 and contained 140 parish churches and many other holy places.

YS

Ys, also known as Is or Ker-Ys in Breton is a mythical city built in the Douarnenez Bay in Brittany by Gradlon, King of Cornouaille for his daughter Dahut. According to legend, Ys was built below sea level and protected from flooding by a dam with the only keys to the dam in Gradlon's possession. However, Satan made Dahut steal them for him and he opened the flood gates, killing all inhabitants except King Gradlon who was saved by Saint Wimwaloe. For further punishment the souls of the dead children were then swallowed by the ocean. Gradlon's statue still survives on horseback looking in the direction of Ys at Saint Corentin Cathedral.

Bretons believed Ys was the most beautiful city in the world and that Lutece was renamed Paris after Ys was destroyed, because Par-Is means 'Similar to Ys' in the Breton language. It is possible that Ys was a real city in the fifth century which was engulfed by the water as several Roman roads actually lead into the sea.

HY BRASIL

Hy Brasil, or Brasil, is a phantom island which features in many Irish myths, particularly that of St Brendan who sailed across the Atlantic in a coracle about 1,500 years ago. It was cloaked in mist except for one day every seven years when it became visible but could not be reached. The name probably comes from the Irish Ui Breasail, meaning descendants of the clan of Breasal. Belief in the island continued until the nineteenth century with the last alleged sighting being in 1872. In earlier centuries several expeditions left Ireland to search for it, the last led by John Cabot.

Maps depicted the island as circular with a river running across its diameter. On maps it was situated south west of Galway Bay from 1325 until 1865, by which time it was called Brazil Rock. In his 'Underworld', Graham Hancock reproduces a bathymetric map of the area which shows that an island the size of Hy Brasil exists under about 55 meters of water off the coast of Ireland. It would have been above sea level around 12,000 years ago. (p 502)

In 1684 the Irish historian O'Flaherty spoke of the enchanted island of Hy Brasil.

"From the Isles of Arran and the west continent often appears visible that enchanted island called O'Brasail and, in Irish, Beg Ara.

"Whether it be real and firm land kept hidden by the special ordnance of God, or the terrestrial paradise, or else some illusion of airy clouds appearing on the surface of the sea, or the craft of evil spirits, is more than our judgments can pound out.

"There is now living, Murrough O'Ley, who imagines he was himself personally in O'Brasail for two days and saw out of it the Isles of Arran, Golam Head, Iross-beg Hill, and other places on the western continent which he was acquainted with. The manner of it he relates, that being in Iross-Ainhagh, in the south side of the Barony of Ballynahinshy, about nine leagues from Galway by sea in the month of April, AD 1668, going alone from one village to another in a melancholy humour upon some discontent of his wife's (!) he was encountered by two or three strangers and forcibly carried by a boat into O'Brasail, as such as were within told him—and they could speak both English and Irish...

"In the western ocean, five or six leagues from the continent there is a sand bank about thirty fathoms deep in the sea. It is called in Irish, Imaire Bay, and in English, the Cod-fishing Bank. From this bank about twenty years ago, a boat was blown southwards by night; next day about noon the occupants spyed land so near them that they could see sheep within it, and yet durst not, for fear of illusions, touch shore, imagining it was O'Brasail, and they were two days coming back towards home..."

http://www.mythicalireland.com/ancientsites/tara/tara-atlantis.php

The legend of Hy Brasil has led some researchers to search for Atlantis in Ireland. Dr Ulf Erlingsson of Uppsala University claims,

"Just like Atlantis, Ireland is 300 miles long, 200 miles wide at the middle. They both feature a central plain that is open to the sea but fringed by mountains. No other island on earth even comes close to this description." Dr Erlingsson claims that the island did not sink, but the Dogger Bank in the North Sea was flooded in prehistoric times which may have inspired the legend of a sunken Atlantis. He believes that royal Tara was the Atlantean capital and other megalithic sites in Europe were part of the Atlantean empire.

His book 'Atlantis from a Geographer's Perspective: Mapping the Fairy Land' was published in 2004.

CANTREF GWAELOD meaning 'The Lowland Hundred' is the legendary sunken kingdom in Cardigan Bay, Wales. According to legend, its capital Caer Wyddno was a walled town which was defended from the sea by a dyke called Sarn Badrig, Saint Patrick's Causeway. One evening during a heavy storm, one of its drunken princes neglected the dykes and the sea swept through the open floodgates, drowning fourteen villages and killing many.

The church bells of Cantref Gwaelod are said to ring out in times of danger.

According to Nigel Pennick in 'Lost Lands and Sunken Cities', manuscript 3514 in the Library of Exeter Cathedral, dated at about 1280, speaks of three lost kingdoms submerged by the sea: "The kingdom of Tewthi, son of Gwynnon, King of Kaerrigog, between Mynwy (St David's) and Ireland. Noone escaped from it, neither man or beast, except Teithi Hen and his horse…The second kingdom was that of Helig, son of Glannawg that was between Cardigan and Bardsey Island and as far as Mynwy. That land was extremely good, fruitful and flat…and stretched from Aber (Abertstwyth) to Lleyn and as far as Aberdyfi. The sea submerged a third, the kingdom of Rhedfoe, son of Rheged…" (D. Childress, 'Lost Cities of Atlantis, Ancient Europe and the Mediterranean' p370)

http://www.bbc.co.uk/legacies/myths_legends/wales/w_mid/article_1.shtml

Although there is no archeological evidence that Cantref Gwaelod ever existed, in about 1770 William Pughe reported seeing ruins about four miles off the Welsh coast, between the rivers Ystwyth and Teifi. These were probably the three huge submerged ridges called sarns which stretch out several miles into Cardigan Bay.

In recent years remains of an ancient forest have been discovered beneath Cardigan Bay, giving credence to the legend of Cantref Gwaelod. In 2006 the BBC reported that a three year study by the Friends of Cardigan Bay would search for the ancient city. The oldest part of the submerged forest dates back to 3500 BC, while other sections at Borth near Aberustwyth probably date back to 1500 BC.

Phil Hughes, chairman of the Friends of Cardigan Bay, said: "There is a lot of evidence to suggest that Cantre'r Gwaelod existed and I believe there was land out there. It will be the first time that it would have been seriously researched from an ecological point of view. The make-up of the area would have provided a natural barrier against raiders and shelter from the weather."

"The primary aim of the project is to study the ecology of the sea bed in the area. We expect the project will last two to three years because the area measures some seven nautical miles."
     http://news.bbc.co.uk/2/hi/uk_news/wales/mid_/5016240.stm

Another legend surrounding Cardigan Bay is that of the lost palace of Helig ap Glannog which was swallowed by a huge flood. Later additions to the legend place it in Conway Bay in the 16th century. Yet another Welsh legend spoke of Caer Aranrhod in Carnarvon Bay which has been associated with a group of stones situated about a mile out to sea. According to Nick Flemming and F.J North, the three legends are based on patches of stones which were deposited by glaciers during the last Ice Age.

REFERENCES: Strabo Book 11, Chapter 5

Polybius 'Histories' Book XXXIV

'Mythical Ireland' http://www.mythicalireland.com/ancientsites/tara/tara-atlantis.php

Cantre'r Gwaelod—The Lost Land , BBC.Co.UK
     http://www.bbc.co.uk/legacies/myths_legends/wales/w_mid/article_1.shtml

BBC News Thursday 25 May, 2006
     http://news.bbc.co.uk/2/hi/uk_news/wales/mid_/5016240.stm

N. Flemming, 'Cities in the Sea'

ATLANTIC ODDITIES

MID ATLANTIC RIDGE

• The first soundings of the Atlantic depths were made by British, American, German and French warships in the nineteenth century. Ignatius Donnelly, the father of modern Atlantology interpreted the results of soundings taken of the Mid Atlantic Ridge in the 1870s as proof that Atlantis existed in this area. Deep sea soundings from the American 'Dolphin', German frigate 'Gazelle' and British ships 'Hydra', 'Porcupine' and 'Challenger' revealed that mountains existed across large sections of the Atlantic Ocean, from the Azores to Tristan d'Acunha which remain as the highest peaks of the lost continent.

• The 'Challenger' discovered the entire mid Atlantic Ridge covered with volcanic deposits, whereas the 'Gettysburg' found evidence of a submarine ridge or plateau connecting Madeira with the coast of Portugal.

• In 1898 when the Trans Atlantic cable was being laid, a breakage forced the cable to be retrieved with various rocks from the bottom of the Atlantic. French Atlantologist Pierre Termier believed that the 15,000 year old lava rocks had formed above water. This belief was confirmed by Dr Maria Klenova, of the Soviet Academy of Science, who examined rocks recovered from near the Azores. She expressed her opinion that the rock had been formed at atmospheric pressure about 15,000 years ago.

• The development of sonar during World War Two allowed scientists to observe mountains and ridges below the surface of the ocean. The presence of submarine flat topped mountains called seamounts or guyots was also discovered. Many Atlantic seamounts, such as the Ampere, are quite close to the surface. Berlitz wrote, "The sonar picture of the submerged islands as indicated on depth maps shows several great landmasses and suggests the presence of large bays, numerous lakes and river systems, indicated by underwater canyons." (C. Berlitz, 'Atlantis, the Lost Continent Revealed' p 16.)

• Other extensive land area existed north of Venezuela to the south Caribbean islands and east of present Central America. Yet another large continent sized underwater plateau extends from Newfoundland to France, the Azores and along the 20 degree line between Mexico and Africa.

• Coral brought up from depths of 3,000 feet near the Great Meteor Seamount and other mid-Atlantic locations indicates that either the sea level has dropped thousands of feet or the sea level has risen dramatically—or both.

• The Swedish research ship 'Albatross' taking cores from a depth of two miles in a fracture zone near the vicinity of St Peter and St Paul Rocks, brought up shallow water micro-organisms preserved in the mud, as well as other debris such as plants and twigs which had descended rapidly into the depths.

• Seabed cores taken from the Ridge in 1957 brought up freshwater plants from a depth of two miles. The Romanche valley has sands which had been formed by weathering when it was above sea level.

• Dr Maurice Ewing, a critic of Atlantis and prominent marine geologist, agreed that the lava at the bottom of the Atlantic had only formed recently in geological terms. "Either the land must have sunk two or three miles or the sea must have been two to three times lower than now. Either conclusion is startling." (Berlitz, ibid p34)

• Dr Kolbe announced the discovery of fresh water diatoms (microscopic plankton) and remains of land plants in cores recovered from two miles on the Mid Atlantic Ridge. (Berlitz ibid, p170)

• A 1969 Duke University research expedition dredged

fifty sites from a ridge running from Venezuela to the Virgin Islands. Granitic rocks which are normally found only on continents were brought up. Dr Bruce Heezen of the Lamont Geological Observatory said, "The occurrence of light coloured granitic rocks may support an old theory that a continent formerly existed in the region of the eastern Caribbean and that these rocks may represent the core of a subsided, lost continent."

• The British Journal New Scientist, June 5, 1975 ran an article 'Concrete Evidence for Atlantis?' on the discovery of "a sunken block of continent" which lies in the middle of the Atlantic Ocean. The discovery comes from dredge samples taken along the Vema offset fault, lying between Africa and South America at 11 degrees north. Not only did they discover shallow water limestone fragments, but also traces of shallow water fossils. The limestone is dated from 70 to 220 million years ago in the Mesozoic era.

THE LOST CITY

In 2000 the discovery of the fabulous 'Lost City' hydrothermal field at 30 degrees north on the Atlantic Massif excited the scientific community. Only nine miles from the Mid-Atlantic ridge, carbonate chimneys towered about 180 feet (60 m) above the seafloor, venting methane and other fluids at temperatures up to 90 degrees centigrade. The manned submersible 'Alvin' dived there in 2000 and 2003 and discovered it was unlike any other hydrothermal field ever discovered. Dense microbial communities which fed on the methane lived in the porous interior of the chimneys.

In 2005 another expedition from the NOAA research vessel the 'Ronald H Brown' dived to 700 meters (2,100 feet). Nearly every monolith in the Lost City was visited and photographed in detail.

HOLE IN THE CRUST

On March 1, 2007 Dr Chris MacLeod from Cardiff University was reported by the BBC as saying that the Earth's crust appeared to be missing across an area of several thousand square km on the mid Atlantic Ridge between the Cape Verde Islands and the Caribbean.

The hole, which lies at a depth of about 5,000 m, has a diameter of 3,000 to 4,000 m. Its depth is unknown, although it does lie in an undersea mountain range.

This hole in the crust is the largest ever discovered and does not seem to be repairing itself. Generally the oceanic crust is between 6 and 7 km thick. According to tectonic theory, this hole is anomalous. "Usually the plates are pulled apart and to fill the gap the mantle underneath has to rise up. As it comes up it starts to melt. That forms the magma," Dr McLeod said.

"Effectively it's a huge rupture —one side is being pulled away from the other. It's created a rupture so big it's actually pulled the entire crust away. We also think the mantle did not melt as much as usual and that the normal amount of mantle was not produced."

As a result, the mantle is exposed to seawater, creating a rock called serpentinite.

British scientists have embarked on a six week mission to study this anomaly on the RRS 'James Cook'. The survey voyage, costing $1m (£510,000), will be led by marine geophysicist Professor Roger Searle, from Durham University and sail from Tenerife. He has said, "We don't know why that is. Because of this gap we can see directly into the Earth's mantle."

The team intends to use sonar to build up an image of the seafloor and take rock cores using a robotic seabed drill.

REFERENCE: **http://news.bbc.co.uk/go/pr/fr/-/2/hi/uk_news/ wales/6405667.stm**

MYSTERIOUS ATLANTIC ISLANDS

- The island of Asmaida was discovered off the Azores in 1447 by the Portuguese. It was settled by colonists who established farms and built towns and harbors. However, after 1555 they were forced to abandon the island when it began to collapse into the sea after a volcanic eruption. For the next 260 years the remaining portion was known as Barenetha Rock but it too vanished and is now identified as the Milne Seamount.
- In 1622 the city of Villa Franca on the Azorian island of

Sao Miguel was buried in an earthquake. Great faults in the land and tsunamis resulted from this catastrophe.

• Islands have appeared and disappeared over the years. In 1811 a large volcanic island appeared in the Azores which suddenly disappeared after being charted as Sabrina.

• Nyey Island was discovered between Greenland and Iceland in 1783, but disappeared in 1830.

• The British merchant ship 'Jesmond' witnessed the birth of an island in the Atlantic in March 1882. At the coordinates of 31 degrees 25 inches N, 28 degrees, 40 inches west, about two hundred miles from both Madeira and the Azores, an island appeared from the depths in a cloud of smoke and mass of dead fish. Captain Robson and his party went ashore the new island which had no vegetation or sand, merely volcanic debris.

"While examining the base of the cliff where the rock was fractured and twisted as if by some tremendous convulsion, and disclosed a bed of breccia, a surprising discovery was made by one of the sailors. On thrusting a prong of a boat hook into the loosened mass of gravel, he dislodged a stone arrowhead. Excited by this incident the search was continued, and other articles of stone were discovered. A large excavation was made, and it was ascertained that the opening led between the crumbling remains of what must have been massive walls. A number of articles were exhumed, such as bronze swords, rings, hammers, carvings of heads and figures of birds and animals, and two vases or jars with fragments of bone, and one cranium almost entire. The most singular thing brought to view was what appeared to be a mummy, contained in a stone case. It was so incrusted with volcanic deposits as to be scarcely distinguished from the rock itself. Much difficulty was experience in dislodging the sarcophagus, which was finally taken out whole and, with the fossils, transported to the steamer."

The article continues: *"The captain thinks that the new land is a section of the immense ridge known to exist in the Atlantic, and of which the Azores and Canaries are a part. He took pleasure in exhibiting the fossils and curious articles of which he was the fortunate finder. The carved heads are in the Egyptian style of sculpturing, being distinguished by the veil or hood, which characterizes Egyptian figures. The urns and vases are spherical with large mouths, and upon them may be discerned inscriptions in hieroglyphics. The edges of the axes and arrow or spear points are blunted and jagged. The sword is a straight weapon of bronze, with a cross-hilt. "That is the mummy," remarked the captain, pointing to that the reporter had taken to be a long block of stone. Scrutinizing closely the lidless case, the outlines of a human figure could be traced through the coating of scoriae and pumice. It will require careful handling to remove the coating. Capt. Robson proposes to present the relics to the British museum at London upon his return to Liverpool."*

Investigations into this story by journalist N.L Hills revealed that it is unlikely that this story was a hoax as there really had been a Jesmond steamer captained by David Amory Robson. Unfortunately the records of this ship were destroyed during the Second World War, although it is known that during 1882 a large swathe of poisonous, volcanic fumes killed thousands of fish in the Atlantic Ocean. The island was never seen again and the British Museum claimed to have no knowledge of Captain Robson's unusual collection of artifacts.

- In 1931 two islands suddenly appeared off the coast of Brazil in the Fernando de Noronha group. Before they could be claimed by any nation, both islands unexpectedly sank between the waves.
- Surtsey rose from the sea off the coast of Iceland in 1963, to be followed by two smaller islands which are still there.
- In the mid 60s two islands rose and fell back into the North Atlantic Ocean. Syrtlingur towered to 210 above sea level and Jolnir spread to 15 square km before disappearing.

REFERENCE: Atlantisite.com **http://geocities.com/MotorCity/ Factory/2583/robson.htm**

MESOLITHIC SITES

NORTH SEA SETTLEMENTS

'The Guardian' reported on Friday September 12, 2003 that Britain's earliest underwater archeological site had been discovered more than 500 meters off the Tyneside coast near Newcastle. Artifacts, including tools and arrowheads, were recovered by a team from the University of Newcastle upon Tyne belonging to the Mesolithic era about 10,000 years ago.

Penny Spikins, who is leading the international submerged prehistoric landscapes project at the university found the artifacts by chance when learning to scuba dive. "To the average person they might appear like ordinary stones you would find on the beach, but to a specialist they were something very exciting indeed," she said.

David Miles, chief archaeologist at English Heritage, said: "We know that there is a prehistoric Atlantis beneath the North Sea, where an area equal to the size of Britain attached us to the continent. This discovery gives us a stepping stone into this unknown world."

Scientists at the University of Birmingham have been using seismic data to reveal the prehistoric landscape of the North Sea sections which were above water more than 10,000 years ago. With the aid of high powered computing facilities at the University's HP VISTA Centre, a team of archeologists, geologists and engineers explored a landscape where humans once hunted animals and gathered plants.

The team has made the fascinating discovery of a large river, comparable in size to the Thames or Rhine when its valley was flooded about 7,000 years ago due to glacial melting. The river's channel was over 600 meters wide and has been traced to a length of 27.5 km travelling in a northwest to southeasterly direction.

Dr Vincent Gaffney, Director of the University's Institute of Archaeology and Antiquity commented, "This pilot project has great significance to the whole of the quaternary research community, both in its environmental, geological & archaeological forms. We intend to extend the project to visualise the whole of the now submerged land bridge that previously joined Britain to Northern Europe as one land mass, providing scientists with a new insight into the previous human occupation of the North Sea."

On April 24, 2007 'The Guardian' reported that scientists had compiled 3D records from oil prospecting vessels working in the North Sea to piece together a landscape covering 23,000 sq km stretching from the coast of East Anglia in the UK to the edge of northern Europe. Scars left by ancient river beds and lakes up to 25 km across, salt marshes and valleys were identified.

Vince Gaffney, who led the project said, "This is the best preserved prehistoric landscape, certainly in the whole of Europe and possibly the world."

http://www.guardian.co.uk/science/story/0,,2064221,00.html?gusrc=ticker-103704

ISLE OF WIGHT

On July 31, 2007 it was announced that excavations of an 8,000 year old site were taking place at the National Oceanography Centre, Southampton. Maritime archeologists from the Hampshire and Wight Trust for Marine Archeology (HWTMA) were diving at a site just off the Isle of Wight which was beneath eleven meters of water.

The site was discovered about ten years ago when lobsters disturbed a cache of Mesolithic flints, prompting further excavations that uncovered two hearths dangling from the edge of an underwater cliff.

The divers raised sections of the seabed for study at the NOCS laboratories. They were transported in specially designed boxes and then pieced together before being examined and dated in the lab.

Garry Momber, director of HWTMA commented that the site was important because it reveals a time before the English Channel existed and Britain was linked to Europe. "Earlier excavations have produced flint tools, pristine 8,000 year old organic material such as acorns, charcoal and worked pieces of wood showing evidence of extensive human activity. This is the only site of its kind in Britain and is extremely important to our understanding of our Stone Age ancestors from the lesser-known Mesolithic period...We are finding evidence of hearths and ovens so it appears to be an extensive settlement."

Garry Momber has recruited students from the University of Southampton to help with the work. "A good chunk of the material left behind from this cultural period is eventually going to be found underwater…With underwater sites, all the trappings of society are going to remain, not just the stone."

http://www.msnbc.msn.com/id/20215343

REFERENCES: Guardian.co.uk April 24, 2007

http://www.guardian.co.uk/science/story/0,,2064221,00.html?gusrc=ticker-103704

msnbc 'Stone Age Settlement found in English Channel, Aug 10, 2007 http://www.msnbc.msn.com/id/20215343

SEAHENGE, ENGLAND

A Bronze Age wooden monument was discovered off the coast of Norfolk at Holme in 1998. Its circular shape consists of an outer ring of fifty-five small oak trucks about 7 meters by 6 meters. The trunks had been split in half with the bark facing outwards. There was a large inverted oak stump in the centre of the ring.

Dendrochronology allows Seahenge to be dated to 2049 BC. Between 16 and 26 different trees were used in building the monument which was cut down by at least fifty different axes.

Seahenge was preserved in peat which was gradually worn down by the tide on Holme Dunes. The logs had survived in an anaerobic waterlogged state for several thousand years. When it was built in the early Bronze Age, the site was probably a saltmarsh environment lying between the sea and forest.

The purpose of Seahenge is unknown although the presence of pottery at the site suggests it was a focal point during the late Bronze Age.

In 1999 British Heritage arranged for the wood to be transported to Flag Fen where it was soaked in wax-emulsified water over years to replace the moisture in the wood with wax. It was later transferred to Portsmouth where it will eventually be recreated at the new Lynn Museum in King's Lynn.

An older ring of two concentric timber circles was found nearby which dates from 2400 BC to 2030 BC. Like Holme 1, Holme 11 is also threatened by the sea but has been left in situ to be exposed to the tides.

REFERENCE: http://en.wikipedia.org/wiki/Seahenge

Photo credit megalithic.co.uk, copyright Andy Burnham

DANISH SETTLEMENTS

The first submerged settlement excavated in Denmark was the Tybrind Vig site off the west coast of the island of Funen in the 1970s. It was discovered three hundred meters from the shore and three meters below the surface. Divers excavated well-preserved artifacts from the late Mesolithic Ertebølle Culture.

In 1975 skin divers discovered an area with large amounts of wood and flint implements which attracted their interest. These divers in 1976 formed the 'Marine Archeological Group' and contacted Assistant Professor Soren Anderson of Arhus University for an evaluation of the material they had recovered. Most of the well preserved organic material derived from the Ertebølle Culture. In 1978 the first proper excavation of the site was arranged with Anderson as the general director of the project. The divers were Danish archeology students as well as foreign students who worked without pay, applied for funding, provided the excavation equipment, organised the camp and took care of diving safety.

The excavations ran each July from 1978 to 1988 and made many discoveries such as:

> • Fishing equipment (wickerwork traps, fish fences, fish hooks and spears).
> • Textiles made from spun plant fibres in the needle netting technique.
> • A grave with a young woman and a child with bone fragments from about three other persons. The female was about 13-14 years old and the baby up to three months old.
> • Boats such as dugouts and paddles made of limewood. At least three boats have their sterns preserved, some with a fireplace in the stern.

http://www.abc.se/~pa/publ/tybrind.htm
Another Mesolithic settlement was excavated in Ronaes Skov in the Gamborg Fjord and the report can be read on http://dendro.de/Unterwasserarchaeologie/NAU%209/Dal.pdf
REFERENCE: Excavating submerged Stone Age sites in Denmark — the Tybrind Vig example
http://www.abc.se/~pa/publ/tybrind.htm

ATLANTIS ON THE CELTIC SHELF
HYPOTHESIS

Viatcheslav Koudriavtsev founded the Russian Institute of Metahistory in 1997 with the aim of searching the Celtic Shelf for the remains of Atlantis. The Celtic Shelf is the huge area of submerged land off the southern coast of Britain, and Koudriavtsev believes that Atlantis existed about 130 miles south west of Cornwall. The capital of Atlantis, he postulates, was in the area known as the Little Sole Bank which was submerged at the end of the last Ice Age.

In his essay 'Atlantis: A New Hypothesis' he examined Plato's descriptions of the fabled land as well as modern theories which seek to validate its existence. He wrote, "In my opinion, the most serious argument in favour of the assumption that Atlantis had not been invented by Plato is that the time when it vanished, as indicated by Plato, and the circumstances of its vanishing described by him, coincide with the data which, no doubt, were inaccessible to Plato, on the time of the end of the last Ice Age and a substantial rise of the level of the world ocean that accompanied it."

Koudriavtsev does not buy into the Thera hypothesis which is founded on the proposition that Plato exaggerated the numbers by tenfold in his Atlantis story. He wrote, "Assertions that Plato had a vague idea of time and chronology do not seem well substantiated. As can be seen from his works, Plato was fairly mathematically minded, since, apparently he was under the influence of the Pythagorean school…Any assertion that Solon may have made a mistake in reading the Egyptian hieroglyphs he did not know sufficiently well, should be discarded as Plato explicitly says that Solon did not read the sacred records himself but was told of their contents by a priest." He found it equally absurd that Plato exaggerated the dimensions of Atlantis by tenfold: "Would it not be easier to cross out Plato's narrative of Atlantis and write their own instead and parameters of which would be acceptable to them, than to logically substantiate the ultimate dotage ascribed to Plato."

He also attacked the notion that the 'Pillars of Hercules' referred to an area in Greece, rather than Gibraltar. "We can only imagine how much the proponents of the Cretan hypothesis must want to

115

adjust Plato's narrative to that hypothesis, to find on the way from Athens to Crete some rocks which were allegedly called the Pillars of Hercules. Had such rocks really existed, and had Crete or Santorin really been Atlantis, then for the Egyptian priest its inhabitants would have been those who lived 'inside the pillars', while the inhabitants of Athens would have been those who lived 'outside the Pillars.'"

The essay continues with a discussion of the Atlantic Ocean and how the continents seem to fit together as a mosaic, making no room for a sunken continent of Plato's magnitude. However, it looks at the sea level of the Atlantic during the last Ice Age when great volumes of water were locked up in glaciation. Using a paper by Richard Fairbanks published in 1989, Koudriavtsev discovered that the sea level was about 121+/- meters lower than at present during the maximum glaciation. About 11 to 12 thousand years ago, when the ice-sheets were melting rapidly, the sea level was still 90-5 meters lower than at present.

The Celtic Shelf was a vast tract of land during this time when northern Europe was covered in a great ice sheet which depressed the land. "Some distance away from it, the crust was uplifted as a result of the so-called isostatic balancing. It is probable that the area of the Celtic Shelf was situated precisely in this uplifted area, so that the relative sea level there was even lower than the mean level by the value of this isostatic uplifting." This shelf could have been a plain precisely about two by three thousand stades.

Koudriavtsev then tackled the definition of the world 'island' or 'nesos' in Greek. After reading Critias's description, he concluded "The only image evoked is that of a city on a hill rising precipitously from the sea, and the flat plan surrounding it, enclosed on three sides by mountains. This description suits in every detail, the land that once existed in the west of Europe: the mountains are the present Ireland, Great Britain, and possibly, the north-western part of France, the plain itself, which now constitutes the Celtic Shelf to the south of the British Isles fits the dimensions specified by Plato, and the edge of the continental platform faces south-southwest. Not far from this edge, at about 48 degrees 16' N and 8 degrees 46-59' W, there is a remarkable underwater hill called the Little Sole Bank marked on sufficiently minute maps. The top of the hill is 57 meters below the sea surface, while the average depth is around 160-70 meters. The hill is located approximately in the middle of the greater length of the plain in question."

Furthermore he wrote, "Nowhere does Plato call Atlantean 'islanders'—as a rule the only specific point he makes is to emphasise the same contrast—that they did not live on the shores of the Mediterranean Sea." He also theorises that since the central part of the city was surrounded by a canal and situated on top of a hill, it would have been called 'island' by the inhabitants and the word would have been transmitted through the generations to Plato.

Koudriavtsev's essay finally tackled the contentious topic of catastrophism—and the skepticism amongst researchers that Atlantis could have been inundated in a single day and night. Without any information on the catastrophic tsunamis which ravaged the Atlantic Ocean, such as the Stormegga Slides, he believed that huge armadas of icebergs discharged during the 'Heinrich events' must have dramatically raised the sea levels. Moreover, when the great Scandinavian icecap started to melt, the land beneath it must have risen and as a compensatory process areas such as the Celtic shelf may have subsided more rapidly.

"Another argument to back the thesis that none other than the rising of the sea level was the catastrophe that Plato described, is that the relief of the plain in point, in the west of Europe, was of such character, that the rising of the sea level by one meter could often have meant the retreat of the coastline by km. I am sure that even if the full submerging of the territory lasted several years, the eyewitnesses and victims, who were on a flat plain, must have perceived it as a very fast sinking of all the land they could see, from horizon to horizon."

Koudriavtsev's Institute of Metahistory was organising an 'Expedition to Verify the Hypothesis' that Atlantis existed on the Celtic Shelf, particularly the Little Sole Bank Area. "The research is to include: a detailed survey of the bottom, using a side-scan sonar or a multi-beam echo-sounder, a profile recorder, satellite and hydro-acoustic navigation systems with a view to building a high resolution digital model of the bottom, on which objects could be singled out that might be the remains of ancient buildings. In case such objects are identified, they can be explored directly, with a remote operated underwater vehicle."

Source 'Atlantis a New Hypothesis' a three part essay in 'New Dawn Magazine', numbers 47, 48, 49 from April to July-August 1998)

Surprisingly, the Institute of Metahistory's website, http://www.imh.ru/about_en.html does not provide any updates, or even a copy of Koudriavtsev's essay.

The Morien Institute provides quotes from this essay which refer to a map of the Little Sole Bank on the Celtic Shelf. In his accompanying analysis of the map Koudriavtsev concluded: "Some paleographic reconstructions of Western Europe at the end of the last glaciations suggest that there had existed a river originating in the area of the modern Irish Sea, which must have flown into the ocean in approximately this area. And if this is indeed the trace of the ancient river bed, then the present Little Sole Bank was not an island or merely a hill on the shore, but a hill at the river mouth, which is a uniquely beneficial position for a city."

The Morien Institute, based in Wales, finds this very interesting because their national epic 'The Mabynogion' describes two rivers as running between Wales and Ireland: "Bendigeidfran and host sailed towards Ireland, and in those days the deep water was not wide. He went by wading. There were but two rivers, the Lli and Archan, but thereafter the deep water grew wider when the deep overflowed the kingdoms."

http://www.morien-institute.org/uwnews1997.html

The Metahistory's website makes no mention of any current or future expedition to the Celtic Shelf, so Koudriavtsev's theory will remain unproven until evidence is provided.

REFERENCES: Morien Institute, http://www.morien-institute.org/uwnews1997.html

Institute of Metahistory, http://www.imh.ru/about_en.html

'Atlantis a New Hypothesis' a three part essay in 'New Dawn Magazine', numbers 47, 48, 49 from April to July-August 1998)

CARNAC, BRITTANY

The famous megaliths of Carnac have been dated to approximately six thousand years old and show evidence of

118

astronomical alignments. There are about three thousand megaliths, mainly menhirs, dolmens and tumuli.

Many of the Carnac stones now trail into the sea and some megaliths can be seen at low tide barely rising above the surface. According to a website 'The Stones of Carnac' by R. Cedric Leonard "Several nearby islands exhibit stone circles (cromlechs) which are partially or completely submerged. Pierre Mereaux, a French engineer in thermodynamics who has made a study of the stones, comments: On the Island south of Gavr'Inis in the Gulf of Morbihan there are 2 tangential circles; 28 stones in the north circle, 32 in the south circle; the stones are 2-5 meters high. Half of the north circle and all of the south circle are submerged--evidence that the sea level has risen and the Gulf flooded since the circles were built." (Mereaux, 1992)

http://www.atlantisquest.com/Carnac.html

The islet of Er Lannic, 500 meters south of Garv'Inis, has two stone circles which are half submerged in the Gulf of Morbihan. Made of about 60 stones, the southern circle is entirely submerged. The circle is 65 m (213 feet) in diameter and its stones are 2 to 5.4 m (6.5 to 17.7 ft) high.

Er Lannic was excavated in the 1920s by Zacharie Le Rouzic, who estimated the site to be about 5,000 years old. He discovered around each stone a cist containing charcoal, animal bones, flints, pottery and polished axes. Two stones are carved with axes and a yoke while one of the stones has cupmarks possibly depicting the constellation of Ursa Minor. The southern submerged stone circle is horseshoe shaped and 61 m (200 ft) in diameter. Two outlying submerged stone lie east and west from the circle. At the southern tip of the submerged horseshoe there was a great pillar called the blacksmith's tone by fishermen. These lines to cardinal points probably had astronomical connections.

http://www.stonepages.com/france/erlannic.html

REFERENCES: The Stones of Carnac http://www.atlantisquest.com/Carnac.html

Er Lannic, Stone circles, Marbihan, Brittany http://www.stonepages.com/france/erlannic.html

GERMANIC AND FRISIAN LEGENDS

The 'Oera Linda' is a medieval book which tells the tale of the Frisian people and describes their origins. According to the text the Frisians had once inhabited an island called Atland which was destroyed by volcanic activity in about 2194 BC. In chapter 22 it says: "During the whole summer the sun had been hidden behind the clouds, as if unwilling to look upon Irtha. There was perpetual calm…the air was heavy and oppressive. In the midst of this stillness Irtha began to tremble as if she was dying. The mountains opened to vomit forth fire and flames. Some sank into the bosom of Irtha, and in other places mountains rose out of the plain. Aldland, called Atland by the navigators, disappeared, and the wild waves rose so high over hill and dale that everything was buried in the sea. Many people were swallowed up by Irtha, and others who had escaped the fire perished in the water." (p148 'A to Z of Atlantis' S. Cox, M. Foster)

The Frisians who survived fled to Scandinavia, Britain or the Mediterranean. The story was compiled orally and possibly first written down in 506 AD and later in 806 before the final version was completed in 1256. The name Atland, the homeland, excites some Atlantologists, while other researchers believe the story pertains to a catastrophic flood or even land collapse which occurred in the North Sea.

Austrian pastor Jurgen Spanuth read the Oera Linda Book and became convinced that Atlantis had existed in the north, in the vicinity of the German archipelago Heligoland. He believed that most of the island sank sometime during the twelfth century BC, leaving only small islands. Survivors of the cataclysm, he believed, became the marauding Sea Peoples who terrorised the Mediterranean during that time.

Using his own funds, Spanuth undertook a series of expeditions into the North Sea and claimed that he had found the remains of a sunken city at the depth of 14 meters (45 feet) about 8 km south of Heligoland. The parallel walls constructed from rocks of red, black and white convinced him that he had discovered Atlantis. He claimed his city had an undamaged wall surrounding it with a circumference of 3,956 feet. He wrote, "Some of their buildings were simple, but

120

in others they put together different stones, which they intermingled for the sake of ornament, to be a natural source of delight." (ibid)

In 1953 he published a book of his theory titled 'Atlantis of the North' based upon this excursion.

Unfortunately Spanuth did not provide any evidence of his discovery such as photographs so his claims are disregarded by archeologists.

REFERENCE: 'A to Z of Atlantis', S. Cox and M. Foster

MID ATLANTIC RUINS?

The following examples are gleaned mainly from Charles Berlitz's fascinating book 'Atlantis, the Lost Continent Revealed' published in 1984. Berlitz, a talented linguist and indefatigable Atlantologist, had been fascinated with archeology all his life. With his unique ability to speak twenty five languages he had access to research to journals and newspapers from many countries, including the Soviet Union. Unfortunately they were not properly referenced, so it is difficult for a researcher to gain access to Berlitz's prime sources.

> • Pilots have reported underwater ruins in the Atlantic Ocean on numerous occasions. World War 11 pilots reported "what looked like clusters of buildings or 'cities' under the ocean surface near St Peter and St Paul's Rocks (1 degree N, 30 degrees W)." Other pilots reported alleged underwater stone walls and ruins at 6 degrees N, 20 degrees W near the Sierra Leone Rise. (Berlitz, pp80-81)
>
> • Captain Reyes Miraga allegedly videotaped miles of pillared buildings, statues and boulevards with smaller avenues branching out from the centre like spokes in a wheel from his salvage ship Talia at the bottom of the Atlantic.

SOVIET EXPLORATIONS

The Russians have had an interest in Atlantis for over a century and maintained a lively presence in the Atlantic Ocean during the Soviet era. Writer Peter James takes a cynical view of Soviet discoveries of underwater ruins in the Atlantic. "Soviet science certainly tolerated, if not encouraged, Atlantis research, because it contradicted the western theory of continental drift. It also provided the Russian navy with a convenient smokescreen for espionage in the Mid Atlantic, where they were searching for places to park nuclear submarines." (P. James, 'The Sunken Kingdom—The Atlantis Mystery Solved' 1995)

• Dr Nicolai Zhirov, a member of the Soviet Academy of Science, is known as the Father of Russian Atlantology. His 1964 book 'Atlantis' examined the historical references and geographical material on Atlantis and its probable location in the Atlantic. He wrote about limestone discs, known as 'sea biscuits' which were originally discovered on the ocean floor near the Azores and found later in the Bimini area. These discs are approximately six inches in diameter and one and a half inches thick with a depression in the centre of one side, like a plate. They had a smooth surface. Tests determined they were 12,000 years old and were formed on the surface.

• A sunken city was allegedly found 400 miles off the coast of Portugal by Soviet expeditions led by Boris Asturua. He claimed that the buildings were made of extremely strong concrete and plastics and saw the remains of something resembling monorail transportation. He salvaged a statue.

• Soviet oceanographers made several studies of the underwater Horseshoe archipelago, including the underwater shoals Ampere, Josephine, Gettysburg, Dacia, Concepcion, Corall and Sen in the 1970s. In 1962 the Soviet vessel 'Sedov' carefully studied the Gettysburg shoal.

• In 1974 a scientific team of geologists and biologists on the Soviet research vessel 'Academician Petrovsky' were studying the "sandbanks in the shallow waters of the Mediterranean Sea." A member of the USSR Institute of Oceanography, Vladimir Marakuyev, a specialist in underwater photography was also on board. The waters in the vicinity of Gibraltar were exceptionally clear and the team was able to lower special cameras to a depth of about three meters from the seafloor where a series of photographs was taken. The ship began its underwater survey of the Horseshoe archipelago about 300 miles west of Gibraltar in January 1974.

Even though American scientists had taken core samples and photographs of the same area with the conclusion by Dr Maurice Ewing that he had spent "Thirteen years exploring the Mid-Atlantic Ridge but found no trace of sunken cities," (Berlitz, ibid p 84) the Soviets had better luck. Marakuyev observed that the pictures taken on the summit of the Ampere Seamount which is only 200 feet from the surface, showed a number of unexpected features. He claimed, "Nowhere have I seen anything so close to traces of the life and activity of man in places which could have once been dry land."

In an article in 'Znanie-Sila' Number 8, 1979, summarised by M. Barinov, these features were noted: "We can see this wall on the left side of the photograph. Stone blocks on the upper edge of the wall are clearly visible...Taking into account the foreshortening of the photograph and the height of the wall...areas of masonry can be seen quite clearly...One may suggest that the masonry blocks of the wall are up to 1.5 meters high and a little longer in length." A second photo revealed the same wall from a vertical position. "It is not difficult to calculate that the breadth of the wall is about 75 centimeters. The masonry blocks are clearly visible on both sides of the wall." A third photograph of the summit of the Ampere Seamount shows lava and five steps. (Berlitz, ibid p85)

The Soviet photographs of the Ampere Seamount received worldwide publicity through an interview with Professor Andrei Aksyonov, deputy director of the Soviet Academy of Science's Institute of Oceanography. On May 21, 1978 'The New York Times' published this interview with Professor Aksyonov who commented, "I believe that the objects in the pictures once stood on the surface."

Whereas AP released another bulletin in April 1979 about a Russian research ship that had taken photos of "what might be ruins", no other reports were forthcoming. Egerton Sykes, an eminent Atlantologist, was interviewed about this silence in 1982

123

and concluded; "It must have been of considerable importance to them." He believed that the photographs were probably taken off the Azores between Santa Maria and Sao Jorge, near the Formigas Rocks. As the Soviets were not supposed to be in that vicinity, they could not officially report the correct position.

When asked about his opinion of the stones and platforms photographs Sykes commented, "They are very intriguing. The stone staircase that is distinctly visible was evidently cut into the cliff...It was probably a flight of 100 steps or more up a rock face... like the steps on Mayan pyramids. One of the photographs shows a leveled-off stone platform which may be a landing connected to another staircase, as in a step pyramid." (Berlitz, ibid p87).

CANARIES

In 1981 underwater explorer Pippo Cappellano detected and filmed rectilinear artificial stone foundations in around 50 feet of water off the coast of Lanzarote, one of the Canary Islands. Covering about 900 square feet in area, these stones were carefully set with wide stones leading down to a landing block like a staircase. Carvings resemble symbols or letters which can be found on rocks in the Canaries.

Due to the depth of submergence, it is very probable that these ruins date from the Phonecian era or proto-Phonecian era in the first or second millennium BC. However, carvings discovered on the island of Fuerteventura have been dated to 6000 BC by palaentologist Francisco Garcia Talavera of the University of Fierteventura, indicating the possibility that the ruins could be much older. Photos of the ruins appeared in an issue of Hera magazine and in an article by A. Bajocco, 'Lazarote: un Nouveau Bimini?'.

AZORES

Ignatius Donnelly was the first to suggest that Atlantis could be found in the vicinity of the Azores. Dolphin's Ridge is a huge sunken landmass connected to the Azores which lies at a depth of almost 5.5 km. Core samples taken by French geologist Pierre Termier in 1915 indicate that the area was once above water although it was impossible to date its submergence. He wrote: "It would seem a fair conclusion then, that the entire region north of the Azores, or which they may be only the visible ruins, was recently submerged, probably during the epoch which geologists call the present because it is so recent..." (p 98 'A to Z of Atlantis, Cox & Foster.)

In his book 'The Mystery of Atlantis' Charles Berlitz spoke of underwater structures observed from aircraft. "Entire cities in the vicinity of the Azores were reported as far back as 1942, when air ferry pilots flying from Brazil to Dakar glimpsed what seemed to be a submerged city just breaking the surface on the western slope of mountains in the Mid-Atlantic Ridge, of which the Azores are the highest peaks. Such random sightings occur when the sun and surface tension attain optimum condition for underwater sightings. Other sightings of submerged architectural remains of what was perhaps the central Atlantean area have been noted off Boa Vista Island in the Cape Verde Islands, off Fayal in the Azores. Non submerged remains of buildings and cities, perhaps dating from Atlantean times, were found by the early Spanish conquerors of the Canary Islands."

Berlitz believed that the Azores held the key to the Atlantis puzzle and wrote, "Volcanic activity is constantly occurring in the Azores area, where there are still active volcanoes....The islands of Corvo and Flores in the Azores, which have been mapped since 1351, have constantly changed their shape, with large parts of Corvo having disappeared into the sea." (D. Childress, 'Lost Cities of Atlantis, Ancient Europe and the Mediterranean' p276)

However, no concrete evidence of ancient human habitation exists in the Azores although there could be ruins beneath the lava deposits or beneath the waves.

REFERENCES: C. Berlitz, 'The Lost Continent Revealed' MacMillan, London, 1984
P. James, 'The Sunken Kingdom—The Atlantis Mystery Solved' Jonathon Cape, London, 1995
A. Bajocco, 'Hera Magazine', 'Lazarote: un Nouveau Bimini?' Kadath, no 66, p 6 Winter 1987.
'A to Z of Atlantis', Cox & Foster, Mainstream Publishing, 2006
D. Childress, 'Lost Cities of Atlantis, Ancient Europe & the Mediterranean'

SEARCHING FOR ATLANTIS IN
THE ATLANTIC

Long before the Thera-Crete association with the island of Atlantis, other researchers were looking for it in the Atlantic Ocean which stretches from Africa and Europe to North and South America. Various islands such as the Azores, Cape Verde, Canaries and Caribbean have also been identified as Atlantis since medieval times.

The earliest and most famous Atlantologist was Ignatius Donnelly, an American who is known as the Father of Scientific Atlantology. After years as a successful politician, he became increasingly interested in the Atlantis legend and spent many hours of study in the Library of Congress. His first book 'Atlantis the Antediluvial World' was published in 1882 and is still in print today. He came up with 13 theories:

> • There once existed in the Atlantic Ocean, opposite the Mediterranean Sea, a large island which was a remnant of an ancient continent.
> • Plato's description is not a fable but veritable history.
> • Atlantis was the reason why man first rose from barbarism to civilization.
> • "This was the true Antediluvial world, the Garden of Eden, Elysian Fields …representing a universal memory of a great land, where early mankind dwelt for ages in peace and happiness."
> • The gods and goddesses of the ancient world were simply the kings, queens and heroes of Atlantis.
> • The mythology of Egypt and Peru represented the original religion of Atlantis which was sun worship.
> • The oldest colony of Atlantis was Egypt.
> • The Bronze Age in Europe was derived from Atlantis. Atlanteans were the first manufacturers of iron.
> • The Phonecian alphabet was derived from Atlantis and conveyed to the Mayans of Central America.

• Atlantis was the original seat of the Aryan or Indo-European families as well as the Semitic races.

• Atlantis perished in a terrible convulsion of nature when the whole island fell into the ocean and nearly all its inhabitants were killed.

• The few survivors on rafts and ships were carried to nations where their tales of the catastrophe became part of our original Flood legend and other deluge stories around the world.

According to Donnelly, Atlantis was the original motherland of mankind which formed a link between the Old and New world civilizations. The Mayans were also of Atlantean origin and possessed many shared characteristics such as pyramids, metallurgy, ships and pillars. Furthermore, he claimed that linguistics supported his theory with New World languages bearing a similarity to those of the Old World.

Donnelly's book, despite its errors such as a similarity between new and old world alphabets, remains the bible of Atlantology and nearly every subsequent writer has been influenced by him, including the founder of Theosophy, Madame Blavatsky in her 1877 book 'Isis Unveiled'. She wrote, "The perfect identity of the rites, ceremonies, traditions, and even the names of the deities, among the Mexicans and ancient Babylonians and Egyptians, are a sufficient proof of South America being peopled by a colony which mysteriously found its way across the Atlantic. When? at what period? History is silent on that point; but those who consider that there is no tradition, sanctified by ages, without a certain sediment of truth at the bottom of it, believe in the Atlantis-legend. ... There are, scattered throughout the world, a handful of thoughtful and solitary students, who pass their lives in obscurity, ... These men believe the story of the Atlantis to be no fable, but maintain that at different epochs of the past huge islands, and even continents, existed where now there is but a wild waste of waters."

In 'The Secret Doctrine', published in 1891, she claimed that her information had been based upon a mysterious manuscript, the 'Stanzas of Dzyan' which was written in Senza, the language of

Atlantis. This massive tome included a lot more information on the Atlanteans who were the fourth root race possessing psychic powers. The large continent in the Atlantic did not sink all at once. Blavatsky tells us that it began sinking more than 4 million years ago. The major submergence occurred 869,000 years ago, leaving various islands. Finally the last small remnant of an island, called Poseidonis, sunk some 12,000 years ago.

The next writer to achieve acclaim in Atlantology was Theosophist W. Elliott-Scott, a merchant banker and amateur anthropologist who was strongly influenced by Blavatsky and Donnelly's view of Atlantis. Using 'astral clairvoyance' he described the races and sub-races of the Atlanteans, with the Toltecs of Mexico being the primary sub-race. Of gigantic proportions, these people built a magnificent capital the City of the Golden Gates off the coast of West Africa. Possessing advanced science with flying machines, their culture expanded into America, Egypt and Britain, building the pyramids and Stonehenge. However, like Plato's Atlanteans, their decline was due to moral decay, resulting from a misuse of power, and Atlantis succumbed to a series of natural disasters.

In his 1896 book 'The Story of Atlantis. A Geographical, Historical and Ethnological Sketch' which drew together many threads and disciplines, he wrote, "Catastrophes, too, on a scale such as has not yet been experienced during the life of our present Fifth Race, took place on more than one occasion during the progress of the Fourth. The destruction of Atlantis was accomplished by a series of catastrophes varying in character from great cataclysms in which whole territories and populations perished; to comparatively unimportant landslips such as occur on our own coasts to-day. When the destruction was once inaugurated by the first great catastrophe there was no intermission in the minor landslips which continued slowly but steadily to eat away the continent. Four of the great catastrophes stand out above the rest in magnitude. The first took place in the Miocene age, about 800,000 years ago. The second, which was of minor importance, occurred about 200,000 years ago. The third—about 80,000 years ago—was a very great one. It destroyed all that remained of the Atlantean continent, with the exception of the island to which Plato gave the name of

128

Poseidonis, which in its turn was submerged in the fourth and final great catastrophe of 9564 BC."

Lewis Spencer, a Scottish mythologist who launched a short-lived magazine called the 'Atlantis Quarterly', wrote five books on the subject, including his 1924 work 'The Problem of Atlantis'. In this book he set out to prove four main points:

> • A great continent occupied all or most of the north Atlantic and a considerable portion of its southern basin. Over millions of years it experienced many changes such as frequent submergences and emergences.
> • In Miocene times from 25 to 10 million years ago it slowly started to disintegrate owing to volcanic and tectonic forces.
> • This disintegration resulted in two masses, primarily one near the Mediterranean and the other in the Caribbean. These were called Atlantis and Antillia. Communication between them was made possible by smaller islands known as the insular chain.
> • The two island continents and connecting chain of islands persisted until the late Pleistocene times. At about 25,000 years ago Atlantis suffered further disintegration until its final disaster in about 10,000 BC. Antillia, on the other hand, survived more recently and still persists fragmentally in the West Indian Islands.

Spencer had to jettison Plato's assertion that Atlantis disappeared in a day and night and Donnelly's claim that it was the source of all civilization. He believed they were a Stone Age people who were linked to the Cro-Magnons, the Caspian and Azilian races. The Cro-Magnons wiped out the inferior Neanderthals after arriving in Europe about 25,000 years ago. The Azilians, who settled in Europe after the final inundation, founded the civilizations of Crete and Egypt. They also founded the Mayan civilization after spending thousands of years on Antillia.

Rudolph Steiner, Austrian founder of Anthroposophy, believed, like the Theosophists, that the Atlanteans were the fourth root race who did not possess the power of abstract reasoning but had a very strong memory and could utilise the 'life force'. He wrote a lot about the social characteristics of the Atlanteans with information he had gleaned from 'the Akashic Record'.

American psychic Edgar Cayce wrote extensively about Atlantis in his readings which were always conducted under hypnosis. According to him, it was a huge continent that extended from the Gulf of Mexico to the Mediterranean. The continent went through three major periods of inundation, the first two about 15,600 BCE when the mainland was divided into islands. The three main islands were Poseidia, Og and Aryan. The final break up occurred about 10,000 BCE and the last place to sink was the Bahamas.

According to Cayce, evidence of Atlantis could be found in the Pyrenees and Morocco on the one hand, Belize, Yucatan and America on the other side of the Atlantic. The British West Indies also known as the Bahamas are protruding portions of Atlantis as well as the Canaries and Azores. In June 1940 Cayce predicted that the island called Poseidia would rise again in 1968 or 69 in the Bahamas.

Prior to its final inundation of Poseidia, many Atlanteans settled in Egypt and introduced the high culture to this land. Refugees from the sunken Atlantis possessing an advanced technology settled ancient Egypt and pre-Columbian America.

The Atlanteans possessed a highly technical culture and constructed giant laser like crystals for power plants. The final destruction was due in part to the overcharging of the crystal which caused a massive explosion. The society itself had become degenerate and was destroyed as a punishment. The Great Flood is but a memory of the final inundation. Cayce believed that many people living in the twentieth century are the incarnations of Atlantean souls and suffer from the same temptations as before.

In 1931 Cayce set up the not-for-profit Association for Research and Enlightenment (A.R.E) based in Virginia Beach to research and explore subjects such as holistic health, ancient mysteries, personal spirituality, dream interpretation, intuition, philosophy and reincarnation. Apart from conducting research on various subjects, the A.R.E keeps meticulous records on Edgar Cayce's readings.

130

Egerton Sykes (1894-1983) possessed the largest library on Atlantis in the world and was an accomplished writer, amateur archeologist and mythologist. He founded the 'Atlantis Research Organisation' which investigated the possibility that Atlantis was the original source of culture in Europe and the Americas. Sykes' conclusions about Atlantis were based on a comprehensive study of ancient maps, a world survey of submerged cities, studies of rock magnetism, petroglyphs and cave paintings, linguistics, historic and mythic records of the event, physical remains of contemporary cultures, early trans-Atlantic movements and astronomy.

Sykes' research convinced him that Atlantis was situated between the West Indies and the Canaries, stretching from the Azores to Ascension Island with a possible northern extension towards Greenland. The whole landmass was about one and a half million square miles. His contribution to the subject was enormous and upon his passing, the huge book collection was housed by the A.R.E at Virginia Beach, VA.

OTHER LANDMARKS IN ATLANTOLOGY

Despite the fame of the Atlantologists who relied on a mystical interpretation of the continent, there were also many scholars, scientists and archeologists who have tried to discover the lost continent. A brief description of these people includes:

- In 1907 Etienne Felix Berlioux wrote a series of scholastic papers linking Morocco with Atlantis for the Academy of Sciences at Lyons.
- Professor Vladimir Bogachev was a Russian geologist sometimes known as the Russian father of Atlantology. In 1912 he published a brochure Atlantida, the first work on the geology of Atlantis to be published.
- In the French language Pierre Termier's 'Atlantide' (1913) and 'La Derive des Continents' (1924) were important scientific contributions to Atlantology.
- In 1925 F. Butavand wrote 'La Veritable Histoire de l'Atlantide' which proposed that Atlantis had been a series of islands, now submerged, lying off the Tunisian coast in

the vicinity of the Punic city of Carthage.

• In 1926 R.M Gattefosse, Jean Gattefosse and Claudius Roux published the 'Bibliographe de l'Atlantide.'

• German Professor Paul Borchardt of Munich, a geographer, claimed to have found Atlantis in North Africa near Tunisia.

• Deep sea samples extracted from the Mid-Atlantic ridge by expeditions have indicated that this area was above water 15,000 years ago. These include Professor Hans Petersson, leader of the Swedish 'Albatross' expedition in the 1930s and Maurice Piggot's famous US Coast and Geodetic Survey of deep core soundings in 1936.

• Italian scholars concentrated on the Tyrrhenian Sea and North Africa as the location of Atlantis. The group 'Centro Culturale Atlantide' in Genoa published 'La Voce d'Atlantide' edited by Gianni Belli from 1956 to 58. In 1963 'The Italian Atlantis' was published in Genoa by Leonardo Bettini, a member of the Atlantis Research Centre.

• A French North African organisation, 'L'Atlantide de Demain' headed by Amedee Guiraud published a quarterly journal 'En L'Atlantide' which had the aim of establishing a link between northern Africa and Atlantis.

• Bulgarian Professor N. Boneff, head of the Department of Astronomy at Sofia University wrote 'Une Application de la Theorie des Marees au Probleme de L'Atlantide' a mathematical thesis on the destruction of Atlantis.

• In 1949 Pastor Jurgen Spanuth claimed that he had located Atlantis five miles south of Helgoland (Heligoland) in the North Sea.

• Professor Hagemeister of Tallin in the USSR wrote an article (1955) for the Soviet Academy of Sciences, Priroda, which stated the Gulf Stream had only come into existence 12,000 years ago, based on the disintegration of ionium at various depths of the Atlantic Ocean. He concluded that the end of the Ice Age, destruction of Atlantis and formation of the Gulf Stream, all occurred at the same time.

• Dr Michael Kamienski, Professor of Astronomy at

Krakow University believed that Halley's comet broke off and plunged into the western Atlantic Ocean in 9542 BC, causing tsunamis which inundated Atlantis.

• Another theory proposed by German Otto Mück in the 1950s that an asteroid hit the earth in 8498 BC, was introduced to the English speaking world in his 1978 book 'The Secret of Atlantis'. He believed this gigantic asteroid caused massive seismic upheavals when it crashed into the Atlantic at the close of the Ice Age. He also believed that the Azores were the remnants of Atlantis.

• Professor Dimitry G. Panov was a Doctor of Geographical Science and the editor of Zhirov's book 'Atlantida' which was published in Moscow in 1964. His own book 'The Origin of the Continents and Oceans' (1961) mentioned his belief in the reality of Atlantis.

• Italian Alf Bajocco published 'The Early Inhabitants of the Canary Islands' in which he proposed that the indigenous Canary Islanders were Berbers, descendants of Atlanteans.

• Professor N. Zhirov of the Soviet Union stated in his 1970 book 'Atlantology; Basic Problems' that the Mid-Atlantic's Dolphin Ridge was above sea level in 10,000 BC. He reviewed hundreds of sources on the formation of continents, mountain structure, seismic processes, cosmological influences, tectonic origins, glaciation and the changes produced by the Gulf Stream in this landmark book.

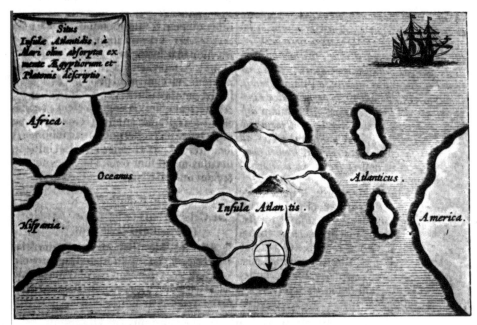

Top: A map of Atlantis, with south at the top, by Athanasius Kircher in 1678.
Below: A map of Atlantis drawn in 1912 by Dr. Paul Schliemann, grandson of
the famous archeologist who discovered Troy.

134

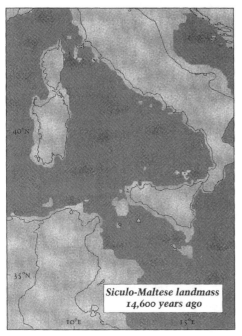

Top: A map of Atlantis drawn by the Greek writer I. Kampanakis in the 1960s showing Atlantis as a bridge continent acros the Atlantic. Below: A map of the ocean levels around Sicily and Malta 14,600 years ago. Courtesy of Graham Hancock.

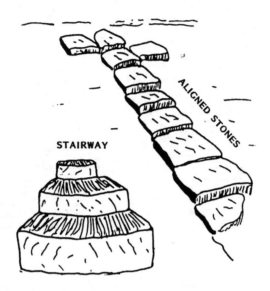

STAIRWAY

ALIGNED STONES

Above: Rock alignment and "stairway" found at a depth of 22 meters off Lanzarote, Canary Islands.

Top: A map of the submerged areas of the North Sea, called Doggerland.

Above:The Swedish physician Olof Rudbeck cuts open a map of the modern world in 1679, revealing the secret history of Scandanavia as Atlantis. The philosopher Plato strains to take a closer look as he stands among the other ancient philosphers and geographers of the ancient world.

PART 5

THE CARIBBEAN SEA
CONTROVERSIAL CARIBBEAN RUINS—
BAHAMAS
BIMINI ROAD
ANDROS ISLAND
CAY SAL
SCOTTS STONES?
OTHER AREAS IN THE BAHAMAS
BERMUDA
RUINS OFF CUBA?
RUINS OFF PUERTO RICO?
MAYAN RUINS OF ISLA CERRITOS, MEXICO

*With the exception of the Mayan ruins in Mexico,
the Caribbean ruins fall into the category of
controversial, as most archeologists do not
acknowledge their artificiality.*

CONTROVERSIAL CARIBBEAN RUINS—
BAHAMAS

THE BIMINI ROAD

In 1940 Edgar Cayce made a startling prediction about the location of Atlantis. "Poseidia will be among the first portions of Atlantis to rise again. Expect it in 68 or 69—not so far away... A portion of the Atlantean temple may yet be discovered under the slime of ages of seawater—near what is known as Bimini, off the coast of Florida."

In the 1950s various reports of structures from the seafloor were reported off the coast of Bimini in the Bahamas. Pilots Trigg Adams and Robert Brush claimed to have spotted a structure near Andros Island in the late 50s.

In September 1968 near Bimini Dr J. Manson Valentine, a Professor of Archeology at Yale University, discovered a giant wall or road several hundred meters in length in shallow waters. On each side it had two perpendicular straight branches made of massive stone blocks measuring five meters. His subsequent explorations revealed a more complex structure which resembled a drowned harbor with quays and a double jetty. He wrote, "I was amazed to discern an extensive pavement of rectangles and occasionally polygonal flat stones of varying size and thickness, obviously arranged and accurately aligned to form convincing engineering courses. These stones had evidently been submerged over a long span of time for the edges of some had become rounded giving the blocks the appearance of giant loaves of bread or pillows. My personal feeling is that the whole fantastic complex represents the intelligent utilization by ancient man of material provided by nature and appropriate for the creation of some sort of ceremonial center."

A photographic survey was then made by Dimitri Rebikoff, a French engineer, inventor, diver and pioneer in the field of underwater photography with his invention of the Pegasus, an underwater platform. Valentine, Rebikoff, Adams and Brush formed the Marine Archeology Research Society (MARS) and sought permission to excavate the formation. Rebikoff, President of the Institute of Underwater Technology, compiled a stereoscopic mosaic survey of the Bimini Road and investigated supporting pillars beneath some of the rocks.

The famous 'Bimini Road' was above sea level until about 6,000 or possibly even 5,000 years ago. Its discovery in 1968 raised the excitement of the A.R.E. foundation which promotes the teachings of Edgar Cayce who had predicted the discovery at Bimini.

142

Unfortunately a 1971 article in 'Nature' by geologist Wyman Harrison reported that the Bimini Road was a natural formation. Marshall McKusik from the University of Iowa wrote in 'Nature' (Vol 287, Sept 4, 1980): "The limestone structures observed off Bimini in 15 feet (5 meters) of sea have all the features of natural bedrock. The limestone is in a narrow band and extends for a considerable distance along a former foreshore... If the stones had been quarried and relaid there is no reason to suppose bedding planes would carry stratigraphically from block to block. The sedimentary laminations clearly show that these were not randomly laid stones but a natural, relatively undisturbed formation... Although under 15 feet of water the beachrock is of recent geological origin. One C14 date on shell has already been published as 2200 plus or minus 150 years BP. Jerry Stipp has run seven bulk samples from cores as a class project and gives slightly older dates for the Bimini submerged beachrock (varying from 2745 – 3510 BC) (Hancock, 'Underworld' p 519).

Valentine and Rebikoff responded in 'Explorers Journal' December 1976 and queried:

> • Why the Bimini stones are of flint hard micrite and not soft bedrock. Micrite will not cleave when hit with a sledge and has a ringing sound when struck.

> • Why the three courses of closely fitted stones are so straight sided, mutually parallel and terminate in corner stones.

> • Why the long avenue lies at a slight angle to others and is composed of a double series of small blocks interrupted by two expansions containing large flat stones.

> • Why the southern end is curved.

> • Why there are so many rectangular shapes, right angles and rectilinear configurations.

Another team, led by geologist John Gifford, discovered a nearby site called the 'Proctor's Road' consisting of stones at intervals running in a straight line for a mile. In 1974 Dr David

143

Zink, an English professor, met Valentine at Bimini and performed the first survey of the road. His Poseidia 1975 Expedition assembled a dozen divers, geologists and archeologists to study the structure. Using professional surveys, side-scan sonar and nuclear activation analysis, he determined that the site was not a road but a megalithic structure. A further expedition in 1976 which included zoologist Dr Doug Richards discovered that there were magnetic anomalies in the Bimini Road.

In 1982 Dr Zink, a pro-Atlantean with ten Bimini expeditions to his credit and author of 'The Stones of Atlantis', questioned the 'Nature' article's dates at a conference on underwater archeology held at the University of Pennsylvania. He claimed that they were unreliable and did not tally with information now available to marine geologists concerning Atlantic sea levels since the end of the Ice Age. His drill cores indicated that the blocks adjacent to one another were not formed side by side but in different chemical environments.

He wrote, (We believe that) "After their original formation in a beach environment, these blocks were removed, shaped and placed above water by human agency. Later as the sea-level continued to rise after the last glacial period, the blocks were again covered and micritization commenced..." ('Underworld' p526)

In 1989 Dr Zink created 'Quest for Atlantis' with Joan Hanley, which included conferences, on-site investigation, underwater exploration and aerial fly-bys. During the 1989 project the group headed out for Paradise Point and were surprised to see the rectangular blocks in neat rows and a fish shaped mound in a mangrove swamp. They also encountered the Legendary Healing Well which seemed to impart a profound sense of peace and balance.

The 1993 Project Alta, funded by the Atlantis Organization, aimed to seek out new sites by means of aerial reconnaissance and side-scan sonar, as well as investigate animal shaped mounds on Bimini. The sonar project resulted in "the discovery of a number of anomalies that included right-angled features and parallel lines. Alta's side scan returns revealed tall spires rising from the ocean floor, a hexagonal feature, an area that had multiple right angled

144

features in association with two concentric circles and parallel lines, a number of rectangles, and a triangular sound shadow about 150 feet in extent in deep water." ('Back to Bimini', W. Donato from Law of One Newsletter, 1997)

In 1996 the Law of One Research Corporation (associated with the A.R.E.) provided funding for a Bimini research project undertaken by Dr Joan Hanley of GAEA Project Inc and Dr Doug Richards of the Meridien Institute. They discovered that there were positional errors on Bimini of approximately 500 meters (1,500 feet). They also discovered that off Bimini there appeared a wave shape with approximately 15 meter undulations in the drop off and 10-15 meter projections that appeared to be both natural and man-made. Man-made objects included wrecks and other debris, but there were also some large shapes of unknown origin.

Frank Joseph, author of 'The Destruction of Atlantis', accompanied William Donato, president of the Atlantis Organisation, on an underwater survey of the Moselle Shoals, a few miles away from Bimini. He wrote, "There we found dozens of rectangular stone columns, averaging 8 feet long, 3 feet wide and weighing about 4 tons each. They resembled the tumbled remains of a monumental edifice thrown into the sea by some geologic violence." (pp72-3) They also saw the wreckage of a sunken trawler which had been salvaging the stones possibly in the 1930s. Apparently most of the upper stones of the Bimini Road had been removed during that time and taken to Miami, as good construction stone was rare in Florida.

Graham Hancock dived the Bimini Road in 1999 assuming that it was a natural formation, but he questioned those assertions. "I still felt the force of the scientific arguments, but now I'd also experienced the force of the great structure underwater and my reaction was not the same reaction as the geologists. Where they'd seen a 'natural' formation of tabular beachrock with uniform particle sizes, constant dip direction and no tool marks, artifacts or other signs of human intervention, I'd seen something that looked like a majestic work of art or sculpture—perhaps a colossal mosaic— something at any rate that felt coherent, organised. Purposive, planned, idiosyncratic and designed. It is true that bedrock does fracture into jointed blocks, and that examples of this process can be seen in Bimini today…However, nothing I have ever seen that is definitely and assailably beachrock, either on Bimini or anywhere else, looks like the Bimini Road." (ibid, p 522)

He observed that some blocks in the 5-15 tonne range were propped up on small vertical supports of a different stone type which resembled stubby pillars. These supports, often five at a time, lifted the stones completely clear of the bedrock foundation. They were probably the 'dolmens' mentioned by Valentine even though they were not proper dolmens.

From late February to early March of 2006, an underwater expedition was conducted to Bimini and the Cay Sal Bank on the 87 ft. research boat, 'Dolphin Dream' with researchers Drs Lora and Greg Little, archeologist William Donato and John and Doris Van Auken of the A.R.E. Accompanying the research team was a production crew from *NBC News* who were making a documentary on the expedition. They were investigating some new discoveries at Bimini, including numerous stone anchors and two dozen pieces of cut grey marble recovered under the Bimini Road blocks. Numerous uniform, rectangular slabs of stone with sharp, angular edges and smooth stones were also photographed. Some of them were seen under huge blocks, acting as leveling stones. A nearby site, called 'Proctor's Road' yielded at least eight stone anchors found on the bottom and at least five stone circles placed at regular intervals.

Later in 2006 the same team returned and began removing rectangular slabs from under huge blocks. They were surprised to see so many slabs in such a confined area. Beneath the stones were several 'wedge stones' which were two by three feet in length and 8 inches wide on one side, tapering to only one inch thick on the other side. The stones are similar to ashlar blocks used in breakwaters to create a quay.

At Proctor's Road, a kilometer from the Bimini Road, they discovered six stone anchors with three large holes and weighing from 70 to 400 pounds. The stones were beachrock limestone and definitely showed evidence of human artifact. One of these anchors is heart shaped, weighs over 400 pounds and is three feet in diameter, making it too heavy for even modern boats to transport. The website **http://www.mysterious-america.net/bimini-caysal200.html** concludes:

"Combined with the May 2005 results, the implications are clear and definitive. The Bimini site was utilized as a harbor at some remote time and a sophisticated maritime culture employed the same construction techniques that have been discovered at ancient Mediterranean harbors. These techniques include the use of smooth rectangular stones and wedge stones utilized for leveling large blocks."

In a press release 'Bimini Harbour: Uncovering the Great Bimini Hoax' by Dr Greg Little, he asserts that "the Bimini formation was once an ancient harbor, nearly identical in size, shape, and construction to many that have been found and verified in the Mediterranean." Furthermore, he accuses archeologists of perpetrating a hoax by claiming the site is natural and ignoring the research of McKusik and Eugene Shinn's original 'Nature' article which concluded that some of the Bimini Road was artificial. Not only did the original skeptics present stones from another site for core sample analysis, but there is little probability that they actually dived on the site at all. Shinn was still actively perpetuating the hoax in his 2004 'Skeptical Enquirer' article.

Long cylindrical columns found near Bimini investigated by Wyman Harrison were made of old cement, while two were fluted marble. In his 2004 Skeptical Inquirer' article, Shinn claimed these columns were made of 'Portland Cement' which had been stored in wooden barrels and dumped overboard in recent times. Little wrote, "They didn't mention the marble columns at all and failed to mention the fact that the idea the cement columns were from barrels dumped in recent times was wild speculation without any basis in fact...There is no evidence whatsoever indicating that wooden barrels were present and the fact that marble columns were also found is simply unacknowledged."

He wrote, "In fact, Eugene Shinn's original 1978 report actually detailed results that point to the Bimini Road being man-made. The documentation of the hoax is clear and definitive, but it is more than likely that skeptics will deride and dismiss the evidence with no investigation. The details of the story are intriguing." He also claimed, "One of the most interesting aspects of the Shinn McKusick Hoax is that it appears to have the active support of the US Geological Survey, mainstream geologists, and certainly academic archeologists. Many scientists have apparently been either duped by secondary sources, simply accepted the skeptical viewpoint because that's what they want to believe, or actively supported the hoax."

He outlined his case of the Bimini Hoax in a free pdf 29 page report which can be found at

http://www.mysterious-america.net/Resources/Bimini%20HarborPrint2.pdf

The official article by the A.R.E. can be found at
http://www.edgarcayce.org/am/bimini2005report.html

In a March 2007 update, Dr Little alluded to enigmatic discoveries made using side-scan sonar and a remote underwater camera. He wrote: "The most interesting finds from the sonar and subsequent follow-ups revealed rectangular formations lying in 100 feet of water off Bimini, several unusual stone formations 20+ miles out on the Great Bahama Bank, and the "rediscovery" of an underwater "mass" of fully dressed marble beams, an exquisite marble building apex, marble columns, and numerous huge, rectangular flat slabs of white marble. The most puzzling results included the discovery of an underwater wall off a small, uninhabited island North of Andros. This wall was constructed from huge blocks and slabs of limestone. One section of the wall remains partially intact and consists of three-to-five layers of stone blocks."

http://mysterious-america.net/bermudatriangle0.html

In the August 2007 issue of Alternative Perceptions Magazine, Dr Little was more forthcoming with information on recent discoveries and provided photographs of enigmatic architectural features such as columns and even architraves.

He presented and refuted the claims of critics that the Bimini road was a natural formation.

Claim 1: There are no slabs of stone sitting squarely on top of each other.

Response: "Our 2005 research proved this was untrue, finding

148

and photographing numerous huge slabs squarely placed into multiple tiers."

Claim 2: There are no tool marks on any of the stones.

Response: "Research by archeologists Bill Donato and a subsequent verificiation in 2005 also showed that this was not true. There are numerous mortise stones present at this site."

Claim 3: There are no prop or leveling blocks under any of the huge blocks.

Response: "Research in 2005 and 2006 also showed this to be false. Under the watchful cameras of a NBC News film crew making a documentary, we removed numerous rectangular slabs of stone from under the large blocks as well as a large wedge stone, which was used as a leveling block. These were later brought to the surface for examination."

Claim 4: Cores from the blocks show the stones are a part of the same massive natural formation.

Response: "Inspection of the actual published reports by the skeptics showed that this was not the actual finding. The initial report clearly indicated that there were great differences between areas of the cores and that they were not, in fact, matched from one stone to the next. We found that the subsequent reports, all of which were subsequently based on the first one, simply altered the description of the findings to fit the idea that all the stones matched."

Claim 5: The Bimini Road stones are beachrock, a naturally occurring limestone.

Response: "The idea that all the thousands of stone blocks at Bimini are beachrock comes from a few stone samples, but has been conclusively disproven by a host of researchers.(Furthermore) ...in the Mediterranean dozens of ancient harborformations ... all used beachrock to construct breakwaters, quays and jetties... The skeptics did not compare any of the ancient harbors in the Mediterranean to the Bimini Road."

http://www.mysterious-america.net/bimini2007.html

A hurricane in 2006 cleared the sand near the Bimini road to reveal additional features, dubbed 'Paradise Point Pier' by the team. This structure appears to be elevated off the bottom and constructed from piled stone blocks with numerous 'columns' on its surface.

In late 2006 and June 2007 two expeditions were conducted at Bimini by Bill Donato. In 2006, the side-scan sonar results found a line of intriguing bottom structures a few miles west of Bimini at a depth of 100 feet. Numerous well aligned rectangular features were sighted, oriented as if they were small buildings sitting by a shoreline. Due to very strong Gulf Stream currents, they were unable to send divers to this site.

The team explored Paradise Point Pier and observed cylinder shaped stones, identical to columns reported at the inlet between North and South Bimini islands. These strongly resembled ancient Roman harbors and breakwaters.

The June 2007 expedition was conducted by Drs Greg and Dora Little as well as Krista and Elsie Brown. Its purpose was to conduct side-scan sonar of the Bimini Road, Paradise Point Pier and Proctor's Road. They also wanted to investigate reports of triangular shaped stones. At Proctor's Road they identified five stone circles and imaged the complete Bimini Road.

The team also visited an area where stone blocks had been reported seven miles north of Bimini. The side-scan sonar revealed that the area was littered with apparent stone forms beneath the sand. These forms had been discovered in 1970 by Richard Wingate who had used a sand blower to reveal three layers of slabs. Beneath the bottom slab he found the remains from an old ship. In 1980 he wrote a book about the marble called 'Lost Outpost of Atlantis'.

Little's team explored the area and saw "numerous rectangular formations on the bottom lying in what looked like a straight line. The rectangular forms sat at the top of a 10 foot drop off which led to a narrow flat area. Then it descended toward the deep Gulf Stream."

They measured the rectangles to be 15 x 30 feet, with most at about 8 x 10 feet. Their depth is at 100 feet which was just above sea level in 10,000 BC. The Browns, who are master divers, reported that the structures were formed from coral encrusted stone. Their photos reveal other stones and possibly pots or amphorae.

ANDROS ISLAND

In 1969 Russian oceanographer Dimitri Rebikoff photographed an anomalous formation, shaped like the cursive letter 'e' off the northwestern shore of Andros. According to author Charles Berlitz, this, and various unusual circular formations found around the island have been used as evidence that underwater structures are present in the area.

In 2003 Greg and Dora Little announced that an underwater three tiered stone platform lying under just ten feet of water was discovered off northern Andros Island. They began a series of research expeditions in February in an attempt to locate numerous underwater formations which had been spotted by pilots over many years. They managed to find all the formations during extensive aerial surveys and concluded that all had natural explanations.

During their March trip to Andros with Dino Keller, an experienced diver, they found the unusual stone platform about 500 yards off shore. It is a gigantic flat stone platform made by thick, mostly rectangular blocks of stone. It is comprised of three tiers which increase in height as they move toward the sea. The blocks on the front edges of each of the three tiers are about 25 to 30 feet. The formation is about 150 feet wide and 450 yards long and encloses a deep water lagoon and harbor at North Andros.

The couple visited Andros in June while filming a documentary for the 'Learning Channel'. In several places they photographed what appear to be paving stones carefully fitted and joined together. Greg claimed that they looked like an ancient Mediterranean quay with breakwaters. In their book 'The A.R.E.'s Search for Atlantis' the Littles speculate that the harbor could have been in use about 8,000 years ago. "The Andros platform could have been used as the massive foundation for buildings. It would have had a commanding view of the entrance into the Tongue of the Ocean, a two mile deep trench running the entire length of the island...It does bear some resemblance to the Bimini Road, but the stones and the structure itself are quite a bit larger."

They located the 'e' shape and dived the twelve feet. About forty feet across, it turned out to be an unusual formation of seaweed, as did many other shapes on the seabed.

151

Drs Greg and Lora Little visited Andros Island in both May and June 2007, taking aerial surveys of the Great Bahama Bank which is only about 25 feet deep. The surveys revealed over thirty unusual dark formations on the banks, most of which were dumped materials. About twenty five percent of the formations turned out to be made from stone blocks which were too large to be ship ballast. Greg wrote, "They could be ruins of buildings which were erected on the Great Bahama Bank when it was above sea level. However, since none of these were clearly definitive, it was decided to spend our time examining as many sites as possible."

http://edgarcayce.org/search_for_atlantis_part3.asp

The coastline along North Andros was examined with a remote underwater video pulled by a cable on the boat. It photographed massive slabs of stone lying on the bottom just off 50 foot high sheer stone cliffs near the 'Tongue of the Ocean' trench. A complete side-scan sonar of the Andros Platform was also made, suggesting that the three tired formation was an ancient breakwater enclosing a harbor at Nicholls Town bay.

The most important archeological find of the Andros expeditions was a stonewall found off an island north of Andros. Interviews with local residents had alerted them to a huge underwater wall in Joulters Cays, about seven miles north of Andros. They managed to photograph the wall, although the residents claimed that a hurricane in the 1990s had destroyed much of it.

The wall is made of square and rectangular limestone blocks ranging from 3-6 feet long to 2-3 feet wide. The blocks are cut and dressed with tool marks visible. The blocks continued off the island for about three hundred yards, although most are completely covered by sand.

The Littles scoured libraries for references to this wall and found nothing, leading them to believe that it was very old.

This article in its entirety can be read on the A.R.E site's 'Search for Atlantis' menu at

http://edgarcayce.org/search_for_atlantis_part3.asp

CAY SAL

Cay Sal is a remote part of the Bahamas near Cuba. It was investigated by the Little team after a satellite image showed an grid like area inside the SE portion of the bank of light and dark spots. When investigated with a remote drop camera, the dark spots were seen to be bottom grass and the light spots were sand.

In the late 1960s an underwater stone formation similar to the Bimini Road was reported off the small island of Anguilla at the extreme SE Cay Sal Bank, 23 miles from Cuba. The Anguilla Arc is in shallow 10-20 feet of water where large deposits of beachrock lie on the sea bottom. The Arc begins on a rocky shoreline and the formation runs fairly straight for a few hundred yards. It is formed by massive slabs of beachrock which has distinctive layers about 1-2 feet in some parts. Beyond this is a curious formation—a rectangular stack of beachrock slabs with four to five layers resting on the bottom. It is approximately 15 by 20 feet in size and at least 8 feet tall and is covered with dense vegetation and coral. About 20 yards further the arc feature reappears and curves back toward land enclosing the remainder of the harbour. It possibly served as a breakwater as it about the same depth as the Bimini Road and Andros Platform.

A stone recovered from the arc is made of limestone with particles of iron and shows no characteristics of beachrock limestone. Dr Dora Little videotaped the entire Anguilla Arc and found what appears to be a stone anchor as well as wedge stones.

The team concluded that "the presence of the various cut rectangular slabs, the wedge stones, the large stone anchors at Bimini point to a maritime culture more sophisticated than the Caribe tribes."

http://geocities.com/MotorCity/Factory/2583/discovery.htm

A huge underwater pyramid to the southwest of the Cay Sal Bank was reported in 1977 by deep sea fishermen. Anecdotal reports by divers of pyramids encouraged Ari Marshall, a Greek industrialist, to mount an expedition in search of them. They took closed circuit footage of a pyramidal mound off the Cay Sal Bank at a depth of 750 feet.

Marshall commented in Berlitz's book about how the compasses were going berserk in the vicinity of the pyramid. "We were right over the pyramid. The top seemed to be about 150 feet from the surface with a total depth of about 650 feet. We lowered the camera and high intensity lights down the side of the mass and suddenly came to an opening. Light flashes or shining white objects were being swept into the opening by turbulence. They may have been gas or some sort of energy crystals. Further down, the same thing happened in reverse. They were coming out again at a lower level It was surprising that the water in this deep area was green instead of black near the pyramid, even at night." (Berlitz op.cit p101)

Because of the extreme depth, divers were not sent to investigate and the resulting footage turned out to be inconclusive. However, large holes on the side of the formation were photographed as well as electrically charged particles passing in and out of them.

SCOTTS STONES?

On June 21, 1997 a press release was made from the Egyptology Society, an alleged affiliate of the Miami Museum of Science announcing "The discovery of tangible archeological evidence which points to the former existence of an advanced civilization which built temples near Bimini which can be geologically dated as being more than twelve thousand years old."

Subsequent press releases in July stated that the 'Scotts Stones', named after a Professor Scott, were constructed of huge blocks of stone, around six feet in thickness and ranging in length from 9-12 feet. They were multicoloured with walls that were covered with metals such as copper, iron and brass. It was revealed that the original structures were more advanced than the Great Pyramid of Giza with casing stones of the same angle. "There are exact orbital plots of the planets and what seem to have been intricate star shafts, metal coated walls, and intermingled stones of various colours (including red, white and black). Other characteristics showed the structure similar to megalithic sites in Mexico, Ireland and Scandinavia.

President Aaron DuVal was contacted by authors Christopher Dunn and Andrew Collins. He promised Dunn that he would reveal the site to him so the author flew to Miami. Dunn suspected that DuVal's stones were actually part of the jetties at Miami which had been built from what some considered to be ancient megaliths. Needless to say, DuVal's megaliths did not materialise and Dunn had the opportunity to examine the jetty blocks, finding nothing to compare them with the quarry marks found in Egypt. Collins also spent a lot of time studying the jetty and came to the conclusion that none of them had been dredged from the Moselle Shoals which had been cited as ancient ruins by mineral prospector Richard Wingate in the 1970s.

'Miami Mirage' issue 13 'Atlantis Rising Magazine'

The 'Scotts Stones' made six press releases, revealing more grandiose 'findings' such as the complete island of Poseidonia, the islands of Og and Aryan, and last, but not least, Edgar Cayce's Hall of Records which were translated with unprecedented rapidity. Not surprisingly, the information they revealed corroborated all of Cayce's insights into Atlantis. Duval had also been offered a large sum to write a book about the 'Scotts Stones' but to date has written nothing. The press releases can be read on this site:

http://www.freddyreyes.com/index.php?option=com_content&task=view&id=24

Ten years after DuVal's first press releases, no findings have been presented, no books written and the so-called Scott Stones need to be treated with extreme skepticism.

OTHER AREAS IN THE BAHAMAS

• Charles Berlitz wrote, "Scores of other examples extend through the waters of the Bahama Banks, sometimes forming great stone circles, like Stonehenge, sometimes connecting existing islands by underwater walls or roads, sometimes consisting of circular walls built around freshwater springs far below the surface, often by a series of straight and intersecting lines along the bottom like the intersecting lines of the Nazca Valley in Peru, and often great rectangular forms traceable in distinct shapes by variations of bottom vegetation, the possible outline of a large platform which has subsided below the ocean floor." (Berlitz, op.cit p95)

• According to an article in Berlitz's book with Dr Manson Valentine, "between Diamond Point and Tongue of the Ocean there is a network of modular straight lines intersecting at right, obtuse and acute angles. I saw a series of enormous rectangles along the sea bottom connected by straight lines between Orange Key and Bimini. At Riding Rocks a vast expanse of shallow water is divided into squares. At Orange Key south of Bimini there is an absolutely straight rectangle the size of a football field. All the way to Bimini there is a succession of architectural patterns, square and rectangular, indicating the size and shape of what lies below."

• In 1982 Herbert Sawinski, an explorer, diver and chairman of the Museum of Science and Archeology in Fort Lauderdale investigated submerged banks between 23 degrees 50 inches N and 80 degrees 30 inches to 79 degrees 40 inches W. According to Berlitz, "Extensive stone pavements were located and photographed at a depth of 25 feet, as well as distinct walls with vestiges of a pavement running along the top. The main wall continues for a quarter of a mile out to sea, where it suddenly disappears into 2,500 feet of water." (p100) This is the area of the famous Blue holes which descend to thousands of feet.

• Pyramids have been sighted from the air and allegedly explored by such divers as Dr Ray Brown. He claimed that near the Berry Islands his compasses were spinning and the magnetometers were malfunctioning. "It was murky but suddenly we could see outlines of buildings under the water. It seemed to be a large exposed area of an underwater city...I turned to look toward the sun through the murky water and saw a pyramid shape shining like a mirror. About thirty five to forty feet from the top was an opening. I was reluctant to go inside...but swam in anyway. The opening was like a shaft debouching into an inner room. I saw something shining. It was a crystal, held by two metallic hands. I had on my gloves and I tried to loosen it. It became loose. As soon as I grabbed it I felt this was the time to get out and not come back. I am not the only person who has seen these ruins—others have seen them from the air and say they are five miles wide and more than that in length." (Berlitz, ibid pp104-5)

• Pilot Ed Wilson encountered an electromagnetic anomaly northeast of Miami, with the water 'opening up'. What he thought was a shipwreck revealed itself to be an enormous building with slanted sides. "The building I was looking at must have been 100 to 250 feet high according to the pattern I could get." (Berlitz p 103) Despite flying over the same coordinates many times, he was never able to see the building under the water again.

• Pilots "have remarked on pyramidal formations, stepped terraces and walls on the ocean floor between the Bahamas and Florida. A Pan American pilot has described seeing an archway in a submerged wall about sixty feet from the surface. Charter pilots have described underwater roads leading eastward out to sea from the coast of Yucatan, which they followed until the roads were lost in deep water, but which presumably continued to other destinations now beneath the sea." (ibid p81) Leicester Hemingway, brother of novelist Ernest, claimed to have seen an expanse of white stone ruins off the northern coast of Cuba.

BERMUDA

• Horace Gouvieva, a follower of Dr Zhirov living in Michigan, explored areas off the coast of Bermuda with scuba equipment in the 1950s. At a depth of 25 feet he claimed to have found stone columns, 24 feet long and 18 inches square resting on their bases, with a layer of additional columns beneath them. He photographed the ruins and reproduced them in a line drawing. A member of his expedition, Dr William Bell found a vertical column rising from the seafloor as well as several stone slabs and a gear like structure. David Zink's book 'The Stones of Atlantis' published some of the pictures.

REFERENCES: G. Hancock, 'Underworld'C. Berlitz, 'Atlantis, the Lost Continent Revealed'

'Back to Bimini', W. Donato from Law of One Newsletter, 1997)

Alternative Perceptions Magazine Issue 100, April 2006

http://www.mysterious-america.net/bimini-caysal200.html

Alternative Perceptions Magazine Issue 106, 2007

http://www.mysterious-america.net/bimini2007.html
Uncovering the Bimini Hoax, Greg Little
http://www.mysterious-america.net/Resources/Bimini%20HarborPrint2.pdf
Updated Report on May 2005 Bimini-Andros Expedition: Bimini Road—an Ancient Harbour, Dr Greg Little http://www.edgarcayce.org/am/bimini2005report.html
Alternative Perceptions, Issue 114, July 2007 http://mysterious-america.net/bermudatriangle0.html
Edgar Cayce's A.R.E http://edgarcayce.org/search_for_atlantis_part3.asp
'Miami Mirage' issue 13 'Atlantis Rising Magazine'

RUINS OFF CUBA?

In his 2000 book 'Gateway to Atlantis', British historian Andrew Collins proposed that Cuba was the flagship of the Atlantean empire. He studied Plato's description in relation to Cuba's geography, matching an island plain of about 540 by 160 km, surrounded on three sides by mountain ranges. This plain, which was drowned at the end of the Ice Age, extended southwards to the Bay of Batabano until about 9,000 years ago.

Cuba has been identified as the mysterious island known as Antillia on Medieval maps as well as the Island of Seven Cities in Moorish and later, Portuguese tradition. Moreover, Antillia's name derives from the Semitic root ATL, 'to elevate'—also associated with Atlas and his island of Atlantis.

The early Mesoamerican people, the Aztecs, Toltecs and Mayans had a myth that their ancestors came from an island paradise in the east, known as Aztlan or Tulan, following a period of darkness when the sun would not appear. They emerged from 'The Seven Caves' and set up Seven Cities. The only site in the Caribbean which bears any resemblance to the Seven Caves is the Punta del Este cave complex at the extreme eastern end of a peninsula on the Isla de Juventud, separated from the southern mainland of Cuba by the Bay of Batabano.

The idea that Cuba was once part of Atlantis can be traced to a two page article which appeared in the February 1952 edition of the magazine ECOS entitled 'Formo Cuba Parte de la Atlandida?' by Francisco Garcia-Juarez. He and other members of the Institute of Cuban Archeology (ICA) were investigating the idea that Atlantean culture might be found in Cuba and Hispaniola as proposed by Egerton Sykes, an Atlantis expert. The ICA had concluded that the most likely location where traces of Atlantean culture might be found on Cuba was the Punta del Este cave complex. Petroglyphs from the caves displayed astronomical information which may have linked them with the origins of the Mayan calendar. Thus Cuba could have been a staging post for the migrations of the Maya into Central America from the island continent.

The petroglyhs also show what appears to be a celestial body, perhaps a comet, breaking up. This fits in with Collins's theory that a comet disintegrated into thousands of fragments which hit the Western Atlantic at the end of the Ice Age. Around 500,000 elliptical craters down the east coast of the USA, known as the Carolina Bays are evidence of this catastrophic event which must have caused massive tsunamis and firestorms upon impact. Collins feels that the Atlantis legend resulted from such a catastrophe.

In 2000 a remarkable discovery lent weight to Collins's theory. Oceanographer and engineer Paulina Zelitsky and her husband Paul Weinzweig, owners of Advanced Digital Communications International Inc, (ADC) were contracted by the Cuban government to take ocean current temperatures at various depths for a global warming study, search for shipwrecks and natural gas deposits. Their ship 'Bic Ulises' was equipped to conduct deep ocean surveys in the Caribbean and Gulf of Mexico.

'BIC Ulises' was taking a sonar survey off northeast of Cabo San Antonio in Cuba, towing a boom box sized sonar on a tether and using sound waves to survey the sea bottom on a computer screen. This area is anomalous because geologically it seems to belong to the Yucatan peninsula rather than Cuba itself. While Zelitsky and her husband were watching the screen, the empty sand plain suddenly gave way to highly anomalous images of massive geometric shapes, apparently cut from stone.

"We were shocked, and frankly we were a little frightened," said Zelitsky. "It was a though we should not be seeing what we were seeing. Our first thought was maybe we found some kind of secret military installation."

For the next six months the couple stayed busy with their work for the Cuban government and said little about their discovery. "But I tried to identify what we had seen. Then one day, in our office, I looked up and saw pictures of ancient Mexican ruins on a calendar, and I made the mental connection." (St Petersburg Times, Underwater world: Man's doing or nature? Nov 17, 2002)

In July 2001 they returned to the site with geologist Manuel Iturralde, senior researcher of Cuba's Natural History Museum. They sent down a Remotely Operated Vehicle to examine and videotape the structures which are located in a submerged or submarine valley. Images sent back confirmed the presence of large blocks of stone, about 8 by 10 feet in circular, rectangular and pyramid shapes. Some blocks appeared to be deliberately stacked on top of each other, while others appeared to be isolated.

Their white appearance underwater leads Zelitsky to believe they are constructed of granite, a stone which is alien to Cuba and the Yucatan but prevalent in Central America. Zelitsky and Weinzweig have dubbed their discovery 'Mega' because the stone pieces appear to be megaliths. Others have called it the Lost City of Atlantis, although the couple is not promoting this idea. She believes Atlantis is only a myth. "What we have found is more likely remnants of a local culture" once located on a land bridge which joined Mexico's Yucatan peninsula with Cuba.

Zelitsky feels the megaliths pre date the Mayan culture and perhaps belonged to the Olmec or Totonec peoples. When questioned as to how the ruins came to be over 2,000 feet below the surface, she responded that large scale underground movement of the Earth's tectonic plates and accompanying volcanoes and earthquakes could have sunk the island. "It's a very powerful event which could have happened very quickly," she said. Some megaliths on the sea floor seemed to be organized, while others were not. "Over about 20 square km there are a large number of structures that appear jumbled, disorganized."

Geologist Iturralde had clearly identified the coastal structures of a separated island and large areas of volcanic glass "Which could be generated only on the oxygenated surface." However, he was also conceding that the images could be a creation of nature or natural structures adapted by intelligent beings for religious or dwelling purposes.

In an interview with journalist Linda Moulton Howe, Weinzweig has made these comments:

"We have sonar images which show architectural types of structures with geometry, perpendicular lines, symmetries that one does not tend to find in nature and are not repeated anywhere else in the region. They are extensive and large and we have video, but is suggestive because the stones we have videotaped are very large, very smooth. They do not belong to the local geography at all, according to our ocean bottom survey work and to Dr Iturralde."

He was questioned about the dimensions of the structures and responded:

- The images are up to 120 to 200 meters (492-656 feet) long and up to 50-100 meters (164-328 feet) in width. Their height is difficult to estimate but it could be 15 to 20 meters, with more extensive structures below the sand.
- The megalithic structures could cover more than ten square km.
- Pyramidal shaped stones have been discovered.
- Some of the structures might be coated with metal according to the sonar images which show darker images.
- Estimated age of structures—about 6,000 years at least.

(Update on Deep Water Megalithic Stones and Structures Near Western Cuba' by Linda Moulton Howe 2003)

As can be expected, the discovery of Mega has been criticized by scientists and archeologists. John Echave, senior editor of National Geographic travelled to Cuba to study the sonar images and commented, "They are interesting anomalies, but that's as much as anyone can say right now. I'm no expert on sonar and until we are able to actually go down there and see, it will be difficult to characterize them." A planned National Geographic expedition

161

fizzled out when the correct permits were not received although the magazine did run an article on the structures in 2002.

Dr Robert Ballard, respected underwater explorer who discovered the Titanic in 1985 responded to the discovery with skepticism. "That's too deep," he said of the 2,000 foot deep site. "I'd be surprised if it was human. You have to ask yourself, how did it get there? I've looked at a lot of sonar images in my life and it can be sort of like looking at an ink blot—people can see what they want to see. I'll just wait for a bit more data."

In 2004 another expedition led by Zelitsky had to be abandoned due to problems with the mini submarine Deep Worker. During the twenty five days of work off Cuba they were able to confirm the existence of a pyramid 35 meters high and rocky 'unnatural formations'. In addition, the team managed to extract a carved rock, possibly part of another pyramid, stone with animal fossils, volcanic sand and a bacterium that can be used in vaccines.

Lack of funding has prevented the ADC from doing further research at the site as it would require about $8 or $9 million dollars to do a proper survey.

http://www.altarcheologie.nl/index.html?underwater_ruins/yonaguni/overview.htm

REFERENCES: Update on Deep Water Megalithic Stones and Structures Near Western Cuba' by Linda Moulton Howe 2003
 St Petersburg Times, Underwater world: Man's doing or nature? Nov 17, 2002
' Cuba' http://www.altarcheologie.nl/index.html?underwater_ruins/yonaguni/overview.htm
'Atlantis in Cuba?' http://www.s8int.com/water28.html
'Underwater Cities; Noah's Flood Proof?' http://www.s8int.com/water1.html

RUINS OFF PUERTO RICO?

On September 19, 2005 'The Journal of Hispanic Ufology' reported that an underwater formation, similar to the 'Bimini Road' had been discovered on the shores of La Parguera, Puerto Rico. The new formation was identified using reconnaissance flights and aerial photography.

A small group of researchers spearheaded by Andrew Alvarez and Aldo Acosta have been studying various anomalies on the island and evaluating if they are natural or man-made. Although the vast majority have a natural origin, the La Parguera formation, sitting in less than 20 feet of water has yet to be identified. The apparent structure measures over 250 feet long and lies in an area where ancient structures, such as a stone wall, have been discovered.

The original Spanish source can be found at **http://www.ovni.net**

MAYAN RUINS OF ISLA CERRITOS, MEXICO

Cerritos is located off the coast of Yucatan in a position where the Gulf Stream and Caribbean join. This island was first reported in archeological journals in 1963, and information has been published in specialised articles such as 'Mexicon' and old 'National Geographic Research Reports.' A massive excavation was done in 1984-5 by a team of archeologists who declared it to be a unique Mayan site with 13 separate habitation layers dating from 300 BC to the 1400 AD.

This tiny island, only 650 feet in diameter, was completely covered with 29 buildings and had a seawall encircling its perimeter. According to Dr Greg Little of the A.R.E, "Numerous huge elevated platforms were built into the water from the shore. These were moorings areas and quays. The breakwater, almost all of which has been looted for its huge stone slabs, is all under about a foot of water now, extending up from the bottom about 4-5 feet today. A few remaining slabs of vertical stone stick up above the surface during low tide…"

http://www.mysterious-america.net/islacerritosexpe.html

The island is off limits to Mexicans and lies in a restricted National Nature Reserve. Dr Little was able to visit and observed many structures made from coarse beachrock, a partially intact seawall about four feet high and a breakwater enclosing the harbor1,000 feet long and 15 feet wide. It was made by first

163

sticking slabs of stone (beachrock) into the bottom forming a 15 foot wide enclosure which was filled with smaller stones. Slabs of shaped, flat beachrock were placed on the top forming a massive breakwater enclosure. Most of these stones, which resembled the stones from the Bimini Road and Andros Platform, had already been looted, although the largest ones were about 4 x 6 feet and a foot thick. Originally thousands of such stones had been placed as a breakwater, but only about 40 to 50 remain.

There were at least three openings through the breakwater into the harbour. The ends that formed these openings had large beachrock stones piled together to make an ending for the openings. The largest opening had two large platforms on each side which extended above the waterline. They once had structures erected on them, probably guard towers of lighthouses.

Dr Little was sure that this Mayan breakwater bore a strong resemblance to both ancient Mediterranean breakwaters and the formations at Bimini and Andros.

PRE-MAYAN SKELETON IN YUCATAN CAVE

On September 9, 2004, Associated Press announced that divers in underwater caves near the Caribbean coast have discovered some of the oldest human skeletons in the Americas.

Arturo Gonzalez and his team from Mexico's National Institute of Anthropology and History discovered at least three skeletons along the Yucatan Peninsula in 2001 and 2002. Gonzalez believed the bones must date from before the time the water levels rose about 400 feet, 8,000 to 9,000 years ago.

Tests on charcoal found beside one of the female skeletons dates it to at least 10,000 years old. An expert from the University of California, Riverside, dated it to 11,670 radiocarbon years old, about 13,000 years, placing it within the time span of the famous Clovis culture.

The oldest find was wade 404 yards (123 m) into a cave, more than 65 feet (20m) below sea level. Such excavations were extremely dangerous as divers could only spend 20 minutes in the cave, as well as 80 minutes swimming time and up to 60 minutes of decompression time. Gonzalez had chosen such a difficult environment because cave divers had reported seeing skeletal remains in the water holes of the Yucatan limestone shelf.

It took many trips to record the sites and excavate the bones, which then required two years of preservation. This discovery proves that humans inhabited the Yucatan over five millennia before the Mayans. As the skeleton itself did not resemble a Mayan, it is very possible that a different race occupied Mesoamerica in extremely ancient times.

http://www.msnbc.msn.com/id/5955043/

REFERENCES:

Alternative Perceptions Magazine Issue # 82, August 2004
http://www.mysterious-america.net/islacerritosexpe.html
msnbc 'Divers find traces of ancient Americans' Sept 9, 2004
http://www.msnbc.msn.com/id/5955043/

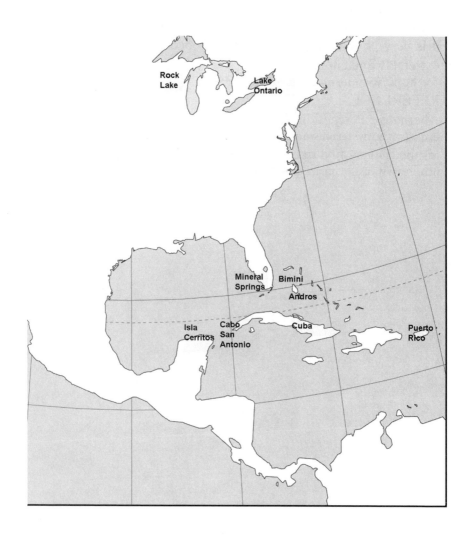

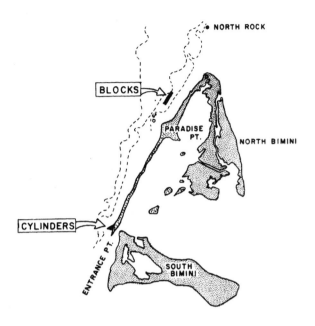

Above: The "Bimini Road" and the mysterious cylinders off the coast of Bimini. Courtesy of William Corliss and the Sourcebook Project.

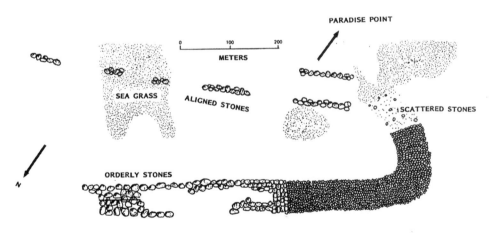

Top: The "Bimini Road" and the curious distribution and organzation of stones off Bimini. Courtesy of William Corliss and the Sourcebook Project.

167

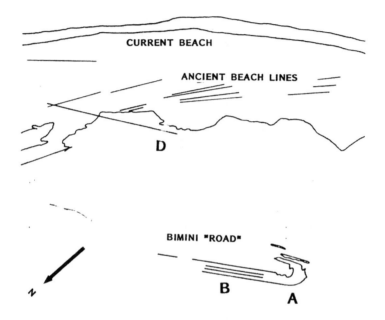

Top: The "Bimini Road" and other puzzling topographic features off the coast of Bimini. Courtesy of William Corliss and the Sourcebook Project.

James Churchward's map of the Amazonian Sea, which he believed was present during the time of Mu an Atlantis.

Top: Basalt logs stacked up in one of Nan Madol's huge walls. Bottom: A diver checks out one of the coral encrusted columns beneath the nearby bay.

PART 6
THE PACIFIC OCEAN
THE LEGEND OF MU
MORE THEORIES & LEGENDS OF A PACIFIC CONTINENT
MYSTERIOUS PACIFIC ISLANDS
LA JOLLA, CALIFORNIA
RUINS OFF PERU?
MICRONESIA, POHNPEI
RYUKYUS ISLANDS, JAPAN — YONAGUNI ISLAND
KERAMA
AGUNI, CHATAN
PESCADORES ISLANDS TAIWAN
MEDIEVAL JAPANESE RUINS?
SUNDALAND

The world's largest ocean may contain many sunken sites, particularly off the coast of Japan, Taiwan and the submerged continent of Sundaland.

THE LEGEND OF MU

In 1864 a French scholar, the Abbe Charles-Etienne Brasseur de Bourbourg came across a treatise on Mayan civilization entitled 'Account of the Affairs of Yucatan' by Diego de Landa, the Bishop of Yucatan who had destroyed most of the Mayan codices in a fit of religious zeal. After almost obliterating the Mayan written language, the bishop was remorseful and tried to learn the language. He provided a Mayan alphabet in his treatise.

Brasseur set out to translate the only three remaining Mayan codices, starting with the Troano Codex. His translation revealed the story of a volcanic catastrophe and a land which sank beneath the waves. The two symbols he could not translate resembled a M and U, so he joined them together to produce Mu, the name he gave to the sunken land.

Unfortunately Brasseur's translation was soon discredited and he shrank into obscurity although his Mu became associated with a lost Pacific continent. Mu also became interchangeable with Lemuria according to many occultists.

The next translation of the Troano Codex came from Augustus Le Plongeon, a physician and archeologist who was the first man to excavate the Mayan ruins in Yucatan. This translation was even more fanciful and retraced the story of Mu with the rivalry between two princes Coh and Aac. During this drama the continent began to sink so many Muvians escaped to Egypt and the Yucatan where they recorded their history and erected temples to their leaders. Le Plongeon's translation said: "In the year 6 Kan, on the 11th Muluc in the month of Zac, there occurred terrible earthquakes, which continued without interruption until the 13th Chuen. The country of the hills of mud, the land of Mu was sacrificed; being twice upheaved it suddenly disappeared during the night, the basin being continually shaken by the volcanic forces. Being confined, these caused the land to sink and to rise several times in various places. At last the surface gave way and ten countries were torn asunder and scattered. Unable to stand the force of the convulsion, they sank with their 64,000,000 inhabitants 8,060 years before writing this book." ('Mysteries of the Lost Lands', E. Van Zandt & R. Stemman)

Like Brasseur, Le Plongeon believed that Mu and Atlantis were the same place, which he assumed to be somewhere in the Gulf of Mexico or Caribbean Sea.

Another Frenchman Louis Jacolliot was writing about a lost continent called Rutas that sank in the Indian Ocean. He believed the legend was referring to the Pacific Ocean and the continent had occupied the Polynesian islands.

Yet another writer, Dr John Ballou Newbrough claimed angelic inspiration for his account of a vanished Pacific continent called Pan. His book 'Oahspe' was published in 1882 and claimed humans were created 72,000 years ago as a result of a union between angels and seal like creatures. His Pan sank 24,000 years ago in the North Pacific and was destined to resurface in 1980.

By far the most famous proponent of a sunken Pacific continent was James Churchward, an Anglo-American in his 70s. His first book 'The Lost Continent of Mu' was published in 1926 and is still in print. He based his theory on two sets of tablets, the 'Nacaal tablets' which are allegedly preserved in an Indian or Tibetan temple, and a collection of 2,500 stone objects recovered in Mexico by William Niven. These objects looked like flattened figurines, but Churchward claimed he could read their bumps and curlicues. He dated the Niven tablets at 12,000 years old and claimed they, and the mysterious Naacal tablets, contained extracts from the Sacred Inspired Writings of Mu.

His first book began with: "The Garden of Eden was not in Asia but on a now sunken continent in the Pacific Ocean. The Biblical story of creation...came not from the peoples of the Nile or the Euphrates valley but from the now submerged continent of Mu—the Motherland of Man.

"These assertions can be proved by the complex records I discovered upon long-forgotten sacred tablets in India, together with records from other countries. They tell of this strange country of 64,000,000 inhabitants, who, 50,000 years ago, had developed a civilization superior in many aspects to our own. They described, among other things, the creation of man in the mysterious land of Mu." (Van Zandt & Stemman ibid p183)

Churchward explained how he saw the sacred Naacal tablets in an Indian temple and the high priest taught him to read the inscriptions on the temple walls. Churchward persuaded the priest to show him the hidden records in the temple's secret archives which had originated in either Burma or Mu itself. These tablets described in detail the Earth's creation and the appearance of man on Mu. "Continuing my researches, I discovered that this lost continent had extended from somewhere north of Hawaii to the south as far as the Fijis and Easter Island, and was undoubtedly the original habitat of man. I learned that in this beautiful country there had lived a people that colonized the earth, and that the land had been obliterated by terrific earthquakes and submersion 12,000 years ago, and had vanished in a vortex of fire and water." (ibid p 184)

Mu was a beautiful tropical country with vast plains and no mountains. Many rivers and streams wound their way around the wooded hills and luxuriant flowers. The happy inhabitants of Mu consisted of ten tribes of different colours, white, yellow, brown and black, with the white race dominating.

The Muvians built a large network of roads from stone and were expert navigators. They set up colonies around the world. Churchward wrote: "While this great land was thus at its zenith, centre of the earth's civilization, learning, trade and commerce, with great stone temples being erected and huge statues and monoliths set up, she received a rude shock; a fearful visitation overtook her." (ibid)

Earthquakes and volcanoes shook the southern part of Mu destroying many cities. Lava piled up into high cones which are seen today as the Pacific Islands. However, a few generations later, a greater catastrophe hit Mu and the whole continent reeled. "With thunderous roarings the doomed land sank. Down, down, down she went, into the mouth of hell—a tank of fire." Over fifty million square miles of water poured over the continent drowning nearly all the noble Muvians.

The few survivors, who had gathered near the lava cones which became islands, eventually became cannibals to survive. The Muvian colonies continued for awhile but without the help of the motherland they eventually disappeared. Atlantis was one of these colonies and suffered a similar fate a thousand years later.

According to Churchward, the Muvians, as well as the ancient Americans, colonised the Pacific Islands, particularly Easter, Tonga, Ponape and the Marianas. "There stand today vestiges of old stone temples and other lithic remains that take us back to the time of Mu. At Uxmal, in Yucatan, a ruined temple bears inscriptions commemorative of the 'Lands of the West' whence we came'; and the striking Mexican pyramid southwest of Mexico City according to its inscriptions, was raised as a monument to the destruction of these same 'Lands of the West'."

Churchward wrote more books on Mu such as 'The Children of Mu', 'The Sacred Symbols of Mu' and 'The Cosmic Forces of Mu Volumes 1 and 11.'

Churchward's map of Mu which looks remarkably like a larger version of the island of New Guinea.

MORE THEORIES & LEGENDS OF A PACIFIC CONTINENT

One of the earliest scholars on the New Zealand Maori, John Macmillan Brown, spent years researching the origins of this Polynesian race. Initially believing that they were a lost 'Aryan' race, which was the prevailing thought of the day, he later thought they came from northern Asia, or even the Americas before settling on the islands. Brown became Chancellor of the University of New Zealand and eventually theorised that there had been a lost continent in the Pacific Ocean. His final book 'The Riddle of the Pacific', published in 1924, claimed that Easter Island was one of the last remnants of the lost continent which had been founded by Aryans from America.

Brown travelled extensively around the Pacific marveling at the stone megaliths on many of the islands. On the enigmatic Easter Island, which possessed the only known script in the Pacific Islands, local tradition claimed that the inhabitants had originated on a sunken land called 'Hiva'.

In addition to the Easter Island archipelago, Brown also believed that land had also been submerged in several other parts of the Pacific within the last few thousand years. The Caroline archipelago with its ruins at Nan Madol, Pohnpei, could be the remains of a vast island-empire in the eastern Central Pacific. Brown figured that to build the fantastic ruins of Pohnpei, the population would need to be ten times larger than it is today.

The Polynesians themselves had legends of a lost land which had sunk beneath the waves. Easter Island legends tell of the first

175

settlers arriving after their native land had been submerged, and of a giant named Uoke who caused the subsidence of a large continent in his rage. Easter Island is the only remnant of this land. Similar traditions of vanished lands are found throughout Polynesia, Micronesia and Melanesia. The Hawaiians also believed that there was once a great continent stretching from Hawaii to New Zealand, its mountain tops surviving today as the Polynesian islands.

HIVA

In his 1965 book 'Mysteries of Easter Island', Francis Mazier explored the legends of the lost land of Hiva. After talking with a man who claimed to be the last initiate of Easter Island's secrets, he learned what had happened to Hiva. "The tradition is clear: there was a cataclysm; and it appears that this continent lay in the vast hinterland that reaches to the Tuamotu archipelago (French Polynesia) to the North West of Easter Island...According to tradition Sala-y-Gomez, an islet some hundred miles from Easter Island, was formerly part of it, and its name. Mutu Motiro Hiva means 'small island near Hiva.'

"Generally accepted geology does not acknowledge a vast upheaval in this part of the world, at least not within the period of human existence. However, there are two recently discovered facts that make the possibility of a sunken continent seem reasonable. When the American submarine 'Nautilis' made her long voyage around the world she called attention to the presence of an exceedingly lofty and still unidentified underwater peak close to Easter Island. And secondly, during his recent studies carried out for the Institute of Marine Resources and the University of California, Professor H.W Menard not only speaks of an exceedingly important fracture zone in the neighbourhood of Easter Island, a zone parallel to that of the Marquesas archipelago, but also the discovery of an immense bank or ridge of sediment." (D. Hatcher Childress, 'Lost Cities of Ancient Lemuria and the Pacific')

Maziere believed in the existence of an archipelago extending south and north of Easter Island between the Marquesas and Galapagos Islands. Easter Island was Sala-y-Gomez, the last peak.

An article in the *National Geographic Magazine* on October 24, 2007 discusses a cataclysm which occurred in the Pacific Ocean 50 million years ago changing its face from Hawaii to Antarctica. The collapse of an underwater mountain range, the mid ocean ridge known as the Izanagi Ridge, led to many changes, such as the location of Australia and the creation of many Pacific islands like Tonga. While this may not have happened in the time of human habitation, it does show that cataclysmic events are capable of changing the face of an ocean as large as the Pacific.

http://news.nationalgeographic.com/news/2007/10/071024-tectonics. html

MYSTERIOUS PACIFIC ISLANDS

The Pacific Ocean is the largest in the world and has its share of mysteries, anomalies and disappearing/reappearing islands. In his fascinating book 'Invisible Horizons' Vincent Gaddis wrote of many islands which have seemingly disappeared or appeared over the centuries. The following examples are from the Pacific Ocean.

• In 1687 Captain Edward Davis discovered a small long island with another huge land mass stretching beyond the horizon at 27 degrees south and five hundred miles west of South America. Davis land was never seen again.

• In 1879 Captain Pinocchio discovered Podesta Island near Easter Island. It appeared on charts but was removed from naval charts in 1935.

• S.S Glewalon sighted an island in 1912 near Easter Island which was never seen again.

• Sarah Ann Island, northwest of Easter Island was removed from naval charts in 1932 after the US Navy failed to locate it.

• Islands such as Bunker, New, Sultan, Eclipse, Roca, Marqueen, Spraque, Favourite, Monks, Dangerous, Duke of York, Grand Duke Alexander, Little Paternoster, Massacre of Mortlock have all disappeared from maps after being identified and mapped!

• Hunter Island at 15 degrees 31 inches South and 176 degrees 11 inches north discovered by Captain Hunter of the Donna Carmelta in 1823 disappeared with its Polynesian population!

• The St Vincents Islands discovered by Antonio Martinus in 1789 at 7 degrees 21 inches North and 127 degrees 4 inches West could not be located in 1825 by Captain Morrell who found discoloured water at 120 fathoms depth at the exact location.

• The low lying Tuanaki Islands near Rarotonga apparently disappeared during an earthquake in the nineteenth century.

• Many islands between Alaska and Japan which were sighted by air during the war disappeared without a trace, as did mysterious lands reported near Hawaii.

In November 2006 a new island was reported off the coast of Tonga as a result of the Curacoa submarine volcano. In the 1970s pumice was first discovered floating in the area; in August of 2006 the crew of the yacht Maiken saw a belt of tightly packed pumice. The following day, crewman Haiken spotted a volcanic island "One mile in diameter and with four peaks and a central crater smoking with steam and once in a while an outburst high in the sky with lava and ashes." **http://www.foxnews.com/story/0,2933,228385,00.html**
REFERENCES: 'Invisible Horizons' Vincent Gaddis
Fox News Nov, 09, 22006
http://www.foxnews.com/story/0,2933,228385,00.html

LA JOLLA, CALIFORNIA
Artifacts were first found off La Jolla's coast (north of San Diego) in the early 1900s when children would find stone bowls on the beach. Since the 1950s more than 2,000 artifacts dating to as early as 5,000 years old have been recovered and at least 34 submerged sites have been recorded from locations as deep as 30 meters. Some people believe there is even a sunken village, particularly archeologist Michael Arubuthnot who is making a movie on his diving expeditions called 'Mysterious Origins of La Jolla's Sunken City'.

Arbuthnot gained access to USGS remote computerised depictions of the ocean floor off La Jolla, allowing him to reconstruct ancient river channels and other submerged features which could indicate where underwater sites could be located.

Using the expertise of Dave Faires to film the event, the divers encountered difficulty with currents and poor visibility. On day two they found a beautiful stone bowl which led to the further discovery of six artifacts in 20 feet of water. Arbuthnot speculates that these artifacts are between 4,000 and 7,000 years old.

The original article can be found at the Team Atlantis website:

http://www.cineform.com/customer/LaJolla/LaJolla.htm

Team Atlantis is a team of experts and enthusiasts who like to dive on ancient sites and shipwrecks.

Mystic Edgar Cayce also spoke of a civilization off the coast of California in one of his readings. "This land…near the present Santa Barbara…that must in the near future fade again into those joining with the land of Mu…where the entity established a temple of worship when Lemuria or lands Mu and Zu were in turmoils for destruction, with the shifting of the earth at that period…" (Reading #509-1)

RUINS OFF PERU?

Edgar Cayce in several readings identified an island of 'Oz' or 'Og' in the vicinity of Peru during Atlantean times. They were said to be the last remnants of the island of Lemuria. In 1947 J. H. Umbgrove in 'Pulse of the Earth' ascertained that the deep Milne-Edward trench South America and at least one other submarine trench show evidence of once being part of a continent.

On April 17, 1966 the 'New York Times' reported that four carved rock columns have been seen and photographed off the coast of Peru. Dr Robert J Menzies, director of Duke University's Oceanographic Program and his colleagues were exploring the 600 mile long Milne-Edward Deep, a trench off Peru on the research ship 'Anton Bruun'. Strange writing was carved on the columns and nearby sonar images detected strange lumps on the level bottom 6,000 feet (1,500m) below the surface, indicating possible ruins. Menzies stated that the find suggested evidence of a sunken city. He took four hundred photos which have not been released to the public.

Apparently there have been no follow up expeditions to study this phenomenon.

MICRONESIA
POHNPEI (PONAPE)

Pohnpei, formerly known as Ponape, is the capital of the independent Federated States of Micronesia and lies about 1,600 km northeast of New Guinea. The partially sunken ruins of Nan Madol on the island of Pohnpei are one of the marvels of the Pacific. According to legend, two brothers Olsihpa and Olsohpa migrated to Pohnpei and established a powerful empire from the royal residence of Nan Madol. Today it exists as a 150 acre complex of stone ruins on the tidal flats off Temwen Island. The ruins consist of a variety of walled constructions built on about ninety rectangular man made islets which are interconnected by a grid of shallow canals.

Dating the ruins has been difficult; radiocarbon dating seems to indicate that the construction of Nan Madol began about 1200 AD, although there are pottery sherds which are at least two thousand years old. The dimensions of the ruins are truly impressive; Nan Douwas possesses fifty feet high walls built of massive prismatic basalt columns which are stacked on top of each other in log cabin style. Most stones at Nan Madol weigh several tons but some of the largest corner stones at Nan Douwas weigh about 50 tons.

It has been difficult to locate the huge quarries required to supply all the basalt stones for this complex. None of the local quarry sites exist on the island so the stones must have been transported some distance to their current location. Perhaps they were floated by raft, although local legend claims the stones were flown over the island by the use of black magic.

Nan Madol was located away from the main island of Pohnpei and extends from the southeast shore of Temwen Island for about

4,600 feet and reaches into the lagoon for about 2,450 feet. The whole area of 200 meters is occupied by the islet, waterways and breakwaters. An artificial island called Nahnningi is located about 2,000 feet south of Nan Madol and is surrounded by stacked prismatic basalt walls several feet high. Another island, Nakapw is a natural island with some stonework and is located across the bay.

Nan Madol consists of 92 artificial islets, many surrounded by retaining walls of immense basalt boulders and stacks of naturally formed prismatic basalt. Some walls extend over 30 feet to form enclosures for mortuaries and residences. Stone pavings and platforms, foundations for residences and meeting houses, walls, tombs, tunnels and other features are also found on the islets.

Not all of Nan Madol's islets are surrounded by basalt retaining walls: Sapwengei, Sapwolos, Sapwenpwe and Sapwuhtik are low lying islets with partly eroded perimeter walls. Most islets are octagonal in plan and have flat platforms which originally supported pole and thatch structures. The spaces between these islets are flooded at high tide, giving Nan Madol the title of Venice of the Pacific.

Nan Madol is divided into two main areas separated by a central waterway. The administrative sector, Madol Pah is the lower town situated in the southwest. To the northeast lies Madol Powe, the mortuary sector where priests dwelled and major tombs were located. At its height, the population of Nan Madol possibly reached between 500 and 1,000 people.

Long seawalls were built although the northern edge of Nan Madol was left open to the elements. These seawalls were built stoutly of huge basalt boulders packed with smaller stones on which prismatic basalt was stacked.

The royal mortuary of Nandauwas is the most imposing structure on Nan Madol. The walls exceed 25 feet in height at their corners and entryways.

There are many romantic tales about Pohnpei which derive from the memoirs of early explorers and native tradition, including a sunken city legend. German archeologist Dr Paul Hambruch excavated Nan Madol at the beginning of the twentieth century and suggested that a sunken city lay around Nakapaw Island, near Nan Madol. These sunken ruins were reportedly explored by the Japanese who administered the islands between the two world wars. They also mentioned the 'platinum coffins' which had been described by German Herbert Rittlinger in 'Der Masslose Ozean', ('The Measureless Ocean') published in 1939. According to Erich von Daniken who quoted from this book, Chinese merchants and pearl divers had discovered well preserved streets, countless stone vaults, pillars and monoliths beneath the waters of Pohnpei. They also discovered skeletons of very large people perhaps as tall as 2.1 meters (seven feet.)

These divers reported vast wealth in precious metals, pearls and bars of silver. The Japanese also recounted that the dead were buried in watertight platinum coffins. However, the Japanese withdrew from the island after the war and their records have not resurfaced about the ruins of Pohnpei.

After the Smithsonian Institute dated the ruins to about 1200 AD, another archeologist, Steven Athens, working for the Pacific Studies Institute in Hawaii, did an extensive survey of Nan Madol in the 1970s, discovering pottery sherds which are at least two thousand years old. He also described the extensive tunnel network throughout Nan Madol which probably connects all the islets together. Most of these tunnels are now blocked, but it has been postulated that they had been used for transportation between the islands. How these tunnels cut into the coral reef were constructed is a mystery, particularly the one which links the islet of Darong with the outer reef.

In his book 'Lost Cities of Ancient Lemurian and the Pacific' David Hatcher Childress described his visit to Pohnpei and his search for the legendary sunken city. An old native told him of two ancient sunken cities which predated the ruins of Nan Madol. "A sunken city lay just off shore of Temwen Island, and to the two brothers it was a sign from the gods to build their great city on top of, or next to the ancient city of the gods. We call this city Kahnihmweso, and it is beneath the waters of Madoenihmw Bay...There is a second sunken city outside the reef from Nan Madol. This city is called Kahnihmw Hamkhet, and is to the east near Nahkapw Island. In a deep and sandy place the gate to the city can be found." (pp 216-17) According to the legend, these cities were built by magic which allowed the stones to fly through the air and dragons to build the canals. The ruins were also reputed to extend all the way to the island of Kosrae.

In 1980 Dr Arthur Saxe published a report on his survey and underwater discoveries around Madolenkhmw Harbour. He had been asked to survey Nan Madol and define its boundaries by the Trust Territory of the Pacific which was about to become independent. He reported the tunnels throughout the complex and made these underwater discoveries:

> • Seven or eight boulders were observed in a line at about 90 feet depth. They were between two and six feet in diameter and covered in coral and orientated on a line between Pieniot and Nahkapw Islands.
> • Two pillars at a depth of 10 and 23 feet.
> • Vertical pillars or columns rising from the sloping bottom which were about 20 feet tall. One pillar was seen to be standing on a flat pedestal on the bottom of the sloping reef drop-off.
> • Four more pillars were located on another dive at about 75 feet. They were about 25 feet tall and 4-5 feet in diameter.

Saxe was aware of legends of the two sunken cities. "One is to the east or under Nahkapw Island, with a gate or entrance outside the reef, at a 'deep and sandy place.' The second city is in the deep channel between Nahkapw Island and Nanmwoluhei, the largest rock in the seawall east of Nan Dowas. This is where we located the columns. It was suggested that we may have seen the gate to this city." (D. Hatcher Childress, 'Lost Cities of Ancient Lemuria and the Pacific.')

Since Saxe's survey two film crews have taken footage of the underwater ruins. A Japanese crew dove and reportedly catalogued twelve columns standing in rows while an Australian crew photographed columns for their film 'Ponape: Island of Mystery.'

Hatcher Childress and his crew dived in the murky harborand

located the pillars and a number of other columns. At other dives around Nahkapw Island they discovered basalt stones with inscriptions such as crosses, squares and rectangles at about three meters in depth. Many of the stones underwater in Nahkapw island weigh about 10 tons and are exposed at low tide. He also noticed straight lines in the coral, indicating that perhaps the coral had grown over walls of stone. Although he failed to locate the underwater castle, city or platinum coffins, he doesn't discount the possibility of the existence of structures in Madolenkhmw Harboror Nahkapw Islands.

REFERENCES: "Pohnpei' http://www.janesoceania.com/micronesia_pohnpei_madol/index.htm

D. Hatcher Childress, 'Lost Cities of Ancient Lemuria and the Pacific'

THE RYUKYUS ISLANDS, JAPAN
YONAGUNI ISLAND

Yonaguni is the westernmost island of Japan and lies 125 km from the east coast of Taiwan. During the last Ice Age it was part of the Asian continent and connected to both Taiwan and the Ryukyu Islands. Today it is ruled by Japan as part of the Okinawa Prefecture.

In 1987 Japanese marine explorer Kihachiro Aratake discovered by chance underwater formations which strongly resemble architectural structures, including a large, terraced monolith. The seabed also contains traces of terrestrial flora, fauna and stalactites that only form on the surface.

Japanese scientists led by Professor Masaaki Kimura of the University of the Ryukyus confirmed that these structures were man-made although other geologists such as Robert Schoch and Wolf Wichmann believe they are basically natural formations. A spirited debate has been raging between proponents of the artificial hypothesis such as Kimura and Graham Hancock, and those who believe them to be natural.

Hancock's 'Underworld' provided a detailed account of his 140 dives on the formations as well as interviews with skeptics such as Dr Wichmann. He studied the legends and architecture of the enigmatic Jomon culture which existed in Japan during the last Ice Age and left statues, pottery and stone structures. The national Japanese epic the 'Nihongi' speaks of the underwater palace of the sea god with "Battlements and turrets, and had stately towers" in the vicinity of the Ryukyus Islands. Yonaguni is at the extreme southwest of this island chain.

'Underworld' examined the arguments of the only three geologists to dive on the structures: Kimura, Schoch and Wichmann.

Dr Kimura and his students have completed hundreds of dives at Yonaguni, particularly around the main terraced structure, measured and mapped it, taken samples of algae, sampled the stone and created a three dimensional model. He believes unequivocally that the monument is man-made and was hewn out of the bedrock when it stood above sea-level possibly 10,000 years ago. His other arguments laid out on pages 597-8 of 'Underworld' are:

- There are holes made by wedge like tools called kusabi in many locations.
- There is a loop road which connects principal areas of the monument. Around this is a wall of neatly stacked rocks placed in a straight line.
- There are traces of repairs along the roadway.
- Stone tools are among artifacts found underwater and on land.
- Carved stone tablets with symbols or letters resembling a 'V' and '+' shape were found. These are similar to symbols found on stone tablets in Okinawa.
- The relief carving of an animal figure was discovered on a huge stone.
- Deep symmetrical trenches on the north of the structure could not have been formed by any natural process.
- Regular steps are found at several places on the monolith.

• Any blocks of stone which had been sheared off by the water currents have not been found beneath the structure leading to the conclusion that they were deliberately cleared away.

• The rock cut pathway at the base of the monument is free from rubble and debris.

Hancock's interview with Dr Kimura reported that the construction had been submerged at least 6,000 years ago according to the coralline algae attaching its walls. The structure itself was possibly built about 9,000 or 10,000 years ago.

Dr Schoch, who dated the sphinx to over 8,000 BP due to water erosion, has also dived at Yonaguni but believes the structure to be primarily natural. He reported, "The geology of the fine mudstones and sandstones of the Yonaguni area, combined with wave and current actions and the lower sea-levels of the area during earlier millennia, were responsible for the formation of the Yonaguni monument about 9,000 to 10,000 years ago." (Hancock ibid p599)

However, in his book 'Voices of the Rocks' Schoch wrote that the structure of the monolith is similar to the architecture of tombs on the island of Yonaguni. "It is possible that humans were imitating the monument in designing the tombs, and it is equally possible that the monument was itself somehow modified by human hands...It is possible that the monument served as a quarry from which blocks were cut, following the natural bedding, joint and fracture planes of the rock, then removed to construct buildings that are now long gone. Since it is located along the coast the Yonaguni monument may have even served as some kind of natural boat dock for early seafaring people...Tools could have been used to modify or reshape the natural stone structures now found underwater off the coast of Yonaguni..." (Hancock, ibid p600)

In a 1999 article 'An Enigmatic Ancient Underwater Structure of the Coast of Yonaguni Island, Japan' Schoch wrote,

"The 'Yonaguni Monument,' as I refer to this structure, superficially has the appearance of a platform-like or partial step-pyramid-like structure. It has been compared to various pyramidal and temple structures in the Americas, such as the ancient 'Temple of the Sun' near Trujillo in northern Peru (Joseph, 1997, pp 4-5). The Yonaguni Monument is over 50 meters long in an east-west direction and over 20 meters wide in a north-south direction. The top of the structure lies about 5 meters below sea level, whereas the base is approximately 25 meters below the surface. It is an asymmetrical structure with what appear to be titanic stone steps exposed on its southern face. These steps range from less than half a meter to several meters in height.

"The rock faces appear to be dressed stone. If this is an artificial, man-made structure then it is reasonable to assume that it was built or carved not underwater but at a time when this area was above sea level. Indeed, this area has experienced major rises in sea levels during and since the Pleistocene ("Ice Age") and based on well-established standard curves of sea-level rises in the region, as recently as 8,000 to 10,000 years ago the Yonaguni Monument may have been above local sea level. Thus we can suggest with some confidence that if the Yonaguni Monument is a man-made construction then it must be at least 8,000 years old."

However, he made these observations: "During my own research on the Yonaguni monument, one of the first things I found is that the structure is, as far as I could determine, composed entirely of solid 'living' bedrock. No part of the monument is constructed of separate blocks or rocks that have been placed into position. This is an important point, for carved and arranged rock blocks would definitively indicate a man-made origin for the structure—yet I could find no such evidence."

He compared the terracing to the formations on the coastline of Yonaguni. "I became convinced that presently, at the surface, natural wave and tidal action is responsible for eroding and removing the sandstones in such a way that very regular step-like and terrace-like structures remain. The more I compared the natural, but highly regular, weathering and erosional features observed on the modern coast of the island with the structural characteristics of the Yonaguni Monument, the more I became convinced that the Yonaguni Monument is primarily the result of natural geological and geomorphological processes at work. On the surface I also found depressions and cavities forming naturally that look exactly like the supposed "post holes" that some researchers have noticed on the underwater Yonaguni Monument."

He concluded, "Based on my preliminary reconnaissance of the Yonaguni Monument, I am not yet absolutely convinced that it is an artificial structure—but in my opinion, even if it is primarily natural, it may have been more modified by human actions in ancient times. This enigmatic structure merits more detailed examination."

http://www.robertschoch.net/Enigmatic%20Yonaguni%20Underwater%20RMS%20CT.htm

The third geologist, Dr Wolf Wichmann, has no qualms about labeling the structure a natural formation. In a 1999 article in 'Der Spiegel', Wichmann, who dived at Yonaguni three times, declared, "I didn't find anything that was man-made." He reported that the steps had been gradually developed in the fracture zones of the rock and the plateaux at the top were typically eroded plains. The plateaux have gradient sections and there is no perpendicular wall. Furthermore, some of the steps seem to end nowhere and have no discernible purpose. Three circular recesses on the topmost plateau are nothing but potholes and not the column foundations ascribed to Dr Kimura.

Wichmann dived at the ruins with Graham Hancock in 2001 and did not change his position about the origin of the structure. "When Wolf and I later discussed the path and the terraces he remained adamant that all the anomalies in these areas could have been produced by the effects of local erosive forces, mainly waves, on the 'layer cake' strata of the Yonaguni mudstones. In short, while he could not absolutely rule out human intervention, he did not feel that it was *necessary* in order to explain anything that we had so far seen underwater." (Hancock ibid p 615)

The only archeologist to visit the structure, Sundaresh from the National Institute of Oceanography in Goa, India has made these points in a 2000 report.

188

• It is a large terraced structure about 250 meters long, 100 meters wide and 25 meters high bounded on the northern side by a road like structure which could be a canal.

• The terraces and attached staircases might have been used for loading and unloading boats sailing through the channel. The whole structure may have been a jetty.

• A large monolith resembling a human head with two eyes and a mouth was studied at Tatigami Iwa Point. Nearby is a large platform.

• Caves near the 'Palace' area were found at depths of 8-10 meters of water. Carvings have been observed on boulders in and near these caves.

• Two rectangular monoliths measuring 6 meters in height and 2.5 m in width have been located between two natural outcrops which can be reached through a tunnel. The shape size and position of these megaliths suggest they are man-made.

• His conclusion stated, "The terraced structures with a canal are undoubtedly man-made, built by cutting an existing huge monolithic outcrop. The rectangular terraced structure and canal might have served as a jetty for handling, loading/unloading small boats before its submergence to present depth. The monolith rock-cut human head and associated platform might have served as an area of worshipping or community gatherings." (Hancock, ibid pp 602-605)

Hancock mentioned other anomalous formations around the waters of Yonaguni such as a one tonne boulder mounted on a 10cm high flat platform at the apex of an enormous rocky slab about 3 meters high, bearing a resemblance to classic 'iwakura' shrine. The 'stadium' is a vast ampitheatre surrounding a stone plain at a depth of 30 meters. Furthermore, there is another area of very large steps much further out to sea in deeper water.

KERAMA

The islands of Kerama were attached to the southern end of Okinawa by a thick tongue of land until about 14,600 years ago. These islands were separated by rising waters about 9,000 to 10,000 years ago.

The Kerama circles lie under about 30 meters of water 10 km off Aka island at latitude 26 degrees 07 minutes north and longitude 127 degrees 17 minutes east. The currents are notoriously strong which makes diving difficult. Three circles have been discovered by divers; two side by side and another about 60 meters away. The Central Circle, about 20 meters wide and 27 meters deep, is made of concentric rings of upright megaliths more than 3 meters tall which have been hewn out of the bedrock surrounding a central menhir.

Hancock and Wichmann dived at the Kerama area for a Channel 4 program. Wichmann scraped off the organisms from one of the monoliths comprising the circle and found ancient coralline limestone beneath. The stones had been quarried in situ out of the bedrock of the ancient mound to which they were still attached at their bases. As with Yonaguni, there was no rock lying around which would be evident if the monoliths were hewn by natural forces. Wichmann, the skeptic, had no natural explanation for the circles of Kerama. "They must have been formatted after the pebbles were laid down on the coralline ground—because some of these pebbles are hanging over the canyons, and they could not have come earlier...But I don't see any force (of nature) which could have shaped these... I won't say anything definite. Much more research must be done. But I agree this is very amazing and very strange, even to me, how these structural buildings could be formed. I haven't seen any such structures done by nature. I won't dare say anything else about human activities because I do not know anything about that." (Hancock ibid p 652)

Hancock pointed out his reasons for believing the Kerama

circles to be man-made.

• Their sense of organisation and structure.

• The ancient Jomon culture, which existed in the Ice Age, built stone circles.

• The Jomon culture existed from 16,000 to 2,000 years ago and could have created the stones when they were above water.

AGUNI

About 60 km north of Kerama, this island has steep cliffs. A small plateau, only 4 meters from the surface lies beneath the cliffs and contains a series of circular holes which are lined with small blocks. The largest and deepest has a diameter of 3 meters and is 10 meters deep: Others are typically 2 to 3 meters in diameter with a depth of less than 7 meters. These features all look man made.

CHATAN, OKINAWA

Less than a kilometer off the coast of the resort area of Chatan lies underwater 'walls', 'battlements' and 'step pyramids' at a depth between 10 -30 meters. Although dismissed as being artifacts of recent military dredging from a USAF base, a Japanese historical researcher, Akira Suzuki has found no such records of US or Japanese operations.

The most striking structure is a wall with its base on the sand which rises to a 'battlement' with a sunken 'walkway' about 10 meters above the sea-bed. At one point the walkway is broken by a vertical U shaped shaft cut through the entire height of the wall. This so called structure bears a resemblance to the Palace of the Sea God which is described in the 'Nihongi', Japan's most ancient chronicle.

REFERENCES: G. Hancock, 'Underworld'

'An Enigmatic Ancient Underwater Structure off the coast of Yonaguni Island', Robert Schoch

http://www.robertschoch.net/Enigmatic%20Yonaguni%20Underwater%

PESCADORES ISLANDS, TAIWAN

Underwater ruins are reputed to lie in the Penghu peninsula, part of the Pescadores Islands which lie between Taiwan and China. Over 13,000 years ago they were joined to China in one mass which later broke up into islands at the end of the Ice Age. Ancient myths of the Pescadores speak of a great red castle with huge walls lying submerged in the area.

In the 1980s Taiwanese diver Steve Shieh discovered what appeared to be walls off the island of Hu-ching, 'Tiger Well'. His discoveries received no publicity in the west, although Graham Hancock met with him and dived at the Tiger Well in 2001. In 'Underworld' he described, "Two immense walls, hundreds of meters in length, one running due north-south and the other running due east-west, crossing the north-south wall at right angles. At the east end of the east-west wall is a large circular enclosure, part of which has completely collapsed. The east-west wall is in relatively shallow water—4 to 6 meters depth. The north-south wall starts at 4 meters depth but can be followed down to 36 meters depth. All the walls are a consistent height 3 meters from the base to the top of the wall; however, some sections are broken." (p 672)

Hancock pointed out that basaltic dykes, which are common around the Pescadores, could account for these walls. These dykes form when a wall like mass of igneous rock intrudes into cracks in older sedimentary rock. However, when Shieh scraped off marine growth from the walls, courses of individual blocks were seen lying side by side. They were able to poke a knife blade between the individual blocks.

Hancock felt that the formations were artificial but concluded 'Underworld' with the comment that much more research was required to "settle the matter."

In 2002 various press reports appeared about underwater walls off the coast of the Penghu Islands. On November 26 the 'China

Post' commented, "Underwater archeologists yesterday announced the discovery of a man-made wall submerged under the waters of the Pescadores Islands that could be at least six or seven thousand years old.

"Steve Shieh, the head of the planning committee for the Taiwan Underwater Archeology Institute, (UAI) said the wall was discovered to the northwest of Tong-chi island in the Pescadores toward the end of September. The wall ran along the ocean floor at depths between 25 and 30 meters, he added....In August, researchers scanning waters in the area with sonar discovered what appeared to be the remnants of four to five man made walls running along the bottom of the sea.

"Despite difficult diving conditions, Shieh said that a team of more than ten specialists was able to ascertain the positions of at least three of the wall sections. The proximity of the wall to a similar structure found in 1976 suggests that it may be further evidence of a prehistorical civilization. British archeologists examined the find and proclaimed the wall was probably made between 7,000 and 12,000 years ago. The current find stands a mere 100 meters from the site of that discovery."

The Taipei Times reported that the stone walls are on average 1 meter high and 50cm wide. The Public Television Service Foundation (PTSF) deployed a team to shoot video footage of the walls. They saw pieces of coral and pebbles at the leeward sides of the walls, strongly indicating that they were not natural formations.

Tian Wen-miin, associated professor from the National Sun Yat-sen University's department of marine environment, presented three sonar graphs at a press conference. "These sonar graphs show the seabed around the site is very even. However, near the walls there are many regular protrusions that look like alleys, staircases, walls and stages," he said.

Shieh commented that the stories of underwater ruins "Are part of Penghu's unwritten history. I've known of other such structures in the area since the late 1970s. But it was in 1992 that I first began to hear stories of a submerged town and the possibilities of an entire temple somewhere in the area."

Other researchers are keen to prove that the lost continent of Mudalu existed. In legend Mudalu stretched from the South China Sea to Hawaii and encompassed many Pacific Islands. Mudalu was supposedly home to some of Asia's earliest peoples, the Ketagalan who lived between 7,000 and 15,000 years ago. According to Chinese legend, the Ketagalan peoples were incredibly advanced with a written language and the ability to construct megaliths and pyramids.

Skeptics point to a lack of man-made objects or human remains near the structures. Linear lava formations are found at Hsishan on Penghu's Hujing Island. However such structures are vertical examples of linear lava flows and bear no resemblance to the horizontal walls. Shieh has responded, "If (the walls) were the result of volcanic activity then we would have an octopus shape on the seabed. The tentacles being the lava flows and in the centre, where the body is, there would be a crater. We didn't find a crater anywhere in the area however. This certainly rules out volcanic activity." (Taipei Times)

http://www.taipeitimes.com/News/feat/archives/2002/12/01/185543

Shieh and the UAI planned to return to the structures in July 2003.

MEDIEVAL JAPANESE RUINS?

On February 4, 2004   Japanese Prefecture archaeologists announced that they had found a one kilometer square area of stone ruins in water off the coast of Atami, in Shizuoka Prefecture, lying about 75 miles south of Tokyo. The ruins are under 60 to 150-feet of water and appear to be clustered in 20 different major sites. Carved stone steps, stone buildings, and building platforms were found.

The site was initially located in 1975 by Hidenori Kunitsugu, a diving instructor who discovered and photographed stone steps, walls, and paving. Tokyo University's underwater archaeologist, Dr. Torao Mozai, has stated that the structures are apparently all man-made.

The age of the ruins is open to speculation, although it is probable that a portion of the Atami ruins site is the remains of a city from the "Kamakura Period," which extended from A.D. 1192 to 1333. Records indicate that a city existed in Sagami Bay until part of it suddenly sank in 1247. However, the researchers also believe that part of the ruins, probably those in the deeper water, are remains of something far older.

Dr Greg Little, a Bimini researcher, believes that the underwater ruins at Atami are very similar to the Andros Platform found in 2003. "The paving stones at Andros appear nearly identical to those at Atami and portions of the foundations at Atami look like the Andros Platform."

Interestingly, some of the photos of the underwater ruins at Atami are strikingly similar to those of the Andros Platform.

REFERENCE: **http://www.mysterious-america.net/newunderwaterrui. html**

SUNDALAND

Sundaland was the huge Pacific-Indian Ocean landmass comprising South East Asia (Thailand, Malaysia, Philippines, Borneo, Sumatra and Java) at the height of the last Ice Age around twenty thousand years ago. This is an area of huge biodiversity and contains rare plants and animals such as tigers, elephants and apes as well as some of the oldest rainforests on earth. Contemporary scholars Steven Oppenheimer, Sunlil Prasannan and Arysio Nunes dos Santos have proposed that Sundaland was the location of Plato's Atlantis.

Stephen Oppenheimer is a medical doctor who has lived in South East Asia for many years. His 1999 book 'Eden in the East: the Drowned Continent of Southeast Asia' concentrates on the drowned areas of Sundaland which he believes were the original Garden of Eden. His book is based on solid research such as genetic, linguistic, archeological and anthropological disciplines. He sees sunken Sundaland as the homeland of the Austronesian languages, agriculture and culture.

Dr. Sunil Prasannan proposes that Sundaland, much of which is underwater today, is the location of Plato's Atlantis. The area was twice the size of India and in close proximity to Sahul, the greater continent of Australia, New Guinea and Tasmania. In an essay on Graham Hancock's website, Prasannan wrote; "As for mountains and rivers, yes, Sundaland would have had them in abundance, the mountains of course still with us today due to their loftiness, in Sumatra, Java and Borneo in particular. Underwater mapping of the Sunda Shelf reveals that modern rivers in Indonesia, Malaysia and Indo-China would have been extended and would often combine to form much bigger rivers in the area inundated. And of course, being smack-bang on the equator, this region must surely have enjoyed a warm climate, for thousands of years either side of LGM. So this must have seemed like a veritable Garden of Eden to the multitude of people who would surely have taken advantage of this Ice Age refugium to settle long term and develop any civilized culture, and consequent technology."

Regarding the timing of the Platonian Atlantis's demise, he wrote; "The bulk of the submerged Sunda Shelf was inundated relatively rapidly between 14,000 and 11,000 years ago. Whilst much of the territory would have been lost in the first of three 'global superfloods', 14,000 years ago, almost all the antediluvian continental shelf would have been inundated during the second flood roughly 11,000 years ago. The only significant event of the third superflood of approximately 7,500 years ago would have been the opening of the Strait of Malacca between Malaya and Sumatra."

Other points of comparison he raised are:

• Both Atlantis and Indonesia possessed abundant forests and elephants.

• The warm climate of Atlantis resembles that of South East Asia.

• Naturna Besar bears a resemblance to the mountain described in 'Critias'.

• Rice cultivation began in South East Asia about nine thousand years ago, at the same time taro was being cultivated in New Guinea.

• Mitochondrial DNA links South East Asian races with those from Polynesia and even the Middle East.

196

• The 1502 Portuguese Cantino map gives an accurate representation of sunken Sundaland.

• Atlanteans possessed quantities of copper and tin, both of which are abundant in Indonesia and Malaysia today.
http://www.grahamhancock.com/underworld/DrSunilAtlantis.php

Professor Arysio Nunes dos Santos of the Federal University of Minas Gerais, Brazil, also claims that Atlantis was located in Sundaland. He believes that Plato was not referring to the Ocean of Atlantis (the Atlantic) but the whole ocean that encircles Eurasia and Africa. He concludes that Atlantis was really located in the Indo-Pacific Ocean.

In his 2005 'Atlantis The Lost Continent Finally Found' he proposed that :

• A catastrophic eruption of Krakatoa sank Atlantis and helped to end the Ice Age.

• Sundaland was larger than Libya and Asia Minor put together just as Plato had described.

• Sundaland was the Lemurian Atlantis.

• Greater India and sunken areas adjoining were the location of the other Atlantis.

• "The Indonesian Islands and the Malay Peninsula that we nowadays observe are the unsunken relics of Lemurian Atlantis, the lofty volcanic mountains that became the volcanic islands of this region, the true site of Paradise in all ancient traditions. The sunken portion of continental extension now forms the muddy, shallow bottoms of the South China Sea." **http://www.lost-civilizations.net/true-history-atlantis.html**

Professor Santos's webpage and book reviews can be found at **http://www.atlan.org/book/**

On July 15, 2005 it was reported on the ABC that an Australian couple was preparing to search for an ancient civilization in Sundaland. Roz and Hans Berekoven believe that the Sunda Shelf in Indonesia holds an unknown underwater city and received support from the Australian Federal Government to undertake

197

an archeological survey expedition from the town of Dampier in Western Australia. Hans, a former sea captain on seismic survey vessels bought the 19 meter 'Southern Sun' to travel the area with his wife and children.

http://www.abc.net.au/news/newsitems/200507/s1415186.htm

Berekoven believes that Sundaland had the world's balmiest climate and would have been the "best piece of real estate on the planet...The prime place for a civilization to take root...Hunters and gatherers were forced south into this tropical zone and I think the concentration of population sparked off animal husbandry and farming-the two greatest inventions of humanity. The reason we haven't found proof of it is because we've been looking on land. The proof is underwater." **http://www.southernsun.info/ourjourney. htm**

Using satellite radar pictures of the sea floor and a bottom profiler, which can see through meters of mud to the underlying landscape, Hans hoped to identify old river valleys and deltas which are now buried under layers of silt in the 40 to 60 meter deep Java Sea. Using side-scan sonar and eventually a remotely operated mini submarine he planned to explore the underwater valleys which would have once been on river mouths and fertile deltas.

On their website **http://www.southernsun.info/ourjourney.htm** the Berekovens give details of their voyage to Indonesia and the disappointment faced when civil unrest and natural disasters in Java thwarted their mission. No updates beyond 2005 are provided.

REFERENCES: **http://www.grahamhancock.com/underworld/ DrSunilAtlantis.php**

'The True History of Atlantis' **http://www.lost-civilizations.net/true- history-atlantis.html**

ABC News online July 15, 2005 **http://www.abc.net.au/news/ newsitems/200507/s1415186.htm**

'Southern Sun' **http://www.southernsun.info/ourjourney.htm**

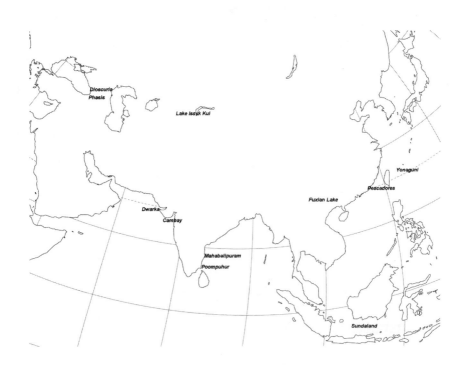

James Churchward's maps of Mu and map of the world including both Mu and Atlantis.

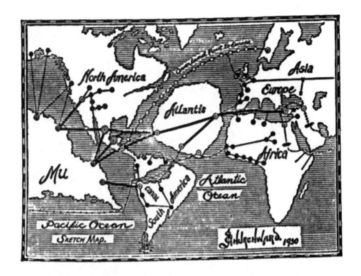

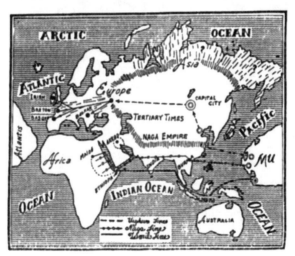

More of James Churchward's speculative maps of Mu and Atlantis.

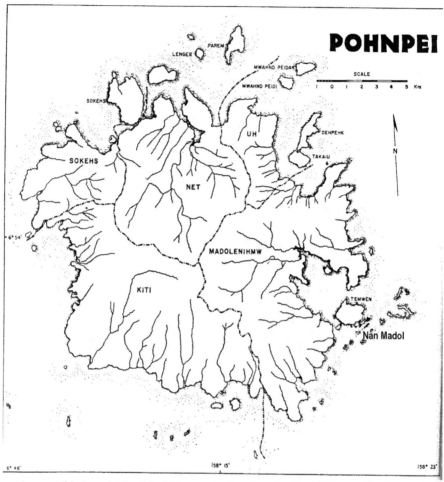

A map of Pohnpei Island in Micronesia showing the five different districts and the location of the megalithic ruins of Nan Madol which lie both above and underwater.

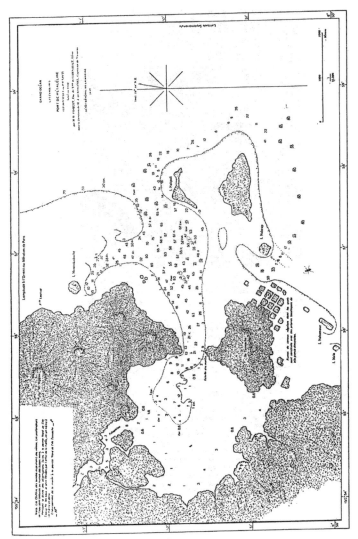

1840 map of Nan Madol, or Metalanim, showing the artificial islands and sunken areas.

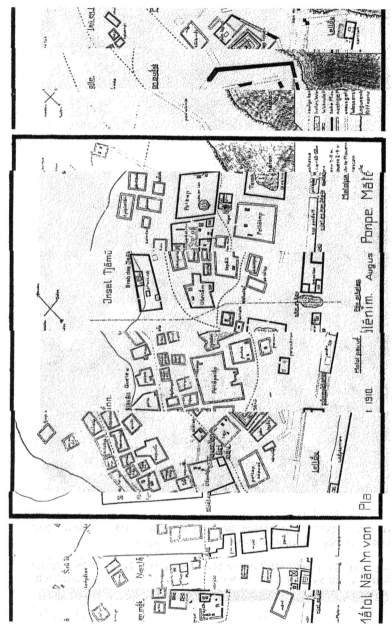

1910 map of Nan Madol, or Metalanim, by Paul Hambruch.

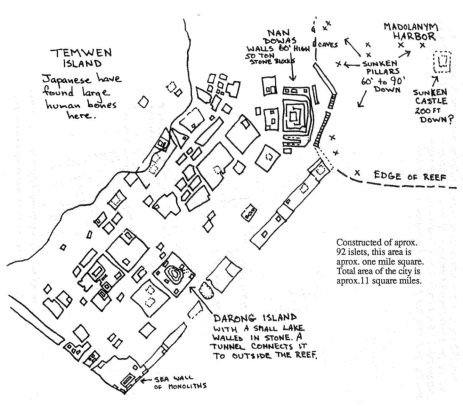

TEMWEN ISLAND

Japanese have found large human bones here.

NAN DOWAS WALLS 60' HIGH 50 TON STONE BLOCKS

CAVES

MADOLANYM HARBOR

SUNKEN PILLARS 60' to 90' DOWN

SUNKEN CASTLE 200 FT DOWN?

EDGE OF REEF

Constructed of aprox. 92 islets, this area is aprox. one mile square. Total area of the city is aprox. 11 square miles.

DARONG ISLAND WITH A SMALL LAKE WALLED IN STONE. A TUNNEL CONNECTS IT TO OUTSIDE THE REEF.

SEA WALL OF MONOLITHS

Top and Right: A map of the seabreak areas of Nan Madol, called Metalanim here.

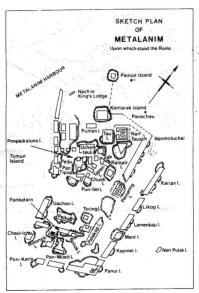

SKETCH PLAN OF METALANIM Upon which stand the Ruins

METALANIM HARBOUR

Painiot Island

Nach or King's Lodge

Kontarak Island

Panachau

Punlan I.

Tau I.

Nan Tauach

Nanmoluchei

Ponpeikaluna i.

Uchen-tau L.

Tomun Island

Peilu

Pan Tipop

Pulak

Rainair

Chuok L.

Pun-iiel I.

Pankatarn

Uachau L.

Peikap

Toring L.

Karian I.

Likop I.

Lemenkau I.

Chau-Ichu

Mant I.

Kapinet I.

Nan Pulak I.

Pon-Karin I.

Pan-Mueit I.

Panui I.

205

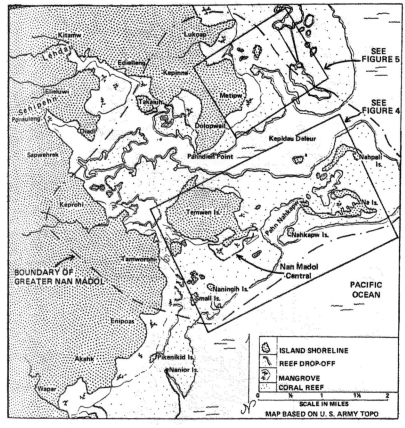

A map of the sunken areas around Nan Madol done by the American archeologist Arthur Saxe who surveyed the extensive complex.

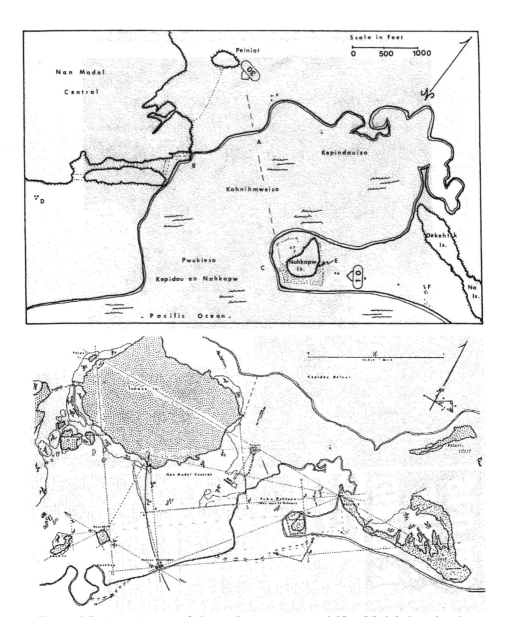

Top and Bottom: A map of the sunken areas around Nan Madol done by the American archeologist Arthur Saxe who noticed certain alignments, including some with possible underwater structures.

207

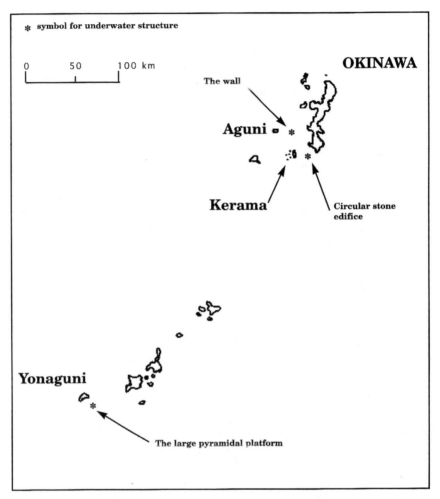

A map of Okinawa, Yonaguni and other islands.

Part of the underwater "structures" near Yonaguni.

Part of the underwater "structures" near Yonaguni.

PART 7
THE INDIAN OCEAN

**LEMURIA
KUMARI KANDAM & RUTAS
THE ANCIENT LAND BRIDGE BETWEEN
INDIA AND SRI LANKA
ANCIENT RUINS OFF INDIA: PART 1 TAMIL
NADU — POOMPUHUR
MAHABALIPURAM
ANCIENT RUINS OFF INDIA: PART 2
GUJARAT — DWARKA
GULF OF CAMBAY
THE SARASVATI RIVER
ANTEDILUVIAL CITIES OF SUMER**

Submerged landmasses off the coast of India may contain sites from the era before the Indus Valley civilization.

LEMURIA

Lemuria is the name of a hypothetical lost continent located originally in the Indian Ocean but sometimes in the Pacific Ocean by occultists. Its origins lie in the nineteenth century with geologist Philip Sclater's article 'The Mammals of Madagascar' in 'The Quarterly Journal of Science' which proposed that India and Madagascar had been part of a larger continent because fossilised lemurs had been discovered in both lands. He named this hypothetical continent Lemuria after the lemurs. Ernst Haeckel, a German taxonomist, proposed Lemuria as an explanation for the absence of 'missing links' in the fossil records. The origin of the human species, he proposed, could exist at the bottom of the Indian Ocean.

Lemuria was popularized by Madame Blavatsky in 'The Secret Doctrine' who claimed that its inhabitants were members of the 'Third Root Race'. They were seven feet tall, sexually hermaphroditic, egg laying and mentally undeveloped but possessing a spiritual purity. Some Lemurians possessed four arms and some had an eye in the back of their heads which gave them psychic powers. Although they only lived in caves and holes in the ground, these inhabitants had strongly developed willpower and could move mountains. These reptilian 'dragon men' eventually turned to black magic and were destroyed in a huge volcanic cataclysm which sank their southern hemisphere continent to the bottom of the ocean. They were replaced by the more intellectual Atlantean fourth root race.

Theosophist W. Scott-Elliot elaborated on Blavatsky's fanciful description of lost Lemuria and its inhabitants. The Manus of the universe chose Lemuria as the location of the evolution of the third root race after Hyperborea broke up. His Lemurians were between twelve and fifteen feet tall with brown skin, flat faces and no foreheads. They had a third eye in the forehead which evolved into the human pineal gland. Originally egg laying hermaphrodites, the Lemurians learnt to reproduce sexually, and interbred with animals, giving birth to apes as their offspring. Eventually they evolved into a seventh subrace, of which Australian aborigines, Andaman Islanders and Lapps are their descendents.

When Lemuria began to sink, a peninsula that extended into the Atlantic Ocean grew into Atlantis and the fourth root race evolved about eight hundred thousand years ago. Eventually Lemurians and Atlanteans fought wars and during one of these conflicts Atlantis split into two islands, Ruta and Daitya.

Scientific evidence has not been able to validate the existence of Lemuria but there is evidence that various areas of the Indian Ocean were once above sea level. In 1961 the research vessel 'Vityaz' ('Errant Knight') which explored the Indian Ocean between Asia, Africa and Australia, discovered an area of 'enormous numbers of sunken islands' near the African coast. Many areas contained extensive elevations and individual mountains as well as ancient animal remains and prehistoric shark's teeth. In 1999 the Joides Resolution research vessel discovered samples of pollen and fragments of wood in 90 million year old sediment from the Indian Ocean, suggesting that a continent sized island called Kerguelen sank about 20 million years ago.

KUMARI KANDAM AND RUTAS

According to the Tamils of India, Kumari Kandam is a sunken kingdom whose oral history includes time spans of thousands of years. Over a period of ten thousand years their kings, the Pandyans, formed three sangams or academies to foster a love of knowledge, literature and poetry. The First Sangam was in a now submerged city called Tenmadurai which survived for 4,440 years. During this time an immense library of poems and literature was codified, including the 'Agattiyam', 'Paripadal', 'Mudunatai', 'Mudukurgu' and 'Kalariyavirai' which are well known amongst Tamils today. At the end of this golden age the First Sangam was destroyed when a deluge or tsunami swallowed Tenmadurai.

Survivors of this cataclysm were able to relocate further north, saving some First Sangam books, and the Second Sangam was established in the city of Kavatpuram. This sangam lasted for 3,700 years and was then lost to the sea as well, with most its literature. Following the inundation of this city the survivors moved northward to Uttara Madurai (Vadamadurai), associated with modern Madurai where the headquarters of the Third Sangam was founded. This sangam survived for a further 1,850 years and was patronised by 49 kings.

Modern historians totally discount the first two sangams and postulate that the third sangam ended between 350 and 550 AD. Graham Hancock, who discussed the Kumari Kandam story in 'Underworld' was surprised to discover that using the time periods provided, the first Sangam was destroyed in 9600 BC, exactly the

213

same time Plato claimed that Atlantis was inundated!

V. Kanakasabhai, a Tamil historian stated, "In former days the land had extended further south and that a mountain called Kumarikoddu, and a large tract of country watered by the river Prahuli had existed south of Cape Kumari. During a violent irruption of the sea, the mountain Kumarikoddu and the whole of the country through which flowed the Prahuli had disappeared." (Hancock, 'Underworld' p 251) Other Tamil poems refer to successive submersions of land to the south of India in the Indian Ocean and the reduction of Tamil land. Scholar T. R Sesha Iyenagar refers to Tamil traditions that part of the mainland of southern India was "overwhelmed and submerged by a huge deluge." (ibid) Furthermore, the Tamil epic 'Manimekalai' speaks of the flooding of a city off the coast of Poompuhur where ruins have been recently discovered.

N. Mahalingam has cited further Tamil sources that speak of even earlier floods at 18,000, 16,000 and 9,600 years ago. According to the tradition, even earlier sangams were destroyed at these times.

Sri Lankan chronicles also spoke of three deluges which destroyed a large area beyond the island. The 'Mahavamasa', 'Dipavamsa' and 'Rajavali' are all based on ancient oral traditions which existed in the fourth century AD when they were compiled by Buddhist monks. According to the 'Rajavali' 100,000 large towns, and over one thousand villages were swallowed by a sea which extended twenty miles inland. The same source also referred to an earlier flood which swallowed the citadel of Ravana with its 25 palaces and 400,000 streets. Surprisingly, maps of the last Ice Age show that this area of northern Sri Lanka was flooded by rising waters about 16,000 years ago.

James Churchward, author of the Mu series, also claimed that there were ruins off the coast of India long before they were discovered. He wrote, "In the Indian Ocean adjoining the west coast of India there exists a large area of submerged lands with structures showing thereon. Like the remains of the South Sea Islands, these structures are prehistoric. These submerged lands commence at about 23 degrees north latitude, or just below the

214

mouth of the river Indus and extend south to about the equator. These submerged lands are apparently of an elongated oval shape. The Laccadive and Maldive groups of low-lying islands are within the boundaries of this oval... These submerged lands are well known to the fishermen along the coast; as a matter of fact, it was through them that I became aware of the submersion. Hindu scientists also know of them; no-one, however, can account for structures being at the bottom of the ocean as the submergence is not spoken of in Hindu history no matter how far one goes back...To my mind, there is not the slightest doubt what caused this submergence and that the present island of Ceylon was raised through it." (D. Hatcher Childress, 'Lost Cities of Ancient Lemuria and the Pacific' p77)

Rutas was a vanished continent in the Indian Ocean according to the French scholar Jacolliot's interpretation of Hindu literature. He later located Rutas in the Pacific Ocean where it became identified with Churchward's Mu.

REFERENCES: G. Hancock, 'Underworld'

D. Hatcher Childress, 'Lost Cities of Ancient Lemuria and the Pacific' p77

.

THE ANCIENT LAND BRIDGE BETWEEN INDIA AND SRI LANKA

In 2002 NASA announced that its space shuttle had imaged a mysterious underwater ancient bridge between India and Sri Lanka, precisely where it was mentioned in the ancient Sanskrit epic 'The Ramayama'. This bridge was named Adam's Bridge and is made of a chain of shoals 30 km long in the Palk Straits between India and Sri Lanka.

The bridge's unique curvature and composition reveals that it is probably man made. Initially the bridge was claimed to be 1,750,000 years old. According to the Ramayama it was built between Rameshwaram in India and Sri Lanka under the supervision of the heroic figure Rama who was an incarnation of a god.

On February 6, 2001 the Express News Service claimed that the Adam's Bridge was only 3,500 years old. Professor S.M Ramasamy of the Centre for Remote Sensing (CRS) of Bharathidasan University, Tiruchi and his team studied the geological changes that occurred along the Tamil Nadu coastline in the past 40,000 years.

The ancient bridge lies between Thirthuraipoondi in Tamil Nadu and Kodiyakari in Sri Lanka. The CRS determined that the Tamil Nadu beach dates back 6,000 years and the Sri Lankan beach was 1,100 years old. Ramasamy explained that the beaches were formed by long shore drifting currents which moved in an anti-clockwise direction in the north and clockwise direction in the south about 3,500 years ago. They believe that the sand was dumped in a linear pattern where corals later accumulated. However, as the age of the bridge corresponds with the dates of the Ramayama, the team decided that more research would need to be conducted.

On March 29, 2007 it was announced that Hindus were launching an international campaign to halt India's plans to create a shipping channel by dredging the sea between India and Sri Lanka. In the Ramayama Lord Rama engaged an army of monkeys under Hanuman to create the bridge so he could rescue his abducted wife Sita from the island of Lanka. They are also protesting on environmental grounds, arguing that the 30-mile string of limestone shoals, also known as Ram Sethu, protected large parts of India from the 2004 tsunami.

Officials argue that the Adam's Bridge is merely a natural formation and its plans to dredge to a depth of 12 meters will not cause serious environmental damage. Hindus however strongly believe it is a sacred site which may have been passable only a few centuries ago. They cite the NASA photographs, although NASA has distanced itself from those claims.

In 2007 a panel of Indian scientists concluded that the bridge was "a geological formation, which took place about 17 million years ago".

REFERENCE: **http://www.timesonline.co.uk/tol/news/world/asia/article1572638.ece**

ANCIENT RUINS OFF INDIA:
PART 1 TAMIL NADU
POOMPUHUR

Poompuhur today is a small fishing village that in ancient times was Kaveripattinam, the port capital of the Cholas as far back as the second century BC. During the reign of Karikala Cholan Poompuhur became a great city and remained so until the Pallava dynasty. Great temples such as the Pallavaneesswaram are but ruins today while others have been reclaimed by the sea and lie a few hundred meters offshore. The ruins of Kaveripattinam exist in the tidal zone and the shallows to three meters in depth. They are believed to be about 2,000 years old and may have been destroyed by an ancient tsunami.

In 1981 geologists from the NIO such as Kamlesh Vora participated in marine archeological explorations of Tamil Nadu, and particularly Poompuhur. They scanned the flat sea-bed using an echo sounder and magnetometer and discovered anomalous features such as oblongs and pinnacles which were raised from 2 to 5 meters above it. Graham Hancock who interviewed Vora for 'Underworld' also spoke with archeologists Sundaresh and Gaur about the 1993 expedition to the ruins off the coast of Poompuhur. Their survey had identified extensive structural remains in the form of heavily eroded and dressed sandstone blocks to a depth of seven meters. At that same depth they had also located several circular cairns made up of rounded and upright stones which were up to ten meters in diameter.

At a depth of 23 meters a curious U-shaped structure and neighbouring mounds appeared. Gaur told Hancock that he assumed the structure was a natural object because "we don't know of any culture 10,000 years ago that could have built it." ('Underworld' p 221) Sundaresh disagreed with his colleague and claimed, "It is definitely man-made. And I have seen a second structure, a mound, about 45 meters away at the same depth where there are perfect cut blocks scattered on the sea-bed." (ibid p222) When questioned about the supposed date of 10,000 years he responded, "Maybe the structures are not that old at all. Maybe there has been some great land subsidence here that we do not know of, or erosion of

217

the coast by the sea."

In February 2001 Hancock, sponsored by Channel 4, dived into the mysterious U shaped structure off Poompuhur. Suffering from a blinding migraine and with only a day to dive the site, he dived with Sundaresh, Gaur and Kamlesh on the mysterious U shaped structure and mounds in the immediate vicinity. Upon descending, his first impression was "that it's a big, squat, powerful-looking structure." The visibility was poor, but the sun broke through the clouds revealing "a massive wall of deeply eroded and pitted stone. Although much broken and ruined, and incorporating a number of jagged vertical protrusions and step-like changes in level, I can see that the wall in general rises about 2 meters above the sea-bed to form the outside edge of an extensive platform." (ibid p293)

Hancock noticed the platform wall was slightly concave or dish like and paved with a mosaic of small stones. The entrance to the platform is about a meter and half wide although it doesn't seem to lead anywhere. The thick retaining wall, about 2 meters high on either side of the gap resembled a pair of gateposts. "It also has a pronounced lip standing proud of the aggregate infill by almost half a meter—weighting the scales ever more in favour of the idea that the U-shaped structure must originally have been designed not as a platform but as an enclosure, and it certainly cannot be a natural formation." (ibid p 294)

On their second dive, the mound was explored. It lay on a plain with no slope or build up. Hancock wrote, "I can make out what seems to be the edge of a wall a meter thick and similar in appearance to the enclosure walls around the U-shaped structure." (ibid p298) When diving on the U-shaped structure again he concluded that it was definitely an enclosure with several internal walls.

On the Graham Hancock website is an article 'A Study of the Poompuhur 'U-Shaped' Object' by Michael Smith who has also dived on it:

http://www.grahamhancock.com/underworld/smithMike_poompuhur.php

Smith wrote a for and against column for the anomaly being man-made.

For:

1. The structure turns by a series of angles which are very sharp and well defined.

2. A second wall can be seen in two places following the inner wall. This rarely occurs in nature.

Against:

> • It has no logical shape or purpose.
>
> • Structures are usually found together and not on their own.
>
> • Natural angles can occur in such places as 'The Giant's Causeway' in Northern Ireland.

Furthermore, the ocean bottom is flat, heavily silted and featureless around the anomaly which is now a coral reef. The poor visibility distorts the shape of the structure which is not really U shaped but definitely has regular shaped angles.

Smith believes the structure is man-made even though the members of the NIO officially claim it is not artificial. However, one told him off the record, "Personally I think it will turn out to be man-made, but until we have the definite proof, we just can't risk saying that!"

REFERENCES: G. Hancock, 'Underworld, Flooded Kingdoms of the Ice Age'

http://www.grahamhancock.com/underworld/smithMike_poompuhur. php

MAHABALIPURAM

According to local legend, there were seven pagodas dating back to the Pallava period in the 7th century AD which were sunk during various deluges at Mahabalipuram, south of Chennai (Madras), in Tamil Nadu. For centuries local fishermen told tales about a great flood which destroyed a fabulous city about 10,000 years ago, according to British explorer J Goldingham in 1798. The seventh pagoda is still sitting on the shore today. Goldingham wrote, "The surf here breaks far out over, as the Brahmins inform you, the ruins of a city which was incredibly large and magnificent…A Brahmin…informed me his grandfather had frequently mentioned having seen the gilt tops of five pagodas in the surf, no longer visible." (Hancock, ibid, p 120)

The legend states that the god Vishnu deposed a wicked king and replaced him with the gentle Prahlada, who reigned with wisdom. His grandson Bali was the founder of the magnificent city of Mahabalipuram and the family line continued to his son Banasura who fought a war against Krishna. Banasura was defeated and several generations later the gods became jealous of the city. "The gods assembled at the court of Indra, their jealousy was so much excited at it that they sent orders to the God of the Sea to let loose his billows and overflow a place which impiously pretended to vie in splendor with their celestial mansions. The command he obeyed, and the city was at once overflowed by that furious element, nor has it ever since been able to rear its head." (ibid p 121)

Graham Hancock took these legends seriously and decided to dive in the area in 2002 with the Indian National Institute of Oceanography (NIO) and UK based Scientific Exploration Society (SES). On April 4, 2002 'The Telegraph' announced, "A mysterious settlement that sank beneath the waves at least 1,200 years ago has been discovered by divers off the south-east coast of India. Granite blocks and walls that lie 20 feet below the surface may be the remains of six 'lost temples' that form part of local mythology."

India's National Institute of Oceanography, believes the ruins at Mahabalipuram, discovered half a mile off the coast, could be 1,200 to 1,500 years old, but Hancock believes that the city could date back to at least 3000 BC. According to Hancock and Geologist Glenn Milne from Durham University, it is possible that the ruins are up to six thousand years old because there has been very little vertical tectonic movement in the area over the past five thousand years and the dominant process driving sea level change was due to the melting of the massive ice sheets at the end of the Pleistocene age.

"The Times of India' reported on July 6, 2002 that the Archeological Survey of India's Underwater Archeology Wing (UAW) had discovered three walls and carved stones from temples running north to south and east to west about 500 meters off shore.

The SES announced, "A joint expedition of 25 divers from the Scientific Exploration Society and India's National Institute of Oceanography led by Monty Halls and accompanied by Graham Hancock, have discovered an extensive area with a series of structures that clearly show man made attributes, at a depth of 5-7 meters off shore of Mahabalipuram in Tamil Nadu. The scale of the submerged ruins, covering several square miles and at distances of up to a mile off shore, ranks this as a major marine archeological discovery as spectacular as the ruined cities submerged off Alexandria In Egypt."

According to NIO:

> • Underwater investigations were carried out at 5 locations in 5-8 meter depths, 500 to 700 meters off Shore temple.
>
> • Each site shows construction of stone masonry, remains of walls, big square cut rocks and a platform leading steps to it amidst naturally formed rocks.
>
> • Most structures are badly damaged and scattered in a vast area and overgrown with organisms.
>
> • The construction pattern and area about 100 m x 50 m is the same at each location. The ruins may extend well beyond the locations explored.
>
> • The ruins probably date to the Pallava dynasty, about 1,500 to 1,200 years ago. Similar rock cut temples are found in Mahabalipuram and Kanchipuram.

(**http://www.india-atlantis.org/**)

Team leader Alok Tripathi, who dived from November 2001 to March 2002 reported, "The walls are made of thick slabs of granite. Two long stone slabs, each with two vertical slits to receive the other stone slabs, were kept upright. Several such blocks arranged in a row formed a wall."

"The remnants are well carved and look like mouldings and pillars of temple. They are similar to the carvings in the existing temples of Mahabalipuram."

Tripathi and his team planned to dive on the ruins in the Tamil month of Tai, which falls between December and January.

Hancock and his wife Santha Faiia's photographs of the ruins off Mahabalipuram can be seen on his website at   **http://www. grahamhancock.com/underworld/mahabalipuram2.php**

221

On December 26, 2004 the great tsunami devastated many coastal areas across the Indian Ocean, including areas of Tamil Nadu. An amazing result of this tsunami is that locals reported seeing a temple structure off the coast of Mahabalipuram when the waters receded before the monstrous waves hit. Other relics were revealed when the powerful waves washed away sand as they smashed into the Tamil Nadu coast. A carved stone house, a rock elephant and two giant granite lions were miraculously revealed on the beach after the tsunami.

The SES site is **http://www.india-atlantis.org/**

ANCIENT RUINS OFF INDIA
PART 2—GUJARAT
DWARKA & BET DWARKA

Dwarka, or Dvaraka in Sanskrit, is the name of an ancient city in the Indian state of Gujarat. This legendary city was the dwelling place of the god Krishna and was submerged six times in the past. According to legend, Dwarka is the seventh city to be built in the area.

Dvaraka was mentioned in the 'Mahabharata', 'Bhagavata Purana', 'Skanda Purana' and 'Vishnu Purana.' Sri Krishna and Yadavas moved the capital city from Mathura to Dvaraka after a series of wars and bloodletting. Land was reclaimed from the sea near Saurashstra and a well planned city was built on the banks of the Gomati River. It had well organised residential and commercial zones, plazas, palaces, wide roads, public halls and public utilities as well as a good harbour. After Krishna left for the heavenly abode, Dvaraka was flooded. Arjuna in the 'Mahabharata' gave this account of the disaster:

"The sea, which had been beating against the shores, suddenly broke the boundary that was imposed on it by nature. The sea rushed into the city. It coursed through the streets and covered everything in the city. I saw the beautiful buildings becoming submerged one by one. In a matter of a few moments it was all over. The sea had now become as placid as a lake. There was no trace of the city. Dvaraka was just a name; just a memory."

On the same day that Krishna departed to his heavenly realm

222

the age of Kali descended. The oceans arose and submerged the whole of Dvaraka, according to the Vishnu Purana. Hindu sages believe that this age began in 3102 BC.

The search for the lost city of Dvaraka has been going on since the 1930s although serious explorations only began in 1983 by the Marine Archeology Unit (MAU) of the National Institute of Oceanography (NIO), under the leadership of marine archeologist Dr S. Rao. Their explorations between 1983 and 1990 revealed a well fortified township of Dvaraka which extended more than a half a mile into the ocean, and just like the legend, the township was built in six sections on land which had been reclaimed from the sea. Accounts of the findings were published in 1987, 'Progress and Prospects of Marine Archeology in India' and in 1988, 'Marine Archeology of Indian Ocean Countries.'

'The Hindu' reported on January 19, 1987 that the fourth underwater expedition had discovered two submerged sea walls, 30-40 feet below the surface. The same source dated the submersion to 3031 BC, the beginning of the age of Kali which resulted from Krishna's departure from Dwarka. It also claimed that a second deluge had destroyed the city in 2700 BC.

On February 7, 1988 'The Hindu' reported on the NIO's sixth marine archeological expedition which uncovered inner and outer gateways, circular bastions built of sandstone, steps, a temple and anchors. Dr Rao discovered an impressive stone wall 550 meters in perimeter not far from Bet Dwark V. Large trapezoidal blocks built course by course formed the outer shell holding together the rubble filling in the core.

At Dwarka, which sits on the Arabian Sea, marine archeologists surveyed a large area covered by 3-12 meters of water. The city was about 1 km long and at least 0.5 km in breadth. Remains of fortification walls which may have been built to protect the city from the ocean have been found, with at least six bastions.

Rao's findings are reproduced by Hancock in 'Underworld' pp211 to 212.

"All six sectors have protective walls built of large well-dressed blocks of sandstone, some as large as 1.5 to 2 m long, 0.5 to 0.75m wide and 0.3 to 0.5 thick. L-shaped joints in the masonry suggest that a proper grip was provided as to withstand the battering of waves and currents. At close intervals semi-circular or circular bastions were built along the fort walls in order to divert the current and to have a proper overview of the incoming and outgoing ships…There are entrance gateways in all sectors as surmised on the basis of the sill of the openings. The fort walls and bastions, built from large blocks which are too heavy to be moved by waves and currents, are in situ up to one or two meters height above the boulder foundation in the sea. In a few places as many as five courses of masonry are visible but in others the wall and bastion have collapsed."

Dvaraka extended to Bet Dwarka in the north (Sankhodhara), Okhamadhi in the south and Pindara in the east. Archeologists have carried out excavations and the most promising are near Bet Dwarka which was a satellite town on an island about 30 km away. In ancient times these two towns may have been connected to each other by a narrow strip of land. Like Dwarka, Bet Dwarka had fortifications around it and seems to have been devoted to trade and ship building, shell-working, pearl-diving and possibly metal working.

Excavations yielding antiquities have been carried out in sites near Bet Dwarka—1, 11, V1 and 1X. The findings are divided into two broad periods: Protohistoric period which includes a seal, two inscriptions, a copper fishhook and late Harappan pottery (c1700 to 1400 BC), and the Historic period consisting of coins and pottery.

Offshore explorations near Bet Dwarka, on the Gulf of Kutch, have discovered a number of stone anchors of different types including triangular, grapnel and ring stones. Some of these anchors weigh up to 100 kilograms, indicating that large ships were berthed there. Roman antiquities such as sherds of amphorae and lead anchors were found with the possibility of a Roman shipwreck in the vicinity.

http://www.arianuova.org/arianuova.it/arianuova.it/Components/
English/A12-Dwaraka.html

Graham Hancock, enchanted by the tales of Krishna's city and the underwater discoveries, decided to dive on the ruins in 2001. He was hoping to prove that some of the ruins dated from the end of the Ice Age and was surprised to hear that Dr Rao did not discount the possibility. "It must have existed. You can't rule that out at all. Particularly, as I have said, since we have found this structure at 23 meters depth. We have photographed it...I do not believe it is an isolated structure, further exploration is likely to reveal others round about." ('Underworld' p 210) Dr Rao also admitted that radiocarbon or thermoluminescence tests have not been possible, nor has any organic matter been found at Dwarka.

Hancock's dives were rather disappointing. "Gone were the lofty turrets, battlements and bastions of Rao's reconstructions and of my imagination. All seemed to have been reduced to a ruin-field of haphazardly strewn stone blocks, the angles and edges of which poked here and there out of the thick sludge of sediment and slimy green weed that carpeted everything." (ibid p213) He was told that the majority of the intact walls that had been photographed before 1994 could not be located or had been destroyed by the sea during recent severe monsoons. On March 17, 2007 it was reported in Indian newspapers that Dwarka was slowly being swallowed by the sea as a result of neglect from authorities.

Hancock was happy to concede that the ruins did not look any older than the late Harappan period, and were probably much younger, although he was fascinated by possible ruins at greater depths. According to legend, Krishna had built his Dvaraka on the ruins of an earlier town Kususthali well before 3100 BC. Furthermore, Glenn Milne, the geologist who mapped antediluvial coastlines around the world for 'Underworld' proved that 16,400 years ago Dwarka was 100 km from the coast and still 20 km inland as late as 10,600 BC.

On his website, Hancock conceded, in response to marine archeologist Nick Flemming's criticism: "What actually happened at Dwarka, over my ten year involvement with the site was that ruins which I had once hoped might be a "Flooded Kingdom of the Ice Age" turned out not even to be as old as the established date of 3,700 years ago and were more likely in fact to be somewhere between 1,200 and just 600 years old."

http://www.grahamhancock.com/underworld/underworld2.php?p=2

In January 2007 the Underwater Archeology Wing of Archeological Survey of India renewed excavations at Dwarka to determine its age. Its age has been hotly debated by historians and archeologists because of its association with the Hindu deity Lord Krishna. On May 4 it was announced that archeologists have discovered a circular wooden structure found underwater offshore of Jamnagar. It is well preserved and surrounded by another structure made of stone blocks.

Superintending Archeologist Alok Tripathi said, "It is significant as scientific dating of wood, which is carbon, is possible. This was not the case with evidences like stone, beads, glass terracotta found earlier." The piece was found during a near shore excavation carried out in the southwest region of Samudranarayan Temple. Tripathi dived in shallow water to study the structure which is made of stone and wood. He studied the blocks which were joined with wooden dowels and nails so well that they remained in position in the heavy surf and currents.

More information : **http://cities.expressindia.com/fullstory. php?newsid=234788**

In early 2007 a group of archeological experts and Indian Navy divers conducted the first scientific survey off the Gujarat coast to establish the validity of the ruins and their association with Krishna's Dwarka.

The Archeological Survey of India (ASI) trained the divers in archeological retrievals and transportation of samples. Alok Tripathi, of the ASI reported, "We found building blocks and collected samples. These have been sent for dating to establish the antiquity of the site."

Before commencing diving operations, a naval hydrographic team surveyed the area off Dwarka with multi-beam and side-scan sonar in the survey ship INS 'Nirdeshak'. They were able to generate a 3D model of the seabed to narrow down the area of research to 50 meters square.

http://www.newkerala.com/july.php?action=fullnews&id=54460

REFERENCES: G. Hancock, 'Underworld'

'Dwaraka a Lost City Discovered'

http://www.arianuova.org/arianuova.it/arianuova.it/Components/English/ A12-Dwaraka.html

http://www.grahamhancock.com/underworld/underworld2.php?p=2

Express News Service May 5, 2007 http://cities.expressindia.com/
fullstory.php?newsid=234788
http://www.newkerala.com/july.php?action=fullnews&id=54460

GULF OF CAMBAY

In 2001 oceanographers from India's National Institute of
Ocean Technology (NIOT) were conducting a survey of pollution
in the Gulf of Cambay, or Khambat, using sidescan sonar. When
studying the images taken over a six month period, they were
amazed to see what appeared to be geometric structures spread
over a nine kilometer stretch beneath the ocean floor at a depth of
120 feet. One of the shapes resembled the great bath seen in the
Harappan city of Mohenjendaro.

Dredging turned up pieces of wood, remains of pots, fossil
bones and possibly construction material off the coast of Surat.

In January 2002 Science and Technology Minister Murli
Monohar Joshi announced the findings in a press conference. He
said, "Some of the artifacts recovered by the NIOT from the site
such as the log of wood date back to 7500 BC, which is indicative
of a very ancient culture in the present Gulf of Cambay."

The age of these artifacts and structures presents orthodox
archeology with a problem as this was supposedly the Neolithic
period and there were no cities in existence. The great Harappan
civilization would not rise for a few more millennia. Furthermore,
the entire Gulf of Cambay was flooded between 6,900 and 7,900
years ago so the remains had to be older. Independent archeologist
S.N Rajguru is quoted as saying: "We can safely say from the
antiquities and the acoustic images of the geometric structures
that there was human activity in the region more than 9,500 years
ago."

Archeologists soon fought back against these claims. Professor
Rao, who discovered Dwarka's underwater ruins, described the
'discovery' as "bunkum", "flippant and premature" that "puts the
credibility of Indian science at stake." He told the Telegraph: "We
need much more evidence, both physical and visual, to confirm
that there were any prehistoric structures on the seabed." When
confronted with the wood sample which was dated to 7500 BC he

responded, "How can one make such a claim without even sending a diver or taking pictures or involving any archeologist?"

Unfortunately the claims by Joshi have also raised allegations by anti-Hindu Revivalist groups that 'Archeology in India has been Saffronized'. They believe that 'saffron archeology' deliberately excavates examples of enduring and culturally specific symbols of Hinduism or 'Indic Culture'. Critics of the 'Ancientness Theory' question the motives of the research project as an attempt to validate the Hindu Nationalists' perspective that Hindu/Sanskrit/ Vedic culture is much older than the accepted 1800 BC ascribed to nineteenth century philologists. The political situation is so sensitive in India that in 2000 a group of 'Leftist' scholars from Muslim and other universities issued a statement recommending that there should be a ban on archeological excavations that could cause communal tensions or validate perspectives of Indian Nationalists.

NIOT's Project Director Dr S. Kathiroli and geological consultant S. Badrinarayan were surprised by the hostility which surrounded the announcement of their findings. Between May and November 2001 they had conducted further research in the area using such equipment as:

- Side-scan sonar for delineating the sea floor surface features.
- Sub Bottom Profiler for cross section of the sub seabed.
- Magnetometer to identify major structural elements.
- Remote controlled videography which is vital as the swift currents of the Gulf of Cambay create high turbidity and low visibility so that optical systems cannot be worked beyond ten meters.

These results confirmed that extensive man-made ruins lie on the sea bed in the Gulf of Cambay at depths of between 25 and 40 meters and at distances of up to 40 km from the modern shoreline. According to Hancock, "The sub-bottom profiles revealed extensive, well-built foundations to the geometrical structures and in some cases walls rising as much as 3 meters above the sea-bed and extending down several meters below. Moreover, as well as the original 'city-complex' covering a rectangular area roughly 9 km long and 2 kms wide, a second city of similar size had been found a little further to the south at similar depths. Both cities lie along the courses of ancient rivers that had flowed here when the area was above water, and in one case the remains of an ancient dam more than 600 meters long have been identified." ('Underworld' p676)

Although the extremely hazardous currents prevented divers from exploring the ruins and remote control vehicles were unable to record clear images, over 2,000 man-made artifacts were recovered by trawls, grabs and vibro-core equipment. The artifacts are typically pre-Harappan and include:

- Round and rectangular pieces of rock and mortar with perfectly shaped holes.
- Cylindrical rods with vertical holes, possibly used as beads for necklaces.
- Rolled rods and well-turned cylindrical rock pieces
- Chert blades cut into long flat pieces.
- Macro tools resembling axes, stone blades, choppers
- Micro tools made of basalt, chalcedony and chert including a pestle and fish hook.
- Ladle shaped objects made of agate or steatite
- Beads made of opal, agate, carnelian, steatite, quartz, malachite and topaz.
- Potsherds including sun-dried grey and kiln-baked red.
- Human and animal (deer and duck) figurines.
- A few fossilized human bones
- A flat rock with what resembles a script.
- Chunk of carbonized teak wood.

The archeological discoveries were no less spectacular:

- Channels 20-40 meters deep and over 9 kms long, adjoined by basement like features in a grid pattern resembling an urban habitation site.
- 40m x 24 m tank-like depression with steps leading to a deeper section.
- 200m x 45m platform like structure.

229

- 79m x 50m buried structure with what appears to be a wall about 3 m above the seabed.

The carbonised teak was dated using C14 by the Birbal Sahni Institute of Paleo Botany, Lucknow, and the National Geophysical Research Institute, Hyderabad, giving a calibrated date of 8150 to 7650 BP. The teak could not have floated to the Gulf as the current patterns indicate that the water circulates within the Gulf and is not exchanged with the Arabian Sea.

http://www.hindunet.org/saraswati/khambat/khambat01.htm#GKCC

Graham Hancock was interested in the Gulf of Cambay long before any ruins were discovered on the seafloor because the Indus Valley civilization city of Lothal on the northern end of the gulf was the greatest port during the third millennium BC. It was excavated by S. Rao, who discovered a giant trapezoid dock, an artificial basin and a walled structure. The sophistication of the dock indicates that a long history of engineering preceded this city even though it had not been discovered in the archeological record. Hancock was convinced that the prehistory of this area lay on the seabed of the flooded Gulf of Cambay. Tying this in with the search for the homeland of the Vedic culture, he wrote, "Never, so far as I am aware, has a reputable scholar, Indian or otherwise—ever suggested a Vedic homeland located not only *within* India, but also *exclusively* on the subcontinent's coastal margins inundated at the end of the Ice Age." (ibid p157)

Hancock used geologist Glenn Milne's maps to illustrate the flooding which inundated the Gulf of Cambay from 17,000 to 7,000 years ago.

- 16,400 years ago the area was a depression, possibly filled by a lake, surrounded by land at least 100 km wide.
- 13,500 years ago the landmass was reduced in area and a large island, almost 500 km long and 100 km wide was marooned off-shore in the Arabian Sea. A marine strait, also 100 kms wide in places, opened up through the basin of the former freshwater lake.
- Between 13,500 and 7,700 years ago the seas rose gradually, eroding the island.

• By 6900 BP the island off the coast of the Gulf was submerged and the Gulf itself was permanently inundated to its modern extent.

Using these dates, he determined that any urban development in the Gulf of Cambay had to be at least 7,000 years old. On Hancock's website message board, researcher Sharif Sakr noted that the data used to recreate the bathymetric maps of Cambay was inaccurate and underestimated the depth of the waters by about 20 meters and thus the age of the inundation, which must have been much earlier. Sakr commented; "If tectonic subsistence has played any role in the subsidence of the cities, then Glenn Milne's later result of 12,000 years would provide an upper limit on the time since they were submerged. Combined with our conservative lower limit of 7,000 years, we would expect the cities to have been submerged at some point between 10,000 and 5000 BC. Indeed the carbon-dating placed a piece of cut wood, recovered from a shallow layer on top of this city, to 7,500 BC (calibrated). Does this mean that the cities themselves are 9,500 years old? Yes — they are very unlikely to significantly younger than that. But, for a number of reasons, we suspect that the cities might turn out to be even older..."

www.grahamhancock.com/underworld/cambay2

REFERENCES: G. Hancock, 'Underworld'
www.grahamhancock.com/underworld/cambay2
http://www.hindunet.org/saraswati/khambat/khambat01.htm#GKCC

THE SARASVATI RIVER

The Sarasvati River is described 72 times in the ancient Sanskrit classic the Rig Veda as the place where the Rishis (wise men) composed their hymns. It was a mighty river flowing through the homeland of the Vedic Aryans from the Himalayas to the ocean. Some descriptions were: "the Seventh, Mother of Floods" (Rigveda 7.36.6) or "best mother, best river, best goddess" (Rig Veda 2.41.16). Originating in the high mountains where she could

"Burst with her strong waves the ridges of the hills" (Rigveda 6.61.2-13), it is also described as a river swollen by many rivers.

The problem today is that there is no such mighty river and until very recently scholars believed it was either mythical or somewhere in central Asia, the supposed homeland of the 'Aryans'. The later epic the Mahabharata says that the Sarasvati dried up in a desert at a place named Vinasana or Adarsana. Other scholars, puzzled at the relationship between the river and goddess Sarasvati, can only conclude that the river was actually the Indus River.

In 2001 satellite images after the Bhuj earthquake revealed a palaeo channel in the Gulf of Cambay which is now about 20 meters below sea level. The mouth of the channel is located about 200 km away from Mumbai and around 150 km from the Saurashtra coast. These images indicate that a large river flowed in this area, although scholars have been reluctant to name it the mythical Sarasvati. "It is too early to say what it is, we need more scientific studies. But it does indicate the likelihood of a river course which could have supported a human settlement in the region," said R. V Karanth, MSU geologist.

In 2002 it was announced that remote sensing satellites had traced the course of the Sarasvati River under the Thar desert in Rajasthan. J. Sharma of the Jodhpur based Remote Sensing Service Centre of the Indian Space Research Organisation (ISRO) and his colleagues A. Gupta and G. Sreenivasan mapped palaeo channels which are relics of ancient rivers. Thirteen bore wells drilled along the river course yielded water at a depth of 35 to 40 meters. They do not believe that the ancient underground river is still flowing, but there is enough to supply good quality ground water.

In 2003 it was reported that the Indian government had started excavating for ancient ruins from the Harappan civilization along the legendary Sarasvati River from Haryana to Gujarat.

REFERENCES: Wikipedia entry on Sarasvati River
Recent Research on Sarasvati River:
http://www.stephen-knapp.com/recent_research_on_the_sarasvati_river.htm

THE ANTEDILUVIAL CITIES OF SUMER

The Sumerian civilization at over 5,000 years old is acknowledged by historians as the most ancient in the world. This amazing civilization in the desert of southern Iraq seemingly sprang up from nowhere with sophisticated architecture, writing, astronomy, political structures and mythology. Their mythology claims that their civilization was "lowered from heaven" by the gods who founded five cult cities — Eridu, Badtibira, Larak, Sippur and Shurrupak. Centuries later, the same gods decided to destroy the cities by flood and warned a man called Zisudra to save his family in a giant boat.

"All the windstorms, exceedingly powerful, attacked as one,

At the same time the flood swept over the cult centres.

For seven days and seven nights the flood swept over the land,

And the huge boat was tossed about by the windstorms on the great waters." (Sumerian tablet, quoted in Hancock's 'Underworld' p27)

According to the single tablet which records this flood, after the deluge, the gods were grateful to Zisudra and granted him eternal life.

From 1922-9 British archeologist Sir Leonard Woolley excavated the Sumerian city of Ur and discovered a layer of silt three meters deep which had been deposited by water. Below this sediment were further habitation records to 3200 BC. He announced that he had discovered Zisudra's flood which was also the biblical flood of Noah. "The deluge was not universal, but a local disaster confined in the lower valley of the Tigris and Euphrates, affecting an area perhaps 400 miles long and 100 miles across, but for the occupants of the valley that was the whole world!" (Hancock, ibid p30)

Woolley's declaration that the flood was riverine and local has influenced archeologists to the point that no-one seriously considers the possibility that other cities may lie beneath the waters of the Persian Gulf. In the 1990s Kurt Lambeck of the Australian National University in Canberra carried out a detailed study of the shorelines of the Persian Gulf over the past 18,000 years and calculated that the modern shoreline was reached about 6,000 years ago and actually flooded by one to two meters above current levels, inundating the low lying areas of Mesopotamia. This marine transgression which occurred between 6000 and 5500 BC also reached the cities of Ur and Eridu where the waters may have risen about three meters before receding. It is very possible that this marine transgression and not a local riverine inundation may have been Woolley's flood.

Other Sumerian cities also show signs of flooding, including Shurrupak on the Euphrates River although this occurred about seven hundred years after Eridu. The remaining antediluvial cities of Badtibira, Sippur and Larak have all been identified and excavated, but show little to indicate their legendary grandeur.

Hancock, using Lambeck's study, has come up with what might become a reinterpretation of early Sumerian history. According to Lambeck, the whole Persian Gulf was dry land between 18,000 and 14,000 years ago. Referring to the puzzle of the Sumerians' origin Lambeck wrote, "A significant element in the puzzle must be the evolution of the physical environment of the Gulf itself." (Hancock, ibid, p43) He saw the dry Gulf as a corridor for migration of peoples into Sumer, whereas Hancock hypothesised that the floor of the Gulf may have been a place of permanent settlement before it was totally flooded 7,000 years ago.

Furthermore, the Gulf was flooded in various stages and the great rivers of Tigris and Euphrates were united as a single river passing through as many as three large freshwater lakes. Even after the Straits of Hormuz were inundated 14,000 years ago, the valley now filled with the Persian Gulf was a very fertile place which may have been the biblical Garden of Eden.

Lambeck wrote, "Until about 11,000 BP the northern part of the Persian Gulf floor would have been a relatively flat but narrow plain, hemmed in between the palaeo-Gulf and the southern foothills of the Zagros mountains forming the present coastline...By about 10,000 BP the north-east margin of the Gulf has approached its present position in several localities, particularly east of the 52 degrees longitude. Much of the southern part of the Gulf remains exposed until about 8,000 BP and areas such as the Great Pearl

Bank are not submerged until shortly after this time." (Hancock, ibid p47)

Hancock has surmised; "That the true story of Sumerian origins may have proved so elusive because it is veiled beneath the waters of the Persian Gulf. In that case, Eridu, and the other four 'antediluvial' cities of Mesopotamia might well bear the same relationship to the original antediluvial cities of the Gulf floor as Halifax Nova Scotia bears to Halifax, England or as Perth Australia bears to Perth Scotland. They could, in other words, have been named in memory of other older cities somewhere else... Moreover, in this case we are not even required to imagine that the migration came from very far away but merely from the flooded lowlands of the Gulf towards the nearest higher and productive ground that was blessed by the same Tigris/Euphrates river system as the floor of the Gulf had once been." (ibid p. 49)

REFERENCE: G. Hancock, 'Underworld'

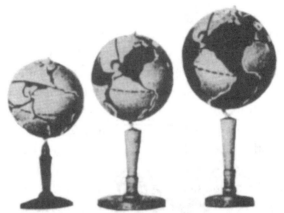

Hilgenberg's 1933 'expanding terellae' – the continents reconstructed on a 3/5 diameter ocean-free globe

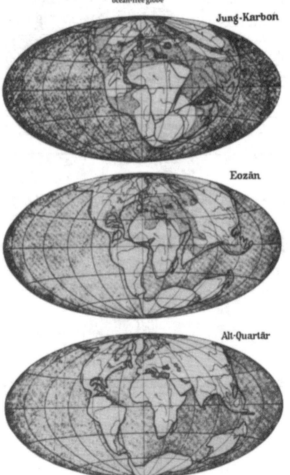

Jung-Karbon

Eozän

Alt-Quartär

Wegener's map of the break-up of Pangaea in the Late Carboniferous, Eocene and Early Quaternary (from the 3rd German edn)

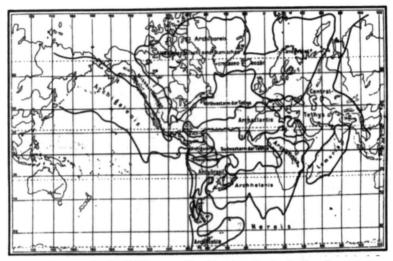

Von Herring's 1907 map of land bridges in the Indian Ocean.

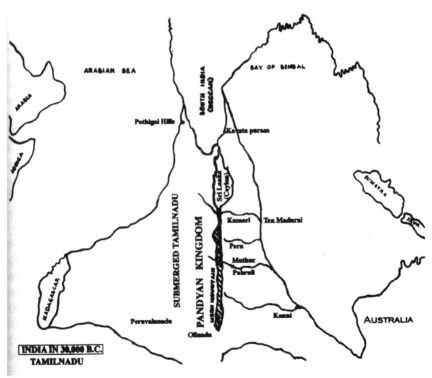

N Mahalingam's map of India circa 30,000 BC showing a sunken Tamilnadu.

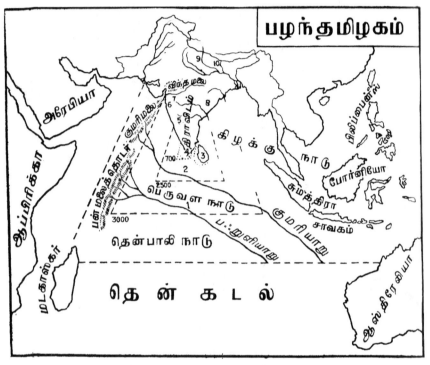

A Tamil language map of Pulavar Kulanthai, Palaiya Tamilakam, the "Ancient Tamil Home-place," showing the modern coastlines and submerged land.

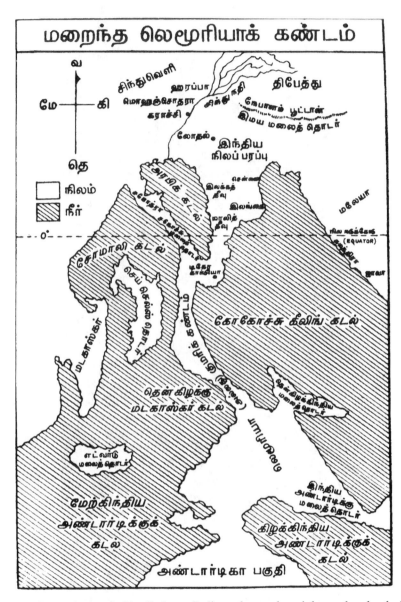

R. Mathivanan's map in Tamil shows India to the north and the sunken land of Lemuria spreading to the south, terminating in Antarctica. The shaded areas are the oceans.

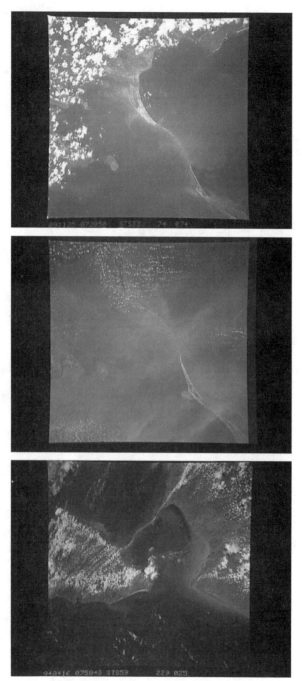

Above: Three satellite photos of the submerged land bridge between the southern end of India and the northern part of Sri Lanka.

PART 8

RUINS & STRUCTURES IN LAKES & INLAND SEAS
EUROPE LAKE DWELLINGS—
SCOTTISH & ORKNEY CRANNOGS
LOCH NESS
THE BLACK SEA
TURKEY
GEORGIA
RUSSIA, KYRGYZSTAN
IRAN
INDIA
FUXIAN LAKE, CHINA
LAKE CHINI, MALAYSIA
LAKE TITICACA
ROCK LAKE, WISCONSIN
FLORIDA LAKES AND CAVES

Fresh bodies of water like lakes and seas also contain sites from lost civilizations.

EUROPE LAKE DWELLINGS

During the Neolithic era in Britain, Ireland and Central Europe, villages were built on piles of wood over lakes. The most famous, the Swiss Lake Village, was discovered in 1854 when the water level lowered in Lake Zurich, revealing wooden posts jutting from the mud with prehistoric artifacts. In 1858 relics turned up in the Robenhausen peat bog on Lake Pfaffker, north of Lake Zurich. In Ireland and Scotland crannogs were also revealing evidence of dwellings.

Archeologists originally believed that these pile villages were built over water on wooden platforms, but by the 1960s it was clear that there was no evidence to support this theory. Excavations at Auvernier and Yerdon on Lake Neuchatel led archeologist Christian Strahm to suggest that the Stone Age villages extended from dry land to a periodically flooded beach. The houses had stood on piles with the floors raised at least 50 centimeters (19 inches). However, in the late 1960s Renato Perini discovered in the peat bog of Flave in Italy that a Bronze Age village had extended up to 15 meters into open water from an island in Lake Carera.

Excavations took place in 1929 in Lake Constance and 1964-5 in Lake Neuchatel, where areas were pumped dry and dammed. On Lake Neuchatel, archeologist Michel Egloff has identified a number of structures by means of aerial photography.

Lake Biel, northwest of Bern, has yielded many artifacts over the past few decades. In Neolithic times villages were built on piles in the once densely populated area of Sutz-Lattrigen. Wooden stakes were driven into the ground to support a platform on which houses and other structures were built. Many of these remains are now underwater.

The latest structure to be discovered dates from 3863 BC and is Switzerland's oldest building. According to Albert Hafner, the leading archeologist, the structure found in late 2006 was a large rectangular building with fish traps discovered nearby. It is likely that the building was used for storing or smoking fish.

The oldest village in the area goes back to the fourth millennium BC. Over 30,000 square meters of the lake bed have now been examined and thousands of artifacts recovered.

REFERENCE:
Swissinfo.ch "Prehistoric find located beneath the waves'
http://www.swissinfo.org/eng/feature/detail/Prehistoric_find_located_beneath_the_waves.html?siteSect=108&sid=8202971&cKey=1189427815000&ty=st

SCOTTISH & ORKNEY CRANNOGS

The Gaelic word crannog indicates a small island that has been built on or created to support one or more huts. Many crannogs have now become totally submerged although some still appear above the water level in most parts of Scotland. Most are difficult to date but a crannog in Milton Loch, Kirkcudbrightshire was dated to the fifth century BC. It is likely that crannogs were built earlier in the Bronze or Neolithic ages and were still being constructed until the Middle Ages.

At first sight, crannogs may appear to be just boulder mounds, but closer inspection reveals structural timberwork surviving underwater. Many are composite structures in which dumped stones were controlled by heavy timberwork and often bound by layers of brushwork packing. Their natural form in a truncated cone whereas wholly artificial islands have a round outline up to 50 meters across.

Cherry Island, in Loch Ness or 'Eileen Mhuireach' is a man-made island which once covered an area of 160 feet by 180 ft (48m by 54m).

Despite lively interest in Edwardian times, the study of crannogs in Scotland is only just recommencing. Underwater excavation in cold climates is a slow and expensive process and it will be a long time before all the sites are excavated.

In recent years archeologists have discovered small artificial islands in Orkney's inland waters which have lain undiscovered for centuries. Bobby Forbes, an underwater archeologist is leading the project in a shallow loch which lies between Stromness and the Loch of Harray. He said, "We were doing some work in the Stenness Loch area and found two small islands with causeways, which were flooded by the sea. People have just not known about these man-made islands. They were not recorded in Orkney's sites and monument record."

One of the newly discovered crannogs in Orkney has the remains of a structure on it with a stone causeway which was once turfed over, leading to the shore. The second crannog has a badly eroded causeway but no surviving structures. The remains of a large 'anomaly' lying further out in the loch has Forbes and his team excited. This skerry like object is only visible when the water in the loch is low and may be natural or artificial. They have also found an old stone quarry near the loch which may have provided material for the causeway and monuments of the area.

It is difficult to date these crannogs as they were built from the Bronze Age until the seventeenth century.

Forbes and his colleagues from the Orkney Archeological Trust hope to conduct a study on the palaeo-archeological core of the loch bottom to see how it has changed since the Ice Age. As a teacher of underwater archeology at Orkney College he has said, "There is a lot known about terrestrial archeology on Orkney but nothing about the archeology of its lochs and inland waters."

LOCH NESS, SCOTLAND

An article entitled 'Ancient Stoneworks Found in Loch Ness' was published in 'Science News' Number 110, 1976. It was reported that scientists searching for the Loch Ness monster found several large, prehistoric manmade stoneworks at the bottom of the loch. "The structures include a stone wall, several ancient mounds (locally called cairns) and possibly and ancient fortified island (called a crannog). Though such cairns and crannogs are common in the area, the discovery of such structures some 30 feet below the Loch's surface indicates the water level has risen sharply over the centuries…The discovery of several apparently intact structures may allow archeologists to learn more about the area's ancient inhabitants.

"The cairns are made of piled stones, varying in size from nearly one foot diameter down to pebbles. Such structures were presumably built as burial and religious mounds three or four thousand years ago. The mounds are generally laid out in a series of concentric circles, as much as 100 feet in diameter, but one complex series stretches 250 feet."

THE BLACK SEA

The Black Sea is basically landlocked with a small strait, the Bosporus, separating the European and Asian continents. Dense salty water flows in to this sea from the Aegean and sinks beneath the surface layer of fresh water from the great rivers of Europe—

the Danube, Don and Dnieper. The deep salty water has become depleted of all oxygen and is completely sterile. The possibilities of ancient marine life being preserved in this anoxic environment have led scientists to study the Black Sea since the cold war.

In 1967 David Ross and Egon Degen from the Woods Hole Oceanographic Institution explored the depths of the Black Sea on the research vessel Atlantis 11 by conducting a survey of the deep sea core samples. They proposed a thesis that the Black Sea had become a freshwater lake during the last Ice Age when the world's oceans dropped dramatically. The melting glaciers carried their clays into the huge lake and deposited them on the floor as a pale grey layer. Gradually, as the sea levels rose, salt water flowed through the Bosporus and the present Black Sea was formed.

Another Woods Hole graduate William Ryan, who cruised the Black Sea aboard the research vessel 'Chain', noted that the Bosporus Strait had slashed a deep chasm through the sediment and bedrock which showed it had been carved with great speed and pressure. He also proposed that the Mediterranean had been dry five million years ago with a natural dam at the straits of Gibraltar. A seismic event had destroyed this dam and the Mediterranean was filled rapidly in a monstrous deluge. Ryan wondered if the breaching of the Bosporus into the Black Sea had caused a flood of cataclysmic proportions which may have been the basis for the story of Noah's flood. With his colleague Walter Pitman, he proposed that from 12,500 BC to 5600 BC the freshwater lake had been isolated from the Mediterranean Sea. One day a tiny channel was cut which became an enormous cascade of water with a force two hundred times greater than Niagara Falls within a matter of weeks.

Over the next two years this torrent caused the Black Sea to rise by about 550 feet (168 meters) above the surface of the landlocked lake. Thousands of acres of pastoral land as well as countless shore dwellers must have been lost in the deluge.

In 1993, after the collapse of the Soviet Union, Pittman and Ryan were able to test their theory with the assistance of a Bulgarian oceanographer, Professor Petko Dimitrov. He had dived in a submersible off the Danube delta and discovered an ancient beach at a depth of 404 feet (123 meters). Shells collected at this time were

245

dated to 9,000 years old. The Russians from the P.P Shirshov Institute of Oceanography in Moscow were also requesting for assistance to track radioactive contamination from the 1986 Chernobyl power plant meltdown. Ryan and Pitman, with geology student Candace Major, volunteered to lend the Russians sophisticated sonar equipment so that they would be able to search for ancient drowned shorelines.

The scientists sailed on the 'Aquanaut' a converted fishing trawler and took sonar scans which revealed a clear profile of ancient beaches and rivers under the bottom sediment. Candace Major found evidence of marine fossils which had existed in a freshwater environment. They had been quickly extinguished by a salt water incursion—thus proving the hypothesis. Dating revealed the shells to be all between 7,580 and 7,470 years old.

Oceanographer Robert Ballard, discoverer of the 'Titanic' and other wrecks, was determined to study the Black Sea as its anoxic depths would preserve ancient shipwrecks. He was fascinated by Ryan and Pitman's account 'Noah's Flood, The New Scientific Discoveries About the Event That Changed History', particularly submerged beach formations at 554 feet (169 m) and shellfish dating from 7,500 years ago.

Ballard believed that the flood waters could have risen only a few inches a day and the beaches could have been preserved underwater. He needed to search in areas away from the river sediment and chose the Turkish city of Sinop as his base. His side-scan sonar found a submerged shoreline which was virtually undisturbed at a depth of 550 feet, while dredging brought up shells and sodden chunks of wood.

In November 1999 Ballard and his colleagues met the press at the headquarters of the National Geographic Society to present the first expedition's findings. They had proved Ryan and Pitman's thesis by discovering freshwater organisms predating saltwater ones. The freshwater ones had become extinct by 5400 BC when a deluge of salt water had killed them, at the time Ryan and Pitman had theorised the Great Flood.

In 2000 another expedition by Ballard and Fredrik Hiebert of the University of Pennsylvania discovered evidence of human habitation on the sunken shores of the Black Sea. They found carved wooden beams, wooden branches and stone tools like chisels at depths of over 300 feet, according to Ballard. Using remote controlled underwater vessels with cameras they located a collapsed structure in an ancient river valley which included preserved wooden beams. The structure resembled stone age dwellings built 7,000 years ago in the interior of Turkey, he claimed, with a hewn beam and wooden branches forming the walls and roof of the structure. "We have also found and photographed stone tools, possibly a chisel or an axe, and ceramic storage vessels, all untouched since the flooding of the Black Sea," he reported in a phone call to the National Geographic Society from the expedition ship Northern Horizon. He was eventually granted permission by the Turkish government to recover some of the wooden artifacts for dating.

In 2003 Ballard used Hercules, an underwater excavator which was able to retrieve artifacts using pincers to revisit the Black Sea. Scientists couldn't arrive at any conclusions about the structure, claiming it had been 'contaminated' by wood which had drifted in. "We were not able to get a smoking gun," said Ballard, but acknowledged the expedition was still a success. He still maintains that the structure was a human dwelling situated on the banks of an ancient river.

REFERENCES: R. Ballard, 'Adventures in Ocean Exploration' National Geographic, 2001

SEVTOPOLIS was the ancient Thracian city in Bulgaria founded in about 320 BC by King Seuthes 111. The city was discovered and excavated in 1948 by Bulgarian archeologists during the construction of the Georgi Dimitrov Reservoir. Unfortunately the ruins were flooded and lie at the bottom of Koprinka Dam.

In 2005 Bulgarian architect Zheko Tilev proposed a project to uncover and reconstruct Sevtopolis by building a dam wall around the ruins. As a UNESCO World Heritage Site it would become a great tourist attraction. Tilev is currently trying to raise funds for the huge project.

TURKEY
TANTALIS (or Tantalus)

In his book 'The Sunken Kingdom—The Atlantis Mystery Solved', historian and archeologist Peter James puts forward the theory that Atlantis was originally the lost city of Tantalis which, according to legend, was destroyed by an earthquake and swallowed by a lake. Similarities between the two legends of Atlas and Tantalis abound, not to mention that Tantalis is an anagram of Atlantis.

According to the ancient Greek legend, Tantalus was a Lydian king who built the earliest city, Tantalis. Powerful amongst mortals, he was also welcomed into the realm of the gods whose secrets he divulged to mortals. As revenge, the gods destroyed his power and swallowed his city in a giant earthquake after which great waves flooded the land. The city of Tantalis was covered by waters and lies beneath a deep lake while the king also lies at the bottom of the lake.

Legend states that the city of Tantalis lies at the bottom of Lake Saloe, which was described as a marsh by the Roman writer Pliny, but James, like explorers before him, was unable to find any corroborating evidence. Lake Saloe was drained in the twentieth century to make room for agriculture. James believes Tantalis may have been a Hittite city destroyed and rebuilt in classical times before being buried under Lake Saloe.

Although James draws many parallels between the story of Tantalus and Atlas, there is no archeological evidence available to support his theory as the former Lake Saloe has never been excavated.

OTHER AREAS OF TURKEY

According to this unreferenced internet report from NTVMSNBC REKLAM, local legend in Turkey claims that there is a 'sunken city' in the location of the healing waters of the Sultaniye Spas on Lake Koycegiz. Locals believe the site became inundated by the lake after an earthquake.

Archeologists under Professor Cengiz Isik began excavations at the underwater site. "The excavations that are being conducted in the waters of the lake, where there is limited visibility, are utilising advanced technology and the support of computer and arithmetic photogrammetry," he is reported to have said.

No further reports have been forthcoming about these excavations.

A five year project mapping Turkey's underwater history has been launched by the Dokuz Eulul University's Marine Sciences and Technologies Institute (DBTE). Since commencing in May 2007, the project has already located over twenty shipwrecks, eight underwater ruins and six sunken locations dating back to the Ottoman era. Project manager Harun Ozdas, said, "So far we have dived to 15 sunken areas between Anamur and Izmir. We came across many sunken places in the Gulf of Gokova."

So far the project is focusing on the Aegean and Mediterranean although they plan to study the Black Sea in the future.
REFERENCE:
http://www.turkishdailynews.com.tr/article.php?enewsid=82558

GEORGIA

Georgia, and other countries on the Black Sea, has experienced subsidence over the centuries. Ancient Greek settlements like Phasis, Dioscouria and Phanagoria have all suffered partial or full submergence. The Greek town of Dioscouria, near Sukhimi, was flourishing until its conquest by Mithridates VI if Ponuts in the 2nd century BC. Under the Roman emperor Augustus, the city assumed the name of Sebastopolis or Savastapolis. A few centuries later the city was deserted and its towers and walls have been discovered underwater dating from the second century AD.

In 1999 it was announced by the Archeological Institute of America that a joint Georgian-American expedition had recovered artifacts from Lake Paliostomi that established the location of the legendary city of Phasis which was the destination of Jason and the Argonauts in their quest for the Golden Fleece.

Underwater archeologists discovered part of a settlement inhabited from at least the fourth century BC to the eighth century AD in the lake on the central coast of the Republic of Georgia. Using reports from ancient scholars such as Strabo, Arrian and Aristotle, they were able to determine that Phasis was located in the general vicinity of Poti, a major Soviet port.

A flourishing city on the Silk Road, Phasis was a primary trading port for goods from Central Asia, the Russian Steppes, Mediterranean and Asia. It was founded by the Greeks in the late seventh century BC at sea level and may have had many canals and moats. Archeologists believe that the city may have sunk gradually into the silt or been inundated by a sea level rise of a few feet during the end of the Byzantine era in the tenth century AD.

The expedition consisted of members from the Institute of Nautical Archeology (INA) at Texas A &M University, the Centre for Archeological Studies of the Georgian Academy of Sciences and the Pipeline Archeology for the Recovery of Knowledge (PARK). They recovered about two thousand cultural items including pottery, coins, glass, bones and building material spanning from the 6th century BC to 8th century AD.

The expedition plans to return to Lake Paliostomi to search for features of Phasis mentioned in ancient sources, such as the temples to Apollo and Artemis, the mint and a famous museum which featured the anchor from Jason's ship the 'Argo'.

LAKE SEIDOZERO, RUSSIA

Mysterious Lake Seidozero, in the Kola Peninsula of Russia above the Arctic Circle, is considered sacred by the native Saami (Lapps) peoples. Difficult to reach, this lake is reputed to have ancient steps with inscriptions, monuments of stacked stones, precision cut megaliths bored by some kind of drill, underground tunnels, strange wells and seven mysterious pillars lined up in a wall.

There are many legends about this lake. One is that it has a false bottom with a huge cave beneath which was explored by the Soviets in the 1920s. Others believe that the Nazis sent an expedition to discover the origins of the Aryan race in the realm of Thule in the 1930s. They believed that the island of Thule may have existed in the Kola peninsula.

An expedition in 1998 by Mikhail Dyomin discovered a ritual well, ruins of an ancient observatory and mysterious writing. In 2001 Dyomin led another expedition which discovered a huge cave on the lakeshore as well as stone panels made with metallic tools which were dated to 8000 BC. An artificial tunnel was said to exist

between this cave and the bottom of the lake.
REFERENCE : http://www.thothweBCom/article-print-1510.html

KYRGYZSTAN

Lake Issyk-Kul in Kyrgyzstan was on the great Silk Road which linked Europe with China from ancient times. When the Mongols, under Genghis Khan (Chingizhan) invaded in the 13th century, many treasures were hidden underground or underwater by the wealthy locals. There are also legends that Khan's treasure and tomb lie at the bottom of the lake. Other treasure hunters believe that the Templars and Nestorians built a castle on one of the lake's islands and transferred the treasures of the Order there.

Today Kyrgyz archeologists are aware of more than ten ancient and medieval settlements that lie beneath the water. Artifacts of the Saki-Usun period (1st millennium BC) such as ceramics, bronzes have been recovered, as well as coins, pottery and metals from the Middle Ages.

On July 21, 2004 UPI reported that a Kyrgyz-Russian expedition was embarking to search for an ancient city covered by Lake Issyk-Kul. According to legend, an island in the lake with fortifications where Tamerlane, the conqueror held prisoners in the 14th century disappeared beneath the waves.

In the middle of the 20th century the Kyrgyz archeologist Dmitry Vinnik discovered the ruins of large buildings of burnt brick near the north coast of the large lake which is 2,250 square miles in area. In 2003 archeologists found two bronze cauldrons used for sacrifice that belonged to ancient tribes living in the territory of modern Issyk-Kul.

Locals call the island Atlantis and have reported seeing stone buildings on the bottom of Issyk-Kul, not far from the mouth of the Tyup River.

Vladimir Poloskih, vice president of the National Academy of Sciences of Kyrgyzstan, was leading the 2006 expedition which included Russian historian Svetlana Lukashova. The Russians were all experienced scuba divers and members of the Russian Confederation of Underwater Sports. In 2006 they worked near the coast at depths of 5 to 10 meters to discover huge walls, some stretching for 500 meters. They also discovered Scythian burial mounds and numerous artifacts such as bronze battleaxes, daggers, casting molds and a faceted gold bar which had been a monetary unit.

Russian and Kyrgyz archeologists have discovered and examined more than ten major inundated urban and rural settlements of varying ages, including a previously unknown culture. They also discovered ritual complexes, dwellings and outhouses. Some of the artifacts include a 2,500 year old ritual bronze cauldron, bronze mirrors, festive horse harnesses, coins and gold wire rings.

REFERENCE: http://en.rian.ru/analysis/20071227/94372640.html

IRAN

An article in the Iran International Magazine on Nov 1, 2004 'Underwater Archeology in Iran' bemoaned the lack of interest from the government in studying and preserving the country's underwater history. According to documents, the ancient city of Kish, the wall of the ancient city of Gorgan, Takht-e Suleiman and part of the Portuguese castle are all submerged in Iran's coastal waters.

The article spoke of fifty years of ignored marine archeology as well as 23 years of unpublished information on exploration. The Iran Cultural Heritage Organisation ICHO has only recently decided to form specialist subgroups in archeology in order to study the rich maritime history of the country. In 1999 the ICHO established an underwater archeology group in line with conventions for preserving underwater heritage sites as a research and field group supervised by the Archeology Research Institute although it only has three archeologists.

In 2006 it was announced that a robotic vehicle was to be sent into the Persian Gulf to search for the drowned port of Siraf. Once a trading centre, the port has been reclaimed by the waters over the past millennium.

"Although the use of robots in underwater archeology is now commonly practiced, this is the first time that the Iranian archeologists have applied such a tool for their research," according to Payvand Iran News :

REFERENCE: http://www.payvand.com/news/06/aug/1118.html

GOVARI RIVER, ORISSA, INDIA

In January 2004 it was reported by the 'Deccan Herald' that a huge Buddhist monastery, measuring 29 meters square, was unearthed from the Govari River in Kantikiari village by researcher Harischandra Prusty.

According to Dr Prusty, his team discovered the site after a local villager had informed him of its presence. The 18 room monastery had walls made of rare bricks. Other artifacts such as rock lamps and cooking pots were also discovered, confirming the spread of early Buddhism in Orissa.

The discovery gives credence to the theory by some Buddhist scholars such as Dr Satyakam Sengupta that the Buddha was born in Kapileswar village Orissa rather than Kapilavastu in Nepal. He supports this theory with evidence that a number of early Buddhist sites have been discovered in Orissa but not Nepal.

FUXIAN LAKE, CHINA

Fuxian Lake, near Kunming, has a surface area of 212 square km and an average depth of 87 meters. According to the history books, the city of Yuyuan in the north of Fuxian Lake once existed but disappeared from records after the Southern and Northern Dynasties (AD 420-589).

In the late 1990s local diver Geng Wei allegedly discovered a large city in the lake thought to span 2.4 square km in area. He claims to have seen many square boulders more than 1.4 meters in size scattered and piled deep underwater. In 2001 the local government launched the first large exploration of the lake which was broadcast live across the nation by China Central Television (CCTV). The submarine detected a 60 meter stone wall and divers unearthed a sherd of pottery embedded in the wall which was found to date back to the Han Dynasty (104 BC to 220 AD.)

In 2005 ten divers began a seven day search for ruins beneath the lake. On the first dive Geng videotaped three notches, each 1.2

253

meters long and 45 centimeters wide on a moss-covered square slate. The 'IY' notches "Support the idea that all the stones were once processed by humans," said Li Kunsheng, director of the Archeological Research Centre of Yunnan University.

Li Qingzhu, director of the Institute of the Chinese Academy of Social Sciences' was more cautious and pointed out that no pictures or evidence about the findings had been provided by the divers. Other dissenters are quick to point out that most buildings in the area were made of bamboo and not stone in ancient times. Li, however, was willing to concede that a city may have sunk during an earthquake in ancient times.

On January 16, 2006 Underwatertimes.com was reporting that Geng Wei had announced the discovery of eight main buildings including a round building and two large buildings with floors which resembled Mayan pyramids. The round building resembles a colosseum like structure with a 37 meter wide base and opening. One of the large buildings has three floors, a 60 meter wide base and lots of small steps linking the floors. Another building is even larger with a 63 meter wide base, five floors and a height of 21 meters. A 300 meter long and 5 to 7 meter wide road connects the two buildings.

http://www.underwatertimes.com/news.php?article_id=21643105879

On July 1, 2006 'Underwater Times' reported another investigation of the lake which started on June 13. As well as the buildings, they discovered numerous regularly placed stones featuring mysterious carvings. The pyramid like structure was reported to have stones ornamented with various designs and symbols. One stone has a small circle surrounded by seven radial lines, resembling the sun, while on the other side of the stone is a similar circle with only four radial lines.

Other carvings resembling masks were found on some of the stones. The flat cheeks and indented teeth of the masks do not resemble any known artistic style of the ancient Chinese.

Signs resembling the letters 'O' and '1' stones with seven holes carved in a design were also found. Some stones had carvings resembling the Roman numeral for '1' and the English letter 'y' arranged in a row. No-one is able to decipher these symbols, but

254

they are possibly older than 4,000 years when Chinese script was first developed.

Near this rock, there was another interesting discovery of a flat rock with many holes. There are five holes lined in a curve on one rock, about 15 to 20 centimeters apart. "They have smooth walls and flat bottoms, suggesting they are human-made," Geng said.

"Over an edge of stone piles, the water suddenly expanded before my eyes. A collapsed but still discernable stone staircase emerged under my body, slanting into deep water," said Zhao Yahui, a reporter with People's Daily who tried a 30-minute dive on the second day. He saw patterns on two or three rocks.

Senior local Archeologist Zhang Xinning thinks the relics may only be several hundred years old, when the place "had lots of stone buildings." He wonders if the relics resulted from one collapse or several collapses over different times.

The latest finds also throws doubts on the theory that the ruins belong to Yuyuan because this city was made of clay and wood, while the submerged ruins are made of stone.

http://www.underwatertimes.com/news.php?article_id=13510490786

According to the 'China Daily' shells attached to stones were carbon tested and estimated to be 1,750 years old. Although Yuyan City was still in existence during the Tang dynasty, the structures bear a resemblance to construction styles of the ancient Dian Country which disappeared after 86 BC. However, it is too early to come to a conclusion on the origins of these stones as long term archeological excavation and careful research are needed.

REFERENCES: 'Mysterious Fuxian Lake's Secrets Told' China Daily, July 8, 2007
http://www.chinadaily.com.cn/ezine/2007-08/17/content_6031188_2.htm
Underwatertimes.com
http://www.underwatertimes.com/news.php?article_id=21643105879
Underwatertimes.com
http://www.underwatertimes.com/news.php?article_id=13510490786
CRIEnglish.com
http://english.cri.cn/3166/2006/06/22/164@105428.htm

NORTHERN CHINA

On May 10, 2006 Associated Press reported that the ruins of a 2000 year old walled city had been found in a reservoir on China's northeastern border with North Korea. The mud covered ruins were exposed when the water level in the Yungfeng Reservoir was lowered for repairs. These ruins, near the present day city of Ji'an, are believed to date from the Han Dynasty, according to Xinhua News Agency.

LAKE CHINI, MALAYSIA

Lake Chini is a body of twelve interconnecting smaller lakes in Malaysia. It has unique waterlilies which are believed by the locals to have originated from Khmers who settled the area over a thousand years ago.

Apart from the myth that the lake contains a dragon like monster, another commonly held belief is that the ruins of an ancient Khmer city can be found beneath the surface of the lake. It is believed that the Khmers from Cambodia swept through Malaysia and Indochina in the fifth century AD and built a city. The local indigenous tribes of the area speak of legends of the city being deliberately flooded to avoid capture by Khmer enemies.

Another local legend states that the lake was originally a mountain called Gunung Chini. An unusual tree trunk oozed liquid when hit by a stick. One villager stuck is walking stick in the tree trunk and when it was retrieved, liquid gushed from it and submerged the mountain. People who had tasted the liquid drowned, but others survived. The liquid became Lake Chini.

Aerial photographs taken of the lake allegedly show "unfamiliar formations on the bottom that suggest the presence of structural foundations or canals." However there have never been any serious archeological studies of the area beyond some pre Islamic discoveries of Khmer pottery.

REFERENCE: http://www.nici.ru.nl/~peterh/srigumum/doc/origin.htm

LAKE TITICACA, BOLIVIA

Lake Titicaca, which straddles both Bolivia and Peru, is the highest navigable lake in the world at over 12,000 feet high. The local people believe that a sunken city called Wanaku lies in the depths of the lake as well as Inca gold which was hidden from the Spaniards. Such tales of treasure lured explorers like Jacques Cousteau to explore the lake in a submarine in 1968 but he only found ancient pottery. Other prospective treasure hunters face the hazards of high altitude diving.

In 2000 the BBC announced that a submerged temple had been discovered beneath the waters of the lake at a depth of thirty meters. An international group of archeologists and scientists from the Akakor Geographic Exploring consist of ten Italians, Germans, Bolivians and Romanians who made over two hundred dives. They claim there is evidence of a temple 200 meters long and 50 meters wide (660 feet by 160 feet), with signs of a paved road. A terrace for crops and an 800 meter long wall have also been sighted. This structure is thought to be 1,000 to 1,500 years old.

Lorenzo Epis, the Italian scientist leading the Atahuallpa 2000 scientific expedition, believes that the ruins are from the Tiwanaku culture. Eduardo Pareja, a Bolivian scientist who was among those who explored the site said the remains contained "conclusive proof" of the existence of a Pre-Columbian temple. Over eighteen days the team conducted and filmed over two hundred dives and were "euphoric" at the find.

However, other archeologists are less enthusiastic. While Bolivia's vice minister for Culture, Antonio Eguino denied the structure was a temple, believing it to be part of a terraced agricultural field, Bolivian archeologist Dr Carlos Ponce was not convinced that any concrete proof of a structure had been discovered.

Local Indian communities were also suspicious of the expedition, believing it was a bad omen to disrespect the lake which is the birthplace of their civilization.

REFERENCES: BBC NEWS, 17 October 2000
http://news.bbc.co.uk/2/hi/americas/976880.stm

BBCNEWS 23 August, 2000 **http://news.bbc.co.uk/2/hi/americas/892616. stm**

ROCK LAKE, WISCONSIN

Stone structures have been reported in Rock Lake, Wisconsin for over a century. The Rock Lake Research Society **http://www.rocklakeresearch.com/history.htm** gives a chronology of the region from the age of copper mining in about 3000 BC until the present. According to this chronology:

- In 1830-40 white settlers saw strange stones sticking out of the water which the Indians refer to as 'rock tepees' of the 'ancient foreigners.'
- A dam caused the lake waters to rise and submerge the structures.
- In 1900 the Wilson brothers spotted mysterious structures underwater while duck hunting. Dozens of people converged on the lake and divers were able to touch a pyramidal structure which is said to be 100 feet long and of undetermined height. A week later the water conditions changed and the lake was permanently silted.
- By the 1930s several divers had located the pyramids but when the state archeologist Charles Brown hired professional divers, nothing was found and cries of fraud abounded.
- Diver Max Nohl tested his earliest scuba invention at Rock Lake and found a tall cone shaped pyramid in the south end of the lake which is made of small stones.
- In 1967 Scuba instructor John Kennedy measured a structure twenty foot high, and about 100 feet long. An article appeared in a 1967 issue of 'Skin Diver' magazine.
- In 1989 author Frank Joseph dived and began with modern electronic sweeps of the lake, finding several anomalies that could be man-made structures.
- In 1991 Joseph published 'The Lost Pyramids of Rock Lake' and 'Atlantis in Wisconsin' although he was unable to provide any clear photographs.
- In 1998 Archie Eschborn and Jack LeTourneau planned an expedition in July including equipment such as side-scan sonar technology, DPGS (Differential Global Positioning

Satellite), underwater infrared video photography cameras as well as a 28 feet research vessel named 'R. V Tyranena'. The group gathered experts and called themselves 'Rock Lake Research Society' with the mission to document and preserve the structures beneath the lake.

• In 1999 three expeditions were completed and the structures were able to be located by Global Positioning Satellites. Several dives under the direction of Dr James Scherz were made to seek new sites and 'The Chicago Tribune' ran a feature story.

• Additional sonar side scan work was completed in May 2000.

• The Rock Lake Research Society conducted extensive aerial photography, capturing new features in the water and on the land, including the 'East Wall Structure'.

• The lake was surveyed by helicopter and sites marked on the surface. The Tyranena was donated to charity and a smaller vessel secured.

• The book 'The Dragon in the Lake' documenting four years of research at Rock Lake was published in December 2004 by Archie Eschborn, the same year a new boat R.V Tyranena 11 was outfitted.

• RLRS acquires its own side-scan sonar which can compare sonar images and GPS data with earlier data for accuracy. The History Channel arrived to shoot a segment for their new series 'Digging for the Truth'. This segment aired in January 2006.

REFERENCE: Rock Lake Research Society **http://www. rocklakeresearch.com/history.htm**
Early drawing of Rock lake structures.

FLORIDA CAVES AND LAKES

At the end of the Ice Age many large mammals persisted in Florida long after they became extinct in the north. As the sea level rose and the groundwater level inland was raised, this in turn raised the water level in rivers, springs, and low lying limestone caves.

Until the 1970s few archeologists believed that drowned land sites containing artifacts could exist. A 1966 paper 'Archeological

Potential of the Atlantic Continental Shelf' by K.O. Emery and R.L Edwards of the Woods Hole Oceanographic Institution reached the conclusion that submerged archeological sites probably lay on the Atlantic Continental Shelf.

The first discovery emerged in 1959 at Warm Mineral Springs when amateur archeologist William Royal discovered a human cranium with intact brain material buried on a ledge 13 feet deep. Although the prevailing attitude was that these were modern remains of a drowned Indian, the Warm Mineral Springs project was initiated in 1973. Archeologists have proved that the burial occurred on a ledge 17 meters (56 feet) above the old water level. About 20 other individuals were buried on this ledge. The sinkhole has also revealed a shell hook from a spear thrower about 10,300 years ago. Animal remains such as turkey, raccoon, cougar, white tailed deer, opossum and others were discovered, while extinct animals such as sabre toothed tiger and ground sloth, were recovered from a lower level.

Various other sites such as Little Salt Springs yielded evidence of an Archaic cemetery on the banks of this water filled, collapsed sinkhole. Archeologist Carl Clausen found a number of human burials on a shallow ledge sloping down to 10 m (33 ft) below the present water level. These skeletons are from 5,000 to 7,000 years old, placing them in the Archaic stage. Douglas Beach has well preserved remains such as Pleistocene tree stumps intact beneath the sand, despite the constant action of the waves. The Tampa Bay is rich in submerged Palaeo-Indian remains such as shells, middens and arrow points. Fish Creek site in this region has revealed projectile points and tools from the Archaic stage.

The Acullia, St Marks, Wakulla and Chipola rivers of northern Florida are reputedly rich in fossil human and animal remains.

On June 4, 2007 the Associated Press published an article on how drought affected Lake Okeechobee had exposed human bone fragments, pottery and even boats. The lake is just about nine feet deep, four to five feet below normal, exposing many areas for the first time in years. More than 17 sites have been identified in Palm Beach County's part of the lake in the past three months. The drought has bared a section of the lake up to a mile and a half wide

260

at some points.

The bones are likely to be five hundred to a thousand years old, or even older. No complete skeletons, skulls or other large fragments have been found, but the boats from modern times are relatively intact. One of these vessels is 50 to 60 feet long; others include a steam powered dredge and a steam ship.

REFERENCE:
http://abcnews.go.com/Technology/wireStory?id=3244104

MACDONALD LAKE, ONTARIO

In 2005 an unusual formation of seven rocks was discovered at a depth of 40 feet in MacDonald Lake, Ontario, Canada. Initially it was considered a complex of glacial rocks but several geologists and archeologists who saw images of the object—a 1,000 pound rock sitting on smaller stones at each end which, in turn, were resting on a massive slab on top of the ledge, thought it might be man-made.

An underwater geologist examined the rock assembly closely and came to the unequivocal conclusion it was an artificial structure even though no signs of tool usage or decorative images were observed. Geologists believe that it was created sometime between 9000 and 7000 BCE when a great drought ensured that the Great Lakes were up to 50 meters lower than at present.

REFERENCE: http://www.stonepages.com/news/archives/002729.html

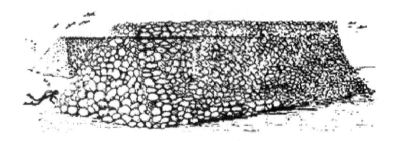

An artist's drawing of the tent-like pyramid structures beneath the waters of Rock Lake, Wisconsin.

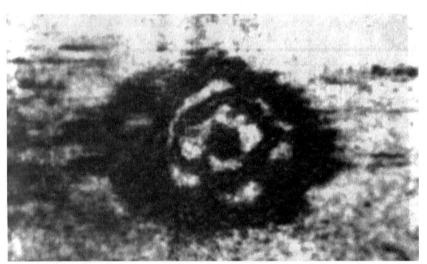

A side-scan sonar image by Martin Klein of stone structures on the bottom of Loch Ness in Scotland.

A Mayan panel from Coba in the Yucatan discovered by the German archeologist Teobert Mahler in the 1930s. It apparently shows the destruction of Atlantis or some lost Caribbean land, in a catastrophe involving an active volcano and water drowning the land. The panel was destroyed during the bombing of Berlin and the destruction of Archeological Museum there.

PART 9
MEDIEVAL AND MODERN SUNKEN RUINS

INUNDATED COASTAL TOWNS OF MEDIEVAL EUROPE
PORT ROYAL, JAMAICA, 1692
BOWOOD, ENGLAND
TOWNS & VILLAGES BENEATH RESERVOIRS
NEW HORIZONS
EVALUATING CONTROVERSIAL SUNKEN CLAIMS
CONFIRMED UNDERWATER SITES

Many medieval to modern settlements and towns now lie underwater due to subsidence, earthquakes and the construction of modern reservoirs.

INUNDATED COASTAL TOWNS OF MEDIEVAL EUROPE

VINETA was an ancient town in either Germany or Poland on the Baltic sea. It has been identified with Wolin, Poland, Usedom island, Germany and Barth in Meclenburg-Vorpommern.

The town was mentioned in several historical sources and reported to be the most powerful port of the Baltic Sea by traders in the 11th and 12th centuries. It was destroyed by the Danish fleet in 1159 although there is a legend that it sank during a storm because of the sinfulness of its inhabitants.

Many archeologists have searched for Vineta on the Baltic Sea with no success and it has been dismissed as a legend by scholars.

DUNWICH, ENGLAND is now a coastal village but during the Middle Ages was a prosperous seaport at the centre of the wool trade. Its natural harbor has been lost to erosion. At its height Dunwich was a large port with a population of around 3,000, five houses of religious orders, three chapels and two hospitals.

In 1286 a large storm inundated much of the town and the Dunwich River was partly silted up. Although residents saved the harbor, it was destroyed by another storm in 1328 which also swept away the nearby village of Newton. Another huge storm destroyed four hundred of the remaining houses and the rest of the town fell into the sea over the next few centuries.

In 1971 historian and diver Stuart Bacon located the remains of All Saints Church off the coast during a diving expedition. In 1973 he also discovered the ruins of St Peters Church which succumbed to the sea in the 18th century. More recently he has located remains of shipbuilding industry on the site.

According to a Wikipedia article, these buildings were lost in Dunwich:

> • St Bartholemew's, St Michael's and the Benedictine Cell were lost in the storm of 1328.
> • St John the Baptist church was a cruciform structure. In 1510 a pier was erected to act as a breakwater from the sea, but it was demolished before falling over the cliffs.
> • St Martin's was lost to the sea between 1335 and 1408.
> • St Peter's lost its east gable in 1688 and the whole building fell off the cliff in 1697.
> • St Francis's Chapel by the Dunwich River and St

Katherine's Chapel were both lost in the 16th century.
- St Anthony's Chapel was lost around 1330.
- Blackfriars Dominican Priory finally fell into the sea in 1717.

http://en.wikipedia.org/wiki/Dunwich

In January 2008 the BBC online posted a story on a forthcoming expedition to explore Dunwich's ruins with hi tech underwater cameras. Stuart Bacon and Professor Sear from the University of Southampton will use the latest sonar, underwater camera and scanning equipment to build up a picture of the sunken Dunwich that lies between 10 ft (3m) and 50 ft (15 m) down.

The dives will take place from June 2008 which money raised from the Esmee Fairburn Foundation.

REFERENCES:

http://news.bbc.co.uk/2/hi/uk_news/england/7187239.stm

RUNGHOLT, GERMANY was a wealthy city which sank between a storm surge in the North Sea on January 16, 1362. Rungholt was situated on the island of Strand which was almost washed away in 1634, with only two small islets as remaining fragments.

In the 1920s and 30s some remains of the city were discovered, suggesting a population of about 2,000, revealing that it was a major port. Relics were being found in the Wadden sea until the late 20th century, but shifting sediments have carried the last of these into the sea.

SAEFTINGHE, NETHERLANDS was a city which existed until 1584 in an area know known as the *Verdronken Land van Saeftinghe* (Drowned Land of Saeftinghe).

Saeftinghe was drained in the 13th century to create a city and until 1570 was a very fertile polder. It was one of the most prosperous areas in the region, along with Namen and Casuwele. In the great All Saint's Flood of 1570 much land, including some in Belguim, was inundated, although Saeftinghe and surrounding land remained dry. In 1587 during the Eighty Years War the Dutch soldiers destroyed the dike and Saeftinghe sunk into the waters of the Scheldt.

Although there have been several attempts to find the city, none have been successful.

REFERENCES: Wikipedia entries on Dunwich, Rungholt and Saeftinghe

BBC NEWS, January 14, 2008

PORT ROYAL JAMAICA QUAKE 1692

Port Royal in Jamaica was renowned in its heyday as the 'toughest and wickedest port' in the western hemisphere. Founded by the Spanish, it was captured by the English in 1655 and fortified to protect the city of Kingston. Hoping to protect their island from the Spanish, the English allowed buccaneers who roamed the Spanish Main to settle in Port Royal. The most famous of them, Henry Morgan, was even knighted by the king and made Lieutenant Governor of Jamaica. Port Royal prospered immensely and the narrow streets were lined with warehouses, slave markets, bars and brothels.

On June 7th 1692, three strong earthquakes struck Port Royal in the space of a few minutes. The sands liquefied, buildings crumbled and the whole shorefront of the town slid about twentyfive feet beneath the waves. Between one and three thousand people, half the population, perished. Eventually a new town of Port Royal was built by the British but it too was destroyed by a devastating quake in 1907 which submerged more areas.

In the early twentieth century Robert Marx of Brooklyn was so intrigued by the story that he was determined to find the sunken city, complete with the church where the skeletons of the congregation still sat. With a mask and fins he failed on his initial attempt to find Port Royal, but after training to become a marine archeologist, he returned to excavate the site. In the meantime underwater explorer Edwin Link had used his salvage vessel 'Sea Diver' and employed US Navy divers to recover a cannon and other artifacts.

Marx was able to map the sunken city which was mostly under mud or encrusted with coral. The church had been covered by so much mud that its site had become dry land again. Marx and his divers had to deal with minimal visibility and mud, suffering many cuts from the coral and sea urchin spines.

Despite the fact that locals had plundered the ruins for centuries, Marx was able to discover many items such as pewter glasses from the tavern, medicine bottles from the druggist's store and fittings located at a shipyard. After over two years of hard work, Marx turned his last finds over to the Jamaican government and departed.

From 1981 to 1990, the Institute of Nautical Archaeology, in cooperation with the Nautical Archaeology Program at Texas A&M University and the Jamaica National Heritage Trust, began underwater archaeological investigations of the submerged portion of Port Royal. They discovered that while the waterfront was submerged by waves, another area sank vertically, and thus the buildings were better preserved in this area. The team also excavated many buildings and has been able to map the original shorefront. The results of their excavations can be found at REFERENCE: **http://nautarch.tamu.edu/portroyal/archhist.htm**

BOWOOD VILLAGE, ENGLAND

On July 18, 2007 the BBC reported that a lost village, which had been deliberately flooded by a lake in the eighteenth century, had been discovered by divers. Old maps showed a community called Manning's Hill where the lake now stands.

Bowood house was built on the site of a hunting lodge in 1725 and the first Marquis of Landsdowne commissioned 'Capability' Brown to create 2000 acres of parkland and wilderness. He created a 45 acre lake from a pond after flooding a valley.

There had been rumours about a flooded village but the current Bowood owner, Lord Landsdowne was unable to locate it with scuba gear twenty years ago.

Diver Jon Dodsworth, leader of the Calne Sub-Aqua Club, led a team which used sonar equipment during the three one hour dives. The team discovered stone walls and the remains of two cottages under the lake. "We pulled up stone with paint on it, and dry stone walls. It was localised rubble, " he said.

The group has no excavation equipment to investigate further.

269

TOWNS AND VILLAGES BENEATH RESERVOIRS

During the twentieth century, large scale hydro projects in the US, UK, Asia, Europe and Australia resulted in many villages and towns being deliberately submerged. This chapter examines a few examples of vanished towns and villages.

UK The Midlands area, centre of the industrial revolution, has seen numerous villages drowned by reservoirs since the nineteenth century.

The Derbyshire area has numerous dams such as Ladybower Dam, Staunton Harold Reservoir, Carsington and Rutland Water. In 1935 construction begun on the Ladybower Dam and was completed in 1943. Two villages, Ashopton and Derwent, were sacrificed, complete with stone cottages, lanes, a seventeenth century church and an old mansion. Derwent Church had to undergo exhumation of its graves for reburial, but its tower was left intact. The Packhorse Bridge at Derwent was moved stone by stone and rebuilt at Slippery Stones near the Howden reservoir. The spire of Derwent Church can sometimes be sighted during times when the water level remains low.

http://www.bbc.co.uk/insideout/eastmidlands/series4/east_midlands_reservoirs.shtml

ITALY—LAGO DI VAGLI Vagli Lake is a hydroelectric basin beneath which the village of Fabbriche di Careggine was submerged in the 1940s. Every ten years the lake is emptied for maintenance work and the phantom village is revealed with its stone buildings.

ARGENTINA, FEDERACION In 1979 the residents of the Argentine city Federacion were relocated so that their city could be demolished and flooded to create a dam on the Uruguay River.

The project, which was carried out during the dictatorship of 1976 to 1983, saw the creation of a new Federacion, 23 km from the original.

When the water is at its normal level main landmarks of the original Federacion can be located by erected posts which identify the main landmarks. Once a year the water drops low enough to allow the residents to walk or drive over the old ruins of the city's streets.

USA—Hundreds of towns and villages have been flooded across the most states of the USA during the past century. A website of the Waterboro Public Library, Drowned Towns has an extensive list of these places.

http://www.waterborolibrary.org/mystlists/drownedtowns.htm#real

Another website **http://www.clui.org/clui_4_1/lotl/v28/b.html** describes some of these doomed settlements, including Elbwoods, North Dakota, Kenneth California, Neversink NY, Enfield MA, Butler, Tennessee and St Thomas, Nevada.

AUSTRALIA, JINDABYNE Old Jindabyne on Lake Jindabyne was one of the three towns (with Talbingo and Adaminaby) which were flooded by the huge Snowy Mountains Hydroelectric Scheme in 1967. The streets and houses were left mainly intact and can still be reached by high altitude divers in the 4,000 feet high artificial lake.

Lake Jindabyne was created by damming the Snowy River. Parts of the original town, including the Catholic church were moved to higher ground in New Jindabyne. The old town existed below the current settlement of East Jindabyne.

The Australian poet Douglas Stewart wrote this poem 'Farewell to Jindabyne' which includes this verse:

"Let us lament for Jindabyne, it is going to be drowned,

Let us shed tears, as many as the occasion warrants;

The Snowy, the Thredbo and the Eucumbene engulf it,

Combining their copious torrents."

The Abyss Diving website has interesting photos and descriptions of dives to old Jindabyne.

REFERENCE: **http://www.abyss.com.au/Jindabine.html**

271

NEW HORIZONS

The new millennium has seen much more interest in underwater archeology in the New World, Australia and even several Middle Eastern countries. Although no concrete evidence of human habitation at underwater sites has been discovered, this neglected area of study is finally gaining credibility and funding.

USA

In March 2007 an expedition of underwater explorers, including geologists, biologists and marine archeologists, failed to locate any evidence of human habitation off the Texas coastline. Led by Robert Ballard and dubbed 'Secrets of the Gulf', the team travelled from Galveston to coral reef Flower Garden banks aboard the SSV 'Carolyn Chousest' with the US Navy's nuclear powered research submarine in tow.

The submarine Argus, with wheels for driving along the seabed, allowed scientists to study the reef from a depth of 40 feet. Unfortunately it was inhibited by bad weather and technical difficulties and was unable to find evidence of ancient habitation along the sunken coastline.

REFERENCE: **http://www.khou.com/news/local/galveston/stories/khou070313_ac_galvexplorers.ad373de.html**

CANADA

A recent theory, that ancient Asian seafarers reached the Americas thousands of years before the Siberians migrated across the Beringia land bridge, is being debated in academic circles. Not only are several sites such as Monte Verde, Chile, older than the Clovis sites, but archeologists now acknowledge that the earliest traces of human habitation may lie underwater.

An article in 'Times Colonist' by Randy Boswell on August 21, 2007 discusses such finds as a 10,000 year old skeleton from an Alaskan cave which is genetically linked to Japanese and Tibetan populations. These genetic traits can be found in aboriginal groups along the west coasts of North and South America.

In 2003 Simon Fraser University scientists reported that

various caves along the British Columbia coast contain 16,000 year old bones of goats and bears, suggesting that humans may have hunted there before the sea levels rose.

Tom Koppel, a Canadian author of 'Lost Worlds—Rewriting Prehistory; How New Science is tracing America's Ice Age Mariners' wrote; "If scientists on the Pacific coast were right, we also became bold seafarers at a very early date, maritime people who built boats and braved the stormy and icebound shores of the North Pacific."

http://www.canada.com/victoriatimescolonist/news/story.
html?id=34805893-6a53-46f5-a864-a96d53991051&k=39922&p=1

BERINGIA

A team of scientists from the University of Florida's Department of Anthropology believe that the North American continent was settled in three phases. Beringia, the now sunken land bridge between Asia and the Americas, provided a 20,000 year layover for migrating tribes who were blocked by large glaciers from heading south.

Beringia was similar to the territories of Siberia or Mongolia, so the migrating tribes may have subsisted by fishing and hunting. During their stay in Beringia many mutations developed in their DNA. According to the theory the tribes moved south after the glaciers melted and their sites were drowned by the rising waters.

According to Andrew Kitchen, a PhD candidate of the anthropology department, "Our theory predicts much of the archeological evidence is underwater. That may explain why scientists hadn't really considered a long-term occupation of Beringia."

http://www.enews20.com/news_People_Entering_the_New_World_
Were_Delayed_by_Glaciers_For_20000_Years_05863.html

AUSTRALIA

Sydney based archeologist Cosmos Coroneos claims that about six thousand years ago the coast of Sydney was about 20-30 km off shore. He believes that there is probably a lot of evidence of Aboriginal occupation that is now underwater and has written a thesis on the subject.

Unfortunately previous attempts to find such submerged sites in Australia have been unsuccessful because of their exposure to wild waves which have washed away sediment. Researchers have decided to focus on sheltered bays in the Sydney area such as Port Hacking which contain underwater caves as likely candidate sites. They hope to obtain permission from the local Aboriginal landowners to collect sediment cores from the caves in the hope of finding stone tools.

Coroneos has worked on submerged archeological sites in the Mediterranean and bemoans that underwater archeology is not taken seriously in Australia.

http://abc.net.au/science/news/stories/2007/2012104.htm

NORTH SEA

In March 2008 a Neanderthal 'treasure trove' from the bottom of the North Sea was announced by archeologists. 28 Neanderthal flint axes recovered off the British East Anglian coast were spotted by an amateur archeologist when a consignment of North Sea gravel arrived at the Dutch port of Flushing. According to 'The Independent': "Archaeologists now suspect that some Neanderthal landscapes have survived under the North Sea. What's more, they are now certain that hundreds or even thousands of square miles of post-Ice Age prehistoric landscapes do survive there. On land they have largely been destroyed or degraded by centuries of agriculture, later human settlement and natural erosion."

http://www.independent.co.uk/news/uk/home-news/neanderthal-treasure-trove-at-bottom-of-sea-793678.html

In the southern North Sea Dutch prehistorians working with North Sea fisherman have identified about 100 Neanderthal flint axes, Palaeolithic bones and flints and the remains of thousands of mammoths, woolly rhinos and other Ice Age animals.

A proposed conference with British and Dutch archeologists will formulate a joint program of North Sea research. It will also included German, Belgian, Danish and Norwegian archeologists.
REFERENCES: Galveston.co 'No signs of underwater human habitation found'
http://www.khou.com/news/local/galveston/stories/khou070313_ac_galvexplorers.ad373de.html

'Times Colonist' August 21, 2007 "Were seafarers living here 16,000 years ago?'
http://www.canada.com/victoriatimescolonist/news/story.html?id=34805893-6a53-46f5-a864-a96d53991051&k=39922&p=1
News in Science, ABC online, 'Treasures may be hiding in sheltered bays' August 24, 2007
http://abc.net.au/science/news/stories/2007/2012104.htm
eNews 2.0 February 16, 2008
http://www.enews20.com/news_People_Entering_the_New_World_Were_Delayed_by_Glaciers_For_20000_Years_05863.html

EVALUATING SUNKEN RUIN CLAIMS

SPARTEL AS ATLANTIS:
ADVOCATES —Jacques Collina-Girard, Dr Gutscher, Georges Diaz-Montexano
PRO – Lies just beyond the Pillars of Hercules as predicted by Plato, sank about 12,000 years ago.
AGAINST – Much smaller than Plato's dimensions, no ruins discovered on surveys.

CADIZ , SPAIN AS ATLANTIS:
ADVOCATES – E.M Whishaw, Dr Maxine Asher, Georgeos Diaz-Montexano, Dr Rainer Kuehne
PRO — Is beyond the Pillars of Hercules, Asher has provided video footage of what appear to be structures from this area.
AGAINST — Her ruins are disputed by archeologists.

TARTESSOS
ADVOCATES — Adolf Schultern believes it can be located in Doñana National Park, the same place that Kuehne believes to be Atlantis.
PRO – Possibility of ruins beneath the wetlands of this national park.
AGAINST – Kuehne relies on only one or two aerial photos of the area to craft his Atlantis in Doñana National Park thesis.

SANTORINI AS ATLANTIS:

ADVOCATES – K.T. Frost, Professor Galanopoulos, James Mavor

PRO – Located near Greece and its Minoan culture has elements of Plato's Atlantis such as bull worship, maritime civilization etc. If Plato's date of 9,000 years is far too old, the Minoan culture existed 900 years before the Greek civilization. There is the possibility that Plato overestimated the age of Atlantis by tenfold. Santorini was destroyed by a massive volcano which created huge tsunamis.

AGAINST – Located in the Mediterranean and not the Atlantic Ocean. It is a stretch to believe that Plato overestimated the age and size of Atlantis tenfold. This is a classical case of facts being altered to fit a theory but this theory has been adopted by mainstream archeologists.

PRE GREEK RUINS IN ALEXANDRIA

ADVOCATES — Jondet, Graham Hancock

PRO — Anomalous ruins beyond the harbor Hellenistic ruins. In July 2007 evidence of pre Hellenistic settlement was discovered in samples recovered from the harbour.

AGAINST – The ruins beneath the Pharos are likely to have come from the legendary lighthouse, not an earlier culture.

ATLANTIS IN CYPRUS CLAIMS

ADVOCATES – Robert Sarmast

PRO – Cyprus was much larger at the end of the Ice Age. Sonar images of the plateau reveal what resembles an artificial platform called the Acropolis.

AGAINST — Critics call his structures mud volcanoes which are 100,000 years old. An expedition in 2007 failed to discover any artificial structures off Cyprus. Sarmast admitted the formations were natural.

ATLANTIS IN MALTA CLAIMS

ADVOCATES —Hubert Zeitlmair and Dr Anton Mifsud. Others amateur archeologists like Shaun Arrigo are convinced there are ruins beneath the seas of Malta.

PRO — Malta was much larger during the last Ice Age and its temples are the oldest in the world. There are enigmatic cart ruts as well as alleged underwater structures at Sliema and Janet Johan. While there is no evidence linking Malta to Atlantis, the claim of unidentified underwater ruins has one of the strongest merits in the Mediterranean.

AGAINST — A total lack of interest by the Maltese archeological authorities points to either a total lack of imagination or a deliberate cover-up.

ATLANTIS ON THE AMPERE SEAMOUNT
ADVOCATES: Vladimir Marakuyev, Andrei Aksyonov

PRO — Photographs taken of stones which resemble artificial features.

AGAINST — Difficult to evaluate Soviet claims. The photos are difficult to interpret. Some people see steps, others see natural features.

ATLANTIS ON THE CELTIC SHELF
ADVOCATES — Viatcheslav Koudriavtsev

PRO — This area was above water during the height of the Ice Age. It fits the geological descriptions given by Plato.

AGAINST — No discoveries of submerged ruins and apparently no follow up expedition to test this thesis.

ATLANTIS IN THE AZORES OR CANARIES
ADVOCATES — Egerton Sykes, Ignatius Donnelly

PRO — In the general location of Plato's Atlantis. The Azores is a volcanic group of islands. Formations resembling ruins have been photographed off Lanzarote Island.

AGAINST — No expedition has located any ruins near the Azores. The Lanzarote ruins are many km away in the Canaries.

RUINS IN BIMINI, ANDROS AND CAY SAL
ADVOCATES — Dr Manson Valentine, Dr Greg Little, Bill Donato

PRO — Was above land 8,000 years ago. Bimini Road has many features of a man-made structure such as a harbour. Recent expeditions have revealed more man-made features on islands of Andros and Cay Sal as well as stone artifacts such as anchors.

AGAINST — Scientists have proclaimed the structures to be natural beachrock.

RUINS OFF CUBA

ADVOCATES — Andrew Collins, Paulina Zelitsky and her husband Paul Weinzweig

PRO — Side-scan sonar and videotape reveals geometric shapes which bear a strong resemblance to Mayan buildings.

AGAINST – No self respecting historian, archeologist or geologist will support any thesis that claims a city could exist over two km beneath the surface of the ocean. No ruins have ever been discovered so deep.

RUINS OFF PERU

ADVOCATES – Robert Menzies

PRO – Claims that architectural features have been photographed in the trench off the coast of Peru.

AGAINST — No supporting evidence has been published.

RUINS AT YONAGUNI ISLAND

ADVOCATES — Graham Hancock, Masaaki Kimura

PRO — Formations with strong architectural features such as steps, right angles, carvings and even a road.

AGAINST – Critics like Robert Schoch and Wolf Wichmann claim these features also appear on the land and can be explained by coastal erosion.

RUINS OFF THE PESCADORES

ADVOCATES – Steve Shin

PRO – Formations strongly resembling walls and other structures.

AGAINST – No supporting historical evidence.

RUINS OFF TAMIL NADU

ADVOCATES — S. Rao, Sundaresh, Gao, Tripoli

PRO — Excavations have been carried out at Poompuhur revealing ancient structures. Excavations at Mahabalipuram also show promise of revealing ancient settlement.

AGAINST — Although Poompuhur is acknowledged as a site, recent monsoons have almost destroyed it.

RUINS IN THE GULF OF CAMBAY

ADVOCATES —Director Dr S. Kathiroli and geological consultant S. Badrinarayan

PRO – Side-scan sonar images, artifacts recovered.

AGAINST – S.Rao and others do not accept any of the findings. This area was above water long before any recorded civilization in India or elsewhere.

FUXIAN LAKE, CHINA

ADVOCATES – Geng Wei

PRO – Reports of stone structures and other artifacts.

AGAINST – No evidence has been presented to archeologists.

LAKE TITICACA, BOLIVIA

ADVOCATES —Akakor Geographic Exploring Team

PRO— Claims of structure (s) from Tiwanaku culture.

AGAINST—No evidence has been presented.

ROCK LAKE WISCONSIN

ADVOCATES — Rock Lake Research Society

PRO—Claims of structures date back over a century. Claims ruins have been mapped and their location recorded.

AGAINST — Archeologists do not accept there are stone ruins beneath a lake in Wisconsin.

CONFIRMED UNDERWATER SITES

According to Nicholas Flemming, there are thousands of prehistoric submerged sites around all inhabited continents. He wrote, "Thousands of Mesolithic settlements have been discovered by the archeologists on the floor of the Baltic, containing hearths, fish weirs, canoes, burials, flint-knapping tools, and artifacts of bone, wood and antlers... Other sites have been discovered around the North Sea, and fishermen continuously retrieve several tons of Pleistocene mammal bones each year from the sediments of the southern North Sea. Large numbers of cold climate fauna bones are retrieved, including mammoth, reindeer, ox, wolf and bear, dating back to 35ky BP." (Submarine Prehistoric archeology of the Indian continental shelf: A potential resource', 'Current Science', Vol. 86, No. 9, (May 2004)

The following is a list of better known excavated sites, particularly from Mesolithic or Classical times. It is by no means comprehensive.

GREECE—Pavlo Petri, Helike, Olous, Kenchreai, Portochele, Plitra, Mochlos, Pseira, Chersonisos, Agaioi Theodoroi
ITALY—Pozzuoli, Baiae, Pyrgi, Spina, Motya, Syracuse
LEBANON—Sidon, Tyre
TURKEY—Kekova,(Simena) Myndos
BLACK SEA—Phasis, Dioscuria
EGYPT—Menouthis, Heraklion
CYPRUS—Akamas, Salamis
ISRAEL – Caesarea, Atlit, Akko
LIBYA – Apollonia, Sabratha, Phycus
TUNISIA—Carthage, Lemta
ALGERIA —Caesarea
SARDINIA —Nora
UK –Tyneside, Isle of Wight, Seahenge
DENMARK – Tybrind Vig, Ronaes Skov
FRANCE – Er Lannic, Gauv'Inis, Fossae Marinae
MEXICO – Isla Cerritas
INDIA – Poompuhur, Mahabalipuram, Dwarka
JAPAN —Tokonami River (Jomon culture)
POHNPEI
SWITZERLAND – Lake Constence, Lake Neuchatel, Lake Biel
RUSSIA Lake Iss

SECRETS OF THE MYSTERIOUS VALLEY
by Christopher O'Brien

No other region in North America features the variety and intensity of unusual phenomena found in the world's largest alpine valley, the San Luis Valley of Colorado and New Mexico. Since 1989, Christopher O'Brien has documented thousands of high-strange accounts that report UFOs, ghosts, crypto-creatures, cattle mutilations, skinwalkers and sorcerers, along with portal areas, secret underground bases and covert military activity. This mysterious region at the top of North America has a higher incidence of UFO reports than any other area of the continent and is the publicized birthplace of the "cattle mutilation" mystery. Hundreds of animals have been found strangely slain during waves of anomalous aerial craft sightings. Is the government directly involved? Are there underground bases here? Does the military fly exotic aerial craft in this valley that are radar-invisible below 18,000 feet? These and many other questions are addressed in this all-new, work by one of America's top paranormal investigators. Take a fantastic journey through one of the world's most enigmatic locales!

460 PAGES. 6x9 PAPERBACK. ILLUSTRATED. BIBLIOGRAPHY. $19.95. CODE: SOMV

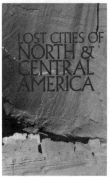

LOST CITIES OF NORTH & CENTRAL AMERICA
by David Hatcher Childress

Down the back roads from coast to coast, maverick archaeologist and adventurer David Hatcher Childress goes deep into unknown America. With this incredible book, you will search for lost Mayan cities and books of gold, discover an ancient canal system in Arizona, climb gigantic pyramids in the Midwest, explore megalithic monuments in New England, and join the astonishing quest for lost cities throughout North America. From the war-torn jungles of Guatemala, Nicaragua and Honduras to the deserts, mountains and fields of Mexico, Canada, and the U.S.A., Childress takes the reader in search of sunken ruins, Viking forts, strange tunnel systems, living dinosaurs, early Chinese explorers, and fantastic lost treasure. Packed with both early and current maps, photos and illustrations.

590 PAGES. 6x9 PAPERBACK. ILLUSTRATED. FOOTNOTES. BIBLIOGRAPHY. INDEX. $16.95. CODE: NCA

LOST CITIES & ANCIENT MYSTERIES OF SOUTH AMERICA
by David Hatcher Childress

Rogue adventurer and maverick archaeologist David Hatcher Childress takes the reader on unforgettable journeys deep into deadly jungles, high up on windswept mountains and across scorching deserts in search of lost civilizations and ancient mysteries. Travel with David and explore stone cities high in mountain forests and hear fantastic tales of Inca treasure, living dinosaurs, and a mysterious tunnel system. Whether he is hopping freight trains, searching for secret cities, or just dealing with the daily problems of food, money, and romance, the author keeps the reader spellbound. Includes both early and current maps, photos, and illustrations, and plenty of advice for the explorer planning his or her own journey of discovery.

381 PAGES. 6x9 PAPERBACK. ILLUSTRATED. FOOTNOTES. BIBLIOGRAPHY. INDEX. $16.95. CODE: SAM

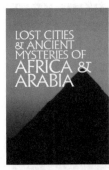

LOST CITIES & ANCIENT MYSTERIES OF AFRICA & ARABIA
by David Hatcher Childress
Childress continues his world-wide quest for lost cities and ancient mysteries. Join him as he discovers forbidden cities in the Empty Quarter of Arabia; "Atlantean" ruins in Egypt and the Kalahari desert; a mysterious, ancient empire in the Sahara; and more. This is the tale of an extraordinary life on the road: across war-torn countries, Childress searches for King Solomon's Mines, living dinosaurs, the Ark of the Covenant and the solutions to some of the fantastic mysteries of the past.
423 PAGES. 6x9 PAPERBACK. ILLUSTRATED. $14.95. CODE: AFA

LOST CITIES OF ATLANTIS, ANCIENT EUROPE & THE MEDITERRANEAN
by David Hatcher Childress
Childress takes the reader in search of sunken cities in the Mediterranean; across the Atlas Mountains in search of Atlantean ruins; to remote islands in search of megalithic ruins; to meet living legends and secret societies. From Ireland to Turkey, Morocco to Eastern Europe, and around the remote islands of the Mediterranean and Atlantic, Childress takes the reader on an astonishing quest for mankind's past. Ancient technology, cataclysms, megalithic construction, lost civilizations and devastating wars of the past are all explored in this book.
524 PAGES. 6x9 PAPERBACK. ILLUSTRATED. $16.95. CODE: MED

LOST CITIES OF CHINA, CENTRAL ASIA & INDIA
by David Hatcher Childress
Like a real life "Indiana Jones," maverick archaeologist David Childress takes the reader on an incredible adventure across some of the world's oldest and most remote countries in search of lost cities and ancient mysteries. Discover ancient cities in the Gobi Desert; hear fantastic tales of lost continents, vanished civilizations and secret societies bent on ruling the world; visit forgotten monasteries in forbidding snow-capped mountains with strange tunnels to mysterious subterranean cities! A unique combination of far-out exploration and practical travel advice, it will astound and delight the experienced traveler or the armchair voyager.
429 PAGES. 6x9 PAPERBACK. ILLUSTRATED. FOOTNOTES & BIBLIOGRAPHY. $14.95. CODE: CHI

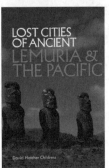

LOST CITIES OF ANCIENT LEMURIA & THE PACIFIC
by David Hatcher Childress
Was there once a continent in the Pacific? Called Lemuria or Pacifica by geologists, Mu or Pan by the mystics, there is now ample mythological, geological and archaeological evidence to "prove" that an advanced and ancient civilization once lived in the central Pacific. Maverick archaeologist and explorer David Hatcher Childress combs the Indian Ocean, Australia and the Pacific in search of the surprising truth about mankind's past. Contains photos of the underwater city on Pohnpei; explanations on how the statues were levitated around Easter Island in a clockwise vortex movement; tales of disappearing islands; Egyptians in Australia; and more.
379 PAGES. 6x9 PAPERBACK. ILLUSTRATED. FOOTNOTES & BIBLIOGRAPHY. $14.95. CODE: LEM

A HITCHHIKER'S GUIDE TO ARMAGEDDON
by David Hatcher Childress

With wit and humor, popular Lost Cities author David Hatcher Childress takes us around the world and back in his trippy finalé to the Lost Cities series. He's off on an adventure in search of the apocalypse and end times. Childress hits the road from the fortress of Megiddo, the legendary citadel in northern Israel where Armageddon is prophesied to start. Hitchhiking around the world, Childress takes us from one adventure to another, to ancient cities in the deserts and the legends of worlds before our own. In the meantime, he becomes a cargo cult god on a remote island off New Guinea, gets dragged into the Kennedy Assassination by one of the "conspirators," investigates a strange power operating out of the Altai Mountains of Mongolia, and discovers how the Knights Templar and their off-shoots have driven the world toward an epic battle centered around Jerusalem and the Middle East.

320 PAGES. 6x9 PAPERBACK. ILLUSTRATED. BIBLIOGRAPHY. INDEX. $16.95. CODE: HGA

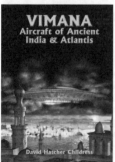

TECHNOLOGY OF THE GODS
The Incredible Sciences of the Ancients
by David Hatcher Childress

Childress looks at the technology that was allegedly used in Atlantis and the theory that the Great Pyramid of Egypt was originally a gigantic power station. He examines tales of ancient flight and the technology that it involved; how the ancients used electricity; megalithic building techniques; the use of crystal lenses and the fire from the gods; evidence of various high tech weapons in the past, including atomic weapons; ancient metallurgy and heavy machinery; the role of modern inventors such as Nikola Tesla in bringing ancient technology back into modern use; impossible artifacts; and more.

356 PAGES. 6x9 PAPERBACK. ILLUSTRATED. BIBLIOGRAPHY. $16.95. CODE: TGOD

VIMANA AIRCRAFT OF ANCIENT INDIA & ATLANTIS
by David Hatcher Childress, introduction by Ivan T. Sanderson

In this incredible volume on ancient India, authentic Indian texts such as the *Ramayana* and the *Mahabharata* are used to prove that ancient aircraft were in use more than four thousand years ago. Included in this book is the entire Fourth Century BC manuscript *Vimaanika Shastra* by the ancient author Maharishi Bharadwaaja. Also included are chapters on Atlantean technology, the incredible Rama Empire of India and the devastating wars that destroyed it.

334 PAGES. 6x9 PAPERBACK. ILLUSTRATED. $15.95. CODE: VAA

LOST CONTINENTS & THE HOLLOW EARTH
I Remember Lemuria and the Shaver Mystery
by David Hatcher Childress & Richard Shaver

Shaver's rare 1948 book *I Remember Lemuria* is reprinted in its entirety, and the book is packed with illustrations from Ray Palmer's *Amazing Stories* magazine of the 1940s. Palmer and Shaver told of tunnels running through the earth—tunnels inhabited by the Deros and Teros, humanoids from an ancient spacefaring race that had inhabited the earth, eventually going underground, hundreds of thousands of years ago. Childress discusses the famous hollow earth books and delves deep into whatever reality may be behind the stories of tunnels in the earth. Operation High Jump to Antarctica in 1947 and Admiral Byrd's bizarre statements, tunnel systems in South America and Tibet, the underground world of Agartha, the belief of UFOs coming from the South Pole, more.

344 PAGES. 6x9 PAPERBACK. ILLUSTRATED. $16.95. CODE: LCHE

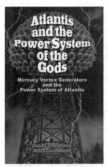

ATLANTIS & THE POWER SYSTEM OF THE GODS
by David Hatcher Childress and Bill Clendenon

Childress' fascinating analysis of Nikola Tesla's broadcast system in light of Edgar Cayce's "Terrible Crystal" and the obelisks of ancient Egypt and Ethiopia. Includes: Atlantis and its crystal power towers that broadcast energy; how these incredible power stations may still exist today; inventor Nikola Tesla's nearly identical system of power transmission; Mercury Proton Gyros and mercury vortex propulsion; more. Richly illustrated, and packed with evidence that Atlantis not only existed—it had a world-wide energy system more sophisticated than ours today.

246 PAGES. 6x9 PAPERBACK. ILLUSTRATED. $15.95. CODE: APSG

THE ANTI-GRAVITY HANDBOOK
edited by David Hatcher Childress

The new expanded compilation of material on Anti-Gravity, Free Energy, Flying Saucer Propulsion, UFOs, Suppressed Technology, NASA Cover-ups and more. Highly illustrated with patents, technical illustrations and photos. This revised and expanded edition has more material, including photos of Area 51, Nevada, the government's secret testing facility. This classic on weird science is back in a new format!

230 PAGES. 7x10 PAPERBACK. ILLUSTRATED. $16.95. CODE: AGH

ANTI–GRAVITY & THE WORLD GRID

Is the earth surrounded by an intricate electromagnetic grid network offering free energy? This compilation of material on ley lines and world power points contains chapters on the geography, mathematics, and light harmonics of the earth grid. Learn the purpose of ley lines and ancient megalithic structures located on the grid. Discover how the grid made the Philadelphia Experiment possible. Explore the Coral Castle and many other mysteries, including acoustic levitation, Tesla Shields and scalar wave weaponry. Browse through the section on anti-gravity patents, and research resources.

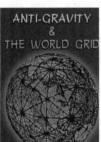

274 PAGES. 7x10 PAPERBACK. ILLUSTRATED. $14.95. CODE: AGW

ANTI–GRAVITY & THE UNIFIED FIELD
edited by David Hatcher Childress

Is Einstein's Unified Field Theory the answer to all of our energy problems? Explored in this compilation of material is how gravity, electricity and magnetism manifest from a unified field around us. Why artificial gravity is possible; secrets of UFO propulsion; free energy; Nikola Tesla and anti-gravity airships of the 20s and 30s; flying saucers as superconducting whirls of plasma; anti-mass generators; vortex propulsion; suppressed technology; government cover-ups; gravitational pulse drive; spacecraft & more.

240 PAGES. 7x10 PAPERBACK. ILLUSTRATED. $14.95. CODE: AGU

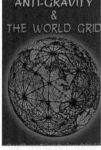

THE TIME TRAVEL HANDBOOK
A Manual of Practical Teleportation & Time Travel
edited by David Hatcher Childress

The Time Travel Handbook takes the reader beyond the government experiments and deep into the uncharted territory of early time travellers such as Nikola Tesla and Guglielmo Marconi and their alleged time travel experiments, as well as the Wilson Brothers of EMI and their connection to the Philadelphia Experiment—the U.S. Navy's forays into invisibility, time travel, and teleportation. Childress looks into the claims of time travelling individuals, and investigates the unusual claim that the pyramids on Mars were built in the future and sent back in time. A highly visual, large format book, with patents, photos and schematics. Be the first on your block to build your own time travel device!

316 PAGES. 7x10 PAPERBACK. ILLUSTRATED. $16.95. CODE: TTH

MAPS OF THE ANCIENT SEA KINGS
Evidence of Advanced Civilization in the Ice Age
by Charles H. Hapgood

Charles Hapgood has found the evidence in the Piri Reis Map that shows Antarctica, the Hadji Ahmed map, the Oronteus Finaeus and other amazing maps. Hapgood concluded that these maps were made from more ancient maps from the various ancient archives around the world, now lost. Not only were these unknown people more advanced in mapmaking than any people prior to the 18th century, it appears they mapped all the continents. The Americas were mapped thousands of years before Columbus. Antarctica was mapped when its coasts were free of ice!

316 PAGES. 7x10 PAPERBACK. ILLUSTRATED. BIBLIOGRAPHY & INDEX. $19.95. CODE: MASK

PATH OF THE POLE
Cataclysmic Pole Shift Geology
by Charles H. Hapgood

Maps of the Ancient Sea Kings author Hapgood's classic book *Path of the Pole* is back in print! Hapgood researched Antarctica, ancient maps and the geological record to conclude that the Earth's crust has slipped on the inner core many times in the past, changing the position of the pole. *Path of the Pole* discusses the various "pole shifts" in Earth's past, giving evidence for each one, and moves on to possible future pole shifts.

356 PAGES. 6x9 PAPERBACK. ILLUSTRATED. $16.95. CODE: POP

SECRETS OF THE HOLY LANCE
The Spear of Destiny in History & Legend
by Jerry E. Smith

Secrets of the Holy Lance traces the Spear from its possession by Constantine, Rome's first Christian Caesar, to Charlemagne's claim that with it he ruled the Holy Roman Empire by Divine Right, and on through two thousand years of kings and emperors, until it came within Hitler's grasp—and beyond! Did it rest for a while in Antarctic ice? Is it now hidden in Europe, awaiting the next person to claim its awesome power? Neither debunking nor worshiping, *Secrets of the Holy Lance* seeks to pierce the veil of myth and mystery around the Spear. Mere belief that it was infused with magic by virtue of its shedding the Savior's blood has made men kings. But what if it's more? What are "the powers it serves"?

312 PAGES. 6x9 PAPERBACK. ILLUSTRATED. BIBLIOGRAPHY. $16.95. CODE: SOHL

THE FANTASTIC INVENTIONS OF NIKOLA TESLA
by Nikola Tesla with additional material by David Hatcher Childress

This book is a readable compendium of patents, diagrams, photos and explanations of the many incredible inventions of the originator of the modern era of electrification. In Tesla's own words are such topics as wireless transmission of power, death rays, and radio-controlled airships. In addition, rare material on a secret city built at a remote jungle site in South America by one of Tesla's students, Guglielmo Marconi. Marconi's secret group claims to have built flying saucers in the 1940s and to have gone to Mars in the early 1950s! Incredible photos of these Tesla craft are included. •His plan to transmit free electricity into the atmosphere. •How electrical devices would work using only small antennas. •Why unlimited power could be utilized anywhere on earth. •How radio and radar technology can be used as death-ray weapons in Star Wars.

342 PAGES. 6x9 PAPERBACK. ILLUSTRATED. $16.95. CODE: FINT

REICH OF THE BLACK SUN
Nazi Secret Weapons & the Cold War Allied Legend
by Joseph P. Farrell

Why were the Allies worried about an atom bomb attack by the Germans in 1944? Why did the Soviets threaten to use poison gas against the Germans? Why did Hitler in 1945 insist that holding Prague could win the war for the Third Reich? Why did US General George Patton's Third Army race for the Skoda works at Pilsen in Czechoslovakia instead of Berlin? Why did the US Army not test the uranium atom bomb it dropped on Hiroshima? Why did the Luftwaffe fly a non-stop round trip mission to within twenty miles of New York City in 1944? *Reich of the Black Sun* takes the reader on a scientific-historical journey in order to answer these questions. Arguing that Nazi Germany actually won the race for the atom bomb in late 1944,

352 PAGES. 6x9 PAPERBACK. ILLUSTRATED. BIBLIOGRAPHY. $16.95. CODE: ROBS

THE GIZA DEATH STAR
The Paleophysics of the Great Pyramid & the Military Complex at Giza
by Joseph P. Farrell

Was the Giza complex part of a military installation over 10,000 years ago? Chapters include: An Archaeology of Mass Destruction, Thoth and Theories; The Machine Hypothesis; Pythagoras, Plato, Planck, and the Pyramid; The Weapon Hypothesis; Encoded Harmonics of the Planck Units in the Great Pyramid; High Freqquency Direct Current "Impulse" Technology; The Grand Gallery and its Crystals: Gravito-acoustic Resonators; The Other Two Large Pyramids; the "Causeways," and the "Temples"; A Phase Conjugate Howitzer; Evidence of the Use of Weapons of Mass Destruction in Ancient Times; more.

290 PAGES. 6x9 PAPERBACK. ILLUSTRATED. $16.95. CODE: GDS

THE GIZA DEATH STAR DEPLOYED
The Physics & Engineering of the Great Pyramid
by Joseph P. Farrell

Farrell expands on his thesis that the Great Pyramid was a maser, designed as a weapon and eventually deployed—with disastrous results to the solar system. Includes: Exploding Planets: A Brief History of the Exoteric and Esoteric Investigations of the Great Pyramid; No Machines, Please!; The Stargate Conspiracy; The Scalar Weapons; Message or Machine?; A Tesla Analysis of the Putative Physics and Engineering of the Giza Death Star; Cohering the Zero Point, Vacuum Energy, Flux: Feedback Loops and Tetrahedral Physics; and more.

290 PAGES. 6x9 PAPERBACK. ILLUSTRATED. $16.95. CODE: GDSD

THE GIZA DEATH STAR DESTROYED
The Ancient War For Future Science
by Joseph P. Farrell

Farrell moves on to events of the final days of the Giza Death Star and its awesome power. These final events, eventually leading up to the destruction of this giant machine, are dissected one by one, leading us to the eventual abandonment of the Giza Military Complex—an event that hurled civilization back into the Stone Age. Chapters include: The Mars-Earth Connection; The Lost "Root Races" and the Moral Reasons for the Flood; The Destruction of Krypton: The Electrodynamic Solar System, Exploding Planets and Ancient Wars; Turning the Stream of the Flood: the Origin of Secret Societies and Esoteric Traditions; The Quest to Recover Ancient Mega-Technology; Non-Equilibrium Paleophysics; Monatomic Paleophysics; Frequencies, Vortices and Mass Particles; "Acoustic" Intensity of Fields; The Pyramid of Crystals; tons more.

292 pages. 6x9 paperback. Illustrated. $16.95. Code: GDES

THE TESLA PAPERS
Nikola Tesla on Free Energy & Wireless Transmission of Power
by Nikola Tesla, edited by David Hatcher Childress

David Hatcher Childress takes us into the incredible world of Nikola Tesla and his amazing inventions. Tesla's fantastic vision of the future, including wireless power, anti-gravity, free energy and highly advanced solar power. Also included are some of the papers, patents and material collected on Tesla at the Colorado Springs Tesla Symposiums, including papers on: •The Secret History of Wireless Transmission •Tesla and the Magnifying Transmitter •Design and Construction of a Half-Wave Tesla Coil •Electrostatics: A Key to Free Energy •Progress in Zero-Point Energy Research •Electromagnetic Energy from Antennas to Atoms •Tesla's Particle Beam Technology •Fundamental Excitatory Modes of the Earth-Ionosphere Cavity

325 PAGES. 8X10 PAPERBACK. ILLUSTRATED. $16.95. CODE: TTP

GRAVITATIONAL MANIPULATION OF DOMED CRAFT
UFO Propulsion Dynamics
by Paul E. Potter

Potter's precise and lavish illustrations allow the reader to enter directly into the realm of the advanced technological engineer and to understand, quite straightforwardly, the aliens' methods of energy manipulation: their methods of electrical power generation; how they purposely designed their craft to employ the kinds of energy dynamics that are exclusive to space (discoverable in our astrophysics) in order that their craft may generate both attractive and repulsive gravitational forces; their control over the mass-density matrix surrounding their craft enabling them to alter their physical dimensions and even manufacture their own frame of reference in respect to time. Includes a 16-page color insert.

624 pages. 7x10 Paperback. Illustrated. References. $24.00. Code: GMDC

TAPPING THE ZERO POINT ENERGY
Free Energy & Anti-Gravity in Today's Physics
by Moray B. King

King explains how free energy and anti-gravity are possible. The theories of the zero point energy maintain there are tremendous fluctuations of electrical field energy imbedded within the fabric of space. This book tells how, in the 1930s, inventor T. Henry Moray could produce a fifty kilowatt "free energy" machine; how an electrified plasma vortex creates anti-gravity; how the Pons/Fleischmann "cold fusion" experiment could produce tremendous heat without fusion; and how certain experiments might produce a gravitational anomaly.

180 PAGES. 5X8 PAPERBACK. ILLUSTRATED. $12.95. CODE: TAP

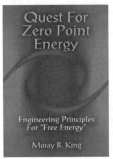

QUEST FOR ZERO-POINT ENERGY
Engineering Principles for "Free Energy"
by Moray B. King

King expands, with diagrams, on how free energy and anti-gravity are possible. The theories of zero point energy maintain there are tremendous fluctuations of electrical field energy embedded within the fabric of space. King explains the following topics: TFundamentals of a Zero-Point Energy Technology; Vacuum Energy Vortices; The Super Tube; Charge Clusters: The Basis of Zero-Point Energy Inventions; Vortex Filaments, Torsion Fields and the Zero-Point Energy; Transforming the Planet with a Zero-Point Energy Experiment; Dual Vortex Forms: The Key to a Large Zero-Point Energy Coherence. Packed with diagrams, patents and photos.

224 PAGES. 6X9 PAPERBACK. ILLUSTRATED. $14.95. CODE: QZPE

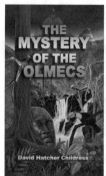

THE MYSTERY OF THE OLMECS
by David Hatcher Childress

The Olmecs were not acknowledged to have existed as a civilization until an international archeological meeting in Mexico City in 1942. Now, the Olmecs are slowly being recognized as the Mother Culture of Mesoamerica, having invented writing, the ball game and the "Mayan" Calendar. But who were the Olmecs? Where did they come from? What happened to them? How sophisticated was their culture? Why are many Olmec statues and figurines seemingly of foreign peoples such as Africans, Europeans and Chinese? Is there a link with Atlantis? In this heavily illustrated book, join Childress in search of the lost cities of the Olmecs! Chapters include: The Mystery of Quizuo; The Mystery of Transoceanic Trade; The Mystery of Cranial Deformation; more.

296 PAGES. 6x9 PAPERBACK. ILLUSTRATED. BIBLIOGRAPHY. COLOR SECTION. $20.00. CODE: MOLM

EYE OF THE PHOENIX
Mysterious Visions and
Secrets of the American Southwest
by Gary David

GaryDavid explores enigmas and anomalies in the vast American Southwest. Contents includes: The Great Pyramids of Arizona; Meteor Crater—Arizona's First Bonanza?; Chaco Canyon—Ancient City of the Dog Star; Phoenix—Masonic Metropolis in the Valley of the Sun; The Flying Shields of the Hopi Katsinam; Is the Starchild a Hopi God?; The Ant People of Orion—Ancient Star Beings of the Hopi; The Nagas—Origin of the Hopi Snake Clan?; The Tau (or T-shaped) Cross—Hopi/Maya/Egyptian Connections; The Hopi Stone Tablets of Techqua Ikachi; The Four Arms of Destiny and more.

348 pages. 6x9 Paperback. Illustrated. Bibliography. $16.95. Code: EOPX

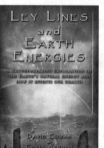

LEY LINE & EARTH ENERGIES
An Extraordinary Journey into the Earth's Natural Energy System
by David Cowan & Chris Arnold

The mysterious standing stones, burial grounds and stone circles that lace Europe, the British Isles and other areas have intrigued scientists, writers, artists and travellers through the centuries. How do ley lines work? How did our ancestors use Earth energy to map their sacred sites and burial grounds? How do ghosts and poltergeists interact with Earth energy? How can Earth spirals and black spots affect our health? This exploration shows how natural forces affect our behavior, how they can be used to enhance our health.

368 PAGES. 6x9 PAPERBACK. ILLUSTRATED. $18.95. CODE: LLEE

OTTO RAHN AND THE QUEST FOR THE HOLY GRAIL
The Amazing Life of the Real "Indiana Jones"
by Nigel Graddon

Otto Rahn led a life of incredible adventure in southern France in the early 1930s. The Hessian language scholar is said to have found runic Grail tablets in the Pyrenean grottoes, and decoded hidden messages within the medieval Grail masterwork *Parsifal*. The artifacts identified by Rahn were believed by Himmler to include the Grail Cup, the Spear of Destiny, the Tablets of Moses, the Ark of the Covenant, the Sword and Harp of David, the Sacred Candelabra and the Golden Urn of Manna. Some believe that Rahn was a Nazi guru who wielded immense influence on his elders and "betters" within the Hitler regime, persuading them that the Grail was the Sacred Book of the Aryans, which, once obtained, would justify their extreme political theories. But things are never as they seem, and as new facts emerge about Rahn a far more extraordinary story unfolds.

450 pages. 6x9 Paperback. Illustrated. Appendix. Index. $18.95. Code: ORQG

THE CRYSTAL SKULLS
Astonishing Portals to Man's Past
by David Hatcher Childress and Stephen S. Mehler

Childress introduces the technology and lore of crystals, and then plunges into the turbulent times of the Mexican Revolution form the backdrop for the rollicking adventures of Ambrose Bierce, the renowned journalist who went missing in the jungles in 1913, and F.A. Mitchell-Hedges, the notorious adventurer who emerged from the jungles with the most famous of the crystal skulls. Mehler shares his extensive knowledge of and experience with crystal skulls. Having been involved in the field since the 1980s, he has personally examined many of the most influential skulls, and has worked with the leaders in crystal skull research, including the inimitable Nick Nocerino, who developed a meticulous methodology for the purpose of examining the skulls.
294 pages. 6x9 Paperback. Illustrated. Bibliography. $18.95. Code: CRSK

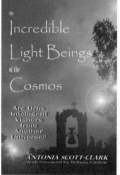

THE INCREDIBLE LIGHT BEINGS OF THE COSMOS
Are Orbs Intelligent Light Beings from the Cosmos?
by Antonia Scott-Clark

Scott-Clark has experienced orbs for many years, but started photographing them in earnest in the year 2000 when the "Light Beings" entered her life. She took these very seriously and set about privately researching orb occurrences. The incredible results of her findings are presented here, along with many of her spectacular photographs. With her friend, GoGos lead singer Belinda Carlisle, Antonia tells of her many adventures with orbs. Find the answers to questions such as: Can you see orbs with the naked eye?; Are orbs intelligent?; Antonia gives detailed instruction on how to photograph orbs, and how to communicate with these Light Beings of the Cosmos.
334 pages. 6x9 Paperback. Illustrated. References. $19.95. Code: ILBC

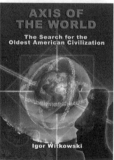

AXIS OF THE WORLD
The Search for the Oldest American Civilization
by Igor Witkowski

Polish author Witkowski's research reveals remnants of a high civilization that was able to exert its influence on almost the entire planet, and did so with full consciousness. Sites around South America show that this was not just one of the places influenced by this culture, but a place where they built their crowning achievements. Easter Island, in the southeastern Pacific, constitutes one of them. The Rongo-Rongo language that developed there points westward to the Indus Valley. Taken together, the facts presented by Witkowski provide a fresh, new proof that an antediluvian, great civilization flourished several millennia ago.
220 pages. 6x9 Paperback. Illustrated. References. $18.95. Code: AXOW

PIRATES & THE LOST TEMPLAR FLEET
by David Hatcher Childress

Childress takes us into the fascinating world of maverick sea captains who were Knights Templar (and later Scottish Rite Free Masons) who battled the ships that sailed for the Pope. The lost Templar fleet was originally based at La Rochelle in southern France, but fled to the deep fiords of Scotland upon the dissolution of the Order by King Phillip. This banned fleet of ships was later commanded by the St. Clair family of Rosslyn Chapel (birthplace of Free Masonry). St. Clair and his Templars made a voyage to Canada in the year 1298 AD, nearly 100 years before Columbus! Later, this fleet of ships and new ones to come, flew the Skull and Crossbones, the symbol of the Knights Templar.
320 PAGES. 6x9 PAPERBACK. ILLUSTRATED. BIBLIOGRAPHY. $16.95. CODE: PLTF

ORDER FORM

10% Discount When You Order 3 or More Items!

One Adventure Place
P.O. Box 74
Kempton, Illinois 60946
United States of America
Tel.: 815-253-6390 • Fax: 815-253-6300
Email: auphq@frontiernet.net
http://www.adventuresunlimitedpress.com

ORDERING INSTRUCTIONS

✓ Remit by USD$ Check, Money Order or Credit Card

✓ Visa, Master Card, Discover & AmEx Accepted

✓ Paypal Payments Can Be Made To:

   info@wexclub.com

✓ Prices May Change Without Notice

✓ 10% Discount for 3 or more Items

SHIPPING CHARGES

United States

✓ Postal Book Rate { $4.00 First Item
   50¢ Each Additional Item

✓ POSTAL BOOK RATE Cannot Be Tracked!

✓ Priority Mail { $5.00 First Item
   $2.00 Each Additional Item

✓ UPS { $6.00 First Item
   $1.50 Each Additional Item

   NOTE: UPS Delivery Available to Mainland USA Only

Canada

✓ Postal Air Mail { $10.00 First Item
   $2.50 Each Additional Item

✓ Personal Checks or Bank Drafts MUST BE

   US$ and Drawn on a US Bank

✓ Canadian Postal Money Orders OK

✓ Payment MUST BE US$

All Other Countries

✓ Sorry, No Surface Delivery!

✓ Postal Air Mail { $16.00 First Item
   $6.00 Each Additional Item

✓ Checks and Money Orders MUST BE US$
   and Drawn on a US Bank or branch.

✓ Paypal Payments Can Be Made in US$ To:
   info@wexclub.com

SPECIAL NOTES

✓ RETAILERS: Standard Discounts Available

✓ BACKORDERS: We Backorder all Out-of-
   Stock Items Unless Otherwise Requested

✓ PRO FORMA INVOICES: Available on Request

ORDER ONLINE AT: www.adventuresunlimitedpress.com

Please check: ✓

☐ This is my first order   ☐ I have ordered before

Name	
Address	
City	
State/Province	Postal Code
Country	
Phone day	Evening
Fax	Email

Item Code	Item Description	Qty	Total

Subtotal ▶

Please check: ✓   Less Discount-10% for 3 or more items ▶

☐ Postal-Surface   Balance ▶

☐ Postal-Air Mail   Illinois Residents 6.25% Sales Tax ▶
   (Priority in USA)   Previous Credit ▶

☐ UPS   Shipping ▶
   (Mainland USA only)   Total (check/MO in USD$ only) ▶

☐ Visa/MasterCard/Discover/American Express

Card Number

Expiration Date

10% Discount When You Order 3 or More Items!